A SIGNET BOOK

CANADIAN CRIMES

Max Haines was born in Antigonish, Nova Scotia. His "Crime Flashback" column made its debut in *The Toronto Sun* in 1972. Since that time, he has researched more than two thousand murder cases from around the world.

Today, "Crime Flashback" appears weekly in *The Toronto Sun* and is syndicated in more than forty newspapers across Canada. Also syndicated in Central and South America, the column has a weekly readership of more than three million and has been translated into Spanish, French and Chinese.

Max is a member of ACTRA, Crime Writers of Canada and the Writers' Union of Canada. He resides in Etobicoke, Ontario , with his wife, Marilyn.

OTHER WORKS BY MAX HAINES

Bothersome Bodies (1977)

Calendar of Criminal Capers (1977)

Crime Flashback #1 (1980)

Crime Flashback #2 (1981)

Crime Flashback #3 (1982)

The Murderous Kind (1983)

Murder & Mayhem (1984)

The Collected Works of Max Haines Vol. I (1985)

That's Life (1986)

True Crime Stories (1987)

True Crime Stories Book II (1988)

True Crime Stories Book III (1989)

True Crime Stories Book IV (1990)

The Collected Works of Max Haines Vol. II (1991)

True Crime Stories Book V (1992)

Doctors Who Kill (1993)

Multiple Murderers (1994)

Multiple Murderers II (1995)

The Collected Works of Max Haines Vol. III (1996)

Celebrity Murders (1996)

Murders Strange But True (1997)

Murder Most Foul (1999)

CANADIAN CRIMES

Max Haines

A SIGNET BOOK

NEW AMERICAN LIBRARY

Published in Canada by
Penguin Books Canada Limited, Toronto, Ontario

SIGNET

Published by the Penguin Group

Penguin Putnam Inc., 375 Hudson Street, New York, New York 10014, U.S.A.
Penguin Books Ltd, 27 Wrights Lane, London w8 5tz, England
Penguin Books Australia Ltd, Ringwood, Victoria, Australia
Penguin Books Canada Ltd, 10 Alcorn Avenue, Toronto, Ontario, Canada m4v 3b2
Penguin Books (nz) Ltd, cnr Rosedale and Airborne Roads, Albany,
Auckland 1310, New Zealand

Penguin Books Ltd, Registered Offices:
Harmondsworth, Middlesex, England

First published in Viking by Penguin Books Canada Limited, 1998

Published in Signet by Penguin Books, 1999

3 5 7 9 10 8 6 4 2

🅞 REGISTERED TRADEMARK — MARCA REGISTRADA

Manufactured in Canada

CANADIAN CATALOGUING IN PUBLICATION DATA

Haines, Max
Canadian Crimes

ISBN 0-451-19673-2

I. Murder–Canada. 2. Criminals–Canada. I. Title.

HV6535.C3H34 1999   364.15′23′0971   C99-930810-6

BOOKS ARE AVAILABLE AT QUANTITY DISCOUNTS WHEN USED TO PROMOTE PRODUCTS
OR SERVICES. FOR INFORMATION PLEASE WRITE TO MARKETING DIVISION, PENGUIN
BOOKS CANADA LTD, 10 ALCORN AVENUE, TORONTO, ONTARIO, CANADA M4V 3B2

Visit Penguin Canada's web site at www.penguin.ca

- CONTENTS -

To Marilyn

– ACKNOWLEDGEMENTS –

A book of this kind requires the contributions of many individuals and organizations.

I am deeply indebted to Julie Kirsh, manager of the *Toronto Sun*'s News Research department and her staff: Susan Dugas, Catherine Flannery, Jillian Goddard, Julie Hornby, Bob Johnson, Anna Morrone, Glenna Tapscott, Joyce Wagler, Kathy Webb Nelson and Barbara White.

Police forces across the country were most cooperative in this endeavour, especially in hunting down old records and transcripts. Alan Cairns, who daily reported on the Bernardo/Homolka case, shared with me the details of the trials. His book, *Deadly Innocence*, co-authored with Scott Burnside, is considered the definitive work on the Bernardo murders.

The staff at Penguin Books has, as always, been tremendously supportive and encouraging, particularly Cynthia Good, Meg Taylor and Jackie Kaiser. The final product would not have been possible without the help of copy editor Liba Berry.

Others who assisted me, and without whose constructive criticism this book would not have become a reality, are Susan Haines, Maureen Hudes and Eleanor Star.

As usual, a woman named Marilyn helped immeasurably.

– CELIA, IKE and AVROM AIRST –

RABBI BENJAMIN FRIEDBERG looked down on his congregation on the eve of Yom Kippur 19 years ago. Three members of his flock were not in attendance. They were dead. Viciously murdered.

Celia and Ike Airst were a wealthy couple who lived on Glencairn Avenue in Toronto's affluent Bathurst-Lawrence area. A son, Avrom, 22, lived at home with his parents. Only one member of the immediate family survived the slaughter: a daughter, Shulamith (Simmie) Moore, 23, who was married to University of Toronto lecturer Bill Moore. They had their own home on Lawrence Avenue West.

Celia, 43, and Ike, 57, had been in the news before the tragedy occurred. In 1971, Celia infiltrated a dinner held by the Canadian Manufacturers Association, at which Alexei Kosygin was giving a speech. During the Soviet premier's speech, Celia and a companion, Albert Appelbaum, unveiled a banner proclaiming "Let My People Go." Police hustled the protesters outside. Celia, then an active member of the millitant Jewish Defence League, told police that at no time had she and Applebaum considered acting violently toward the Soviet leader. They merely wanted him to know that many Canadians opposed the Soviet curbs on immigration to Israel.

Ike had made the newspapers for far different reasons than his wife, although he too was active in Jewish affairs in Toronto. Ike and his brother Herman had been business partners for more than 35 years. They owned scores of properties in the city, mostly small shops and houses. In 1966, Alderman June Marks accused Ike of being a slum-lord. He owned 25 homes, which she considered to be slums.

The Airsts were a close-knit family. They were not Orthodox, but they observed Jewish traditions. I mention the occasions in the past when their names appeared in the paper because these two incidents were thoroughly inves-tigated when Metro homicide detectives searched for a motive for the triple murder of Celia, Ike and Avrom Airst.

It was 1979, in the early morning hours of October 1, when the murders took place. Yom Kippur, the Day of Atonement, the holiest day of the Jewish year, would start that night at sundown.

On the previous evening, the Airsts attended Beth Tzedec synagogue for Saturday-evening services. The family had made plans to go to dinner that night. Ike begged off. He had had a pacemaker implanted years before and opted for a quiet evening at home watching baseball on television. Celia called her daughter, Simmie Moore. She and Avrom met the Moores at the Inn on the Park for dinner. The meal went well.

Avrom wanted to return home. The family decided to drive him back and then take a walk through the pictur-esque Yorkville area. Back at the Glencairn home, the group found Ike in his bathrobe. Avrom mentioned that he would retire for the night.

In Yorkville, Celia, Simmie and Bill dropped into the Park Plaza Hotel for a nightcap. In the hotel's rooftop bar, they met friends, had a drink and headed home. A thick fog enveloped the city. It was approaching 1 a.m.

When they got to Glencairn Avenue, Bill parked his car

and the trio took a 20-minute walk. Afterward, Celia Airst walked the short distance from her daughter and son-in-law's to her front door. Her daughter watched as she disappeared into the fog. Celia may have walked past a hidden assailant. Maybe her killer was parked nearby. Maybe he was already in the house. Homicide detectives theorize that Celia opened the front door of her home and, being security conscious, locked the door as soon as she entered the house. Before she moved out of the hallway, there was someone at the door. Celia either knew the caller or figured it was Simmie who had forgotten something. She opened the door and was attacked immediately with an instrument that was never found. She died on the tile floor of her home from a crushed skull.

The killer or killers made their way upstairs. The thick broadloom silenced their footsteps. Avrom was asleep in his bed. Crushing blows rained down on his head. On to Ike's room, where the process was repeated. The bedrooms were bloody, the house quiet. Three members of one family were dead.

That same Sunday, Simmie and Bill Moore called on the Airsts. Bill stayed in his car. Simmie walked up the steps of her parents' home. She couldn't open the door. Her mother's body lay in the hall, obstructing the door. Simmie summoned help using a neighbour's phone.

Investigating officers discovered the bodies of Ike and Avrom Airst in the upstairs bedrooms.

Initially, the officers focused on the Airst pickup truck, which appeared to be missing. The truck had been used by father and son to check on their properties and carry repair equipment. The vehicle was found in a local garage being repaired and did not figure any further in the investigation.

Why had the Airsts been slaughtered? This was the question facing the police. Ike's real estate holdings were scrutinized. Surely over the years there had been dissatisfied tenants, but using that angle, police were unable to uncover anything approaching a motive for the vicious triple murder. The investigation did not establish a relationship between Celia's political activities and her murder; nor did it reveal any connection between Ike's reputation as a slum landlord and his death.

Each year, as the anniversary date of the murders and that most holy of Jewish holy days draws near, we again wonder who was instrumental in annihilating Celia, Ike and Avrom Airst. Their murders remain unsolved to this day.

– MAY BANNISTER –

IN 1936, THE POPULATION of Pacific Junction, New Brunswick, located about 10 miles outside of Moncton, was an even dozen.

Among those who called Pacific Junction home were the Lake family, consisting of Phil, 30, his wife Bertha, 28, son Jackie, 20 months, and the baby of the family, 4-month-old Betty. The Lakes lived in a 26-by-10-foot home in a little clearing in the woods near the Canadian National Railway tracks.

Eight miles away in Berry Mills lived May Bannister and her four children, Daniel, 20, Arthur, 18, Frances, 14, and Marie, 13. May Bannister had been deserted by her husband shortly after Marie's birth. The family had lived in abject poverty ever since.

They sold blueberries, cut firewood and snared rabbits to eke out a meagre existence. Often, they wandered the streets of Moncton looking for day-old bread. No one in the family could read or write. Both boys were of below-average intelligence.

Strangely enough, the members of these two families would become the main characters in a murder case that would make New Brunswick history and capture the imagination of the entire nation.

On Monday, January 6, 1936, Otto Blakeney was cutting firewood near the Lakes' home. Normally, he ate his midday meal with the Lakes. Otto was shocked to find nothing but a smouldering burnt-out ruin where the Lake home had once stood. Upon closer examination, he made out the horribly burned body of Phil Lake.

Otto scurried down the railway track toward the CNR office. He noticed the droplets of blood that were clearly visible in the fresh snow. Every hundred yards or so there were larger blood smears, as if someone had fallen and risen, only to fall again. Farther on, Otto came across a baby's bottle.

Exactly 471 yards from the Lakes' home he sighted the frozen body of 20-month-old Jackie Lake. A few yards farther was Bertha Lake's almost-nude body. The snow beside the body was disturbed, giving mute evidence that, after dropping her son and falling, Bertha had made vain attempts to rise before dying alone in the snow.

Otto raised the alarm and soon the RCMP was on the scene. An entire family had been wiped out in one night. Although 4-month-old Betty's body was not recovered from the blackened ruins, it was assumed that it had been consumed by the flames. Phil's body, minus his burnt-off arms and legs, was readily identified by his two conspicuous gold teeth. Why had someone annihilated the Lake family? The answer was forthcoming.

Police noted what appeared to be two sets of tracks beginning in the snow where Bertha had died. Wearing snowshoes, the police followed the tracks into the woods. Officers observed small holes in the deep snow beside the tracks, as if someone had used some sort of cane while trudging along.

RCMP Sergeant Bedford Peters, following closely along the trail, found a mitten. It would become the most important piece of evidence in one of the weirdest murder cases in Canadian history.

Meanwhile, CNR employee David Barron told police that around nightfall the day before he had seen one of the Bannister boys walking the tracks. Mounties called on the Bannister home and were greeted by Daniel. Shown the mitten found along the trail, Daniel exclaimed, "Hey, that's mine, where'd you guys get that?" Questioned further, Daniel stated that he had loaned his mittens to his brother, Arthur, on the previous day. David Barron identified Arthur as the man he had seen walking along the tracks. Arthur was arrested and charged with murder.

Arthur confessed, admitting that he had visited the Lakes' home. Daniel and Frances showed up to take him home. Phil Lake made an improper advance to Frances. A brawl ensued, in which Bertha was accidentally struck on the head by a piece of firewood thrown by her husband. Daniel then hit Phil on the head with another piece of firewood, at the same time overturning an oil lamp.

According to Arthur, the three Bannisters took off and never looked back. No doubt Bertha Lake ran from the fire and collapsed, dropping her baby, who froze to death while she died from the wound to her head. In a general way, Frances and Daniel backed up their brother's story. Arthur was taken into custody and charged with murder. Frances was held as a material witness.

The murder victims were duly buried. It was then that the Bannister-Lake case took a bizarre twist. While questioning Milton Trites, a neighbour of the Bannisters', the police learned that there was a baby at the Bannister home. RCMP officers faced May Bannister with this information. Reluctantly, she turned over the baby to the officers. When asked about the identity of the child's mother, she curtly replied, "It's mine." In reality, the baby was 4-month-old Betty Lake, who for a week was believed to be dead.

May had concocted a diabolical plot. In order to make it look as if she had given birth to a baby, she had sometime before purchased a doll at the Metropolitan Store in Moncton. She was seen by several people carrying a bundle, which everyone assumed was a baby. When questioned, all admitted that they had not actually seen the child. Why did May Bannister pose as the mother of a doll, and later somehow come into possession of the Lake baby?

Milton Trites had known the Bannisters for years. He often loaned May small amounts of money. During the previous year she had worked for him as a housekeeper. When she left his employ in November 1935, she told him she was leaving to have his baby. She did in fact go away for some time. When she returned she told Trites she had left their child in Moncton. On the day after the Lake murders she invited Trites to her home to see his baby.

It was also learned that Albert Powell, a CNR freight clerk and part-time Sunday-school teacher, had conducted classes at the Bannister home for about two years. He was often alone in the company of Marie Bannister. May had accused Powell of being responsible for Marie's fictional pregnancy.

It was obvious May Bannister was planning to blackmail two men into supporting two nonexistent babies. There was one tricky detail. At some point May had to produce a real live baby.

Evidence given by Frances Bannister further incriminated her brothers. She stated that, together with Arthur and Daniel, she had arrived at the Lake house around 7 p.m. on the night of the murders. Arthur went into the house. When he came out, he passed her the baby and she started home alone. She heard a scream. Shortly afterward, her two brothers caught up with her.

During their investigation, the RCMP heard persistent rumors that big, tough Phil Lake could not have been overpowered by a boy with a piece of wood. Phil's body was exhumed. Doctors removed a .22-calibre bullet from his brain.

Now the canelike marks in the snow beside the tracks took on a new significance. Maybe they were made by a rifle. Volunteers shovelled tons of snow from the area along the trail. The tedious task paid off. The rifle was recovered and proved to be the murder weapon.

Daniel and Arthur Bannister were tried for the murder of Philip Lake. Both were found guilty and sentenced to death. On September 23, 1936, the two brothers were hanged in the county jail at Dorchester, New Brunswick. No one claimed their bodies.

May Bannister, who no doubt hatched the plot, and ordered her dull, obedient sons to carry out her evil scheme, was found guilty of harbouring a stolen child. She received the maximum sentence of three and a half years' imprisonment. May served her time and returned to Berry Mills, where she was a rather feared curiosity until 1971, when she died of natural causes.

– CYRIL BELSHAW –

WHEN CYRIL AND BETTY BELSHAW took their year-long sabbatical from the University of British Columbia, they had no way of knowing that before the year was out tragedy would descend upon them both, leaving Betty dead and Cyril accused of her murder.

Professor Belshaw, the respected head of the anthropology department of the university, planned to spend the last half of his sabbatical in Montana-Vermala, Switzerland, with his wife of 37 years, Betty, who was also employed at U.B.C., as an English instructor. All went well until early 1979, when the urbane, cultured Belshaws decided to take a trip to Paris.

According to Professor Belshaw, he and Betty left Montana-Vermala on January 13, stopping over that night at the Relais PLM Beaune, arriving at the Novotel Bagnolet in Paris the next day. The Belshaws didn't leave their room for the rest of that day.

On the morning of the fifteenth, Cyril and Betty had a continental breakfast in their room. Betty planned to do research at the Bibliothèque Nationale. Cyril would get in some shopping.

The Canadian couple left the hotel and caught the subway. They separated at Bourse Station when Betty left the subway. Cyril watched her departure. According to the statement he later gave police, he never laid eyes on his wife again.

At 1 p.m. Cyril waited for Betty at their prearranged meeting place, the Galleries Lafayette, Paris's largest department store. Betty didn't show up.

All that day Cyril waited for word from his wife. When he hadn't heard from her by the following day, he reported her missing to the police. He also called on the Canadian Embassy and gave the official all the details of his wife's disappearance. Then he phoned his two adult children back in Canada and advised them of their mother's strange absence. On January 18, Belshaw returned by car to Montana, Switzerland.

This then was the sequence of events later related by Belshaw. Staid, correct Betty Belshaw, who had never been anything but a well-organized, punctual individual, had mysteriously disappeared from the streets of Paris.

On March 28, labourers repairing a road near Le Sepey, Switzerland, found the nude body of a middle-aged woman. The body had been wrapped in garbage bags and tied with twine before being thrown down a ravine that was frequently used as a garbage-disposal site. Animals had mauled the body, making identification extremely difficult.

Initially there was no connection between Betty Belshaw and the decomposed, partially consumed body found at Le Sepey. One must remember that Mrs. Belshaw disappeared in France, while the unidentified body was discovered in Switzerland. Eventually, Interpol inquired if the body could be that of the Canadian woman who had vanished from the streets of Paris.

As a result of this inquiry, Professor Belshaw was asked for his wife's dental charts, which he volunteered to procure himself. Belshaw provided the police with Betty's charts, which were compared with the teeth of the corpse found at Le Sepey. The comparison indicated that the corpse was definitely not that of 55-year-old Betty Belshaw. Professor Belshaw returned to Canada.

Despite this seemingly conclusive proof, Swiss authorities contacted the RCMP in Vancouver and requested Mrs. Belshaw's dental charts to be sent to them directly from her dentist. The RCMP called upon Professor Belshaw to obtain the name of his wife's dentist.

Knowing that precise records would be forwarded to Switzerland, Professor Belshaw wrote out a statement that he delivered to a Vancouver detachment of the RCMP. In the statement he admitted altering the dental charts which he had initially provided to the Swiss police. He gave as his reason the fact that he could not face "the psychological trauma of possibly identifying my wife without the presence of family and friends, or the delays in returning to my home and family after many months of hope that my wife might be found alive." Professor Belshaw further stated that he had acted foolishly and on impulse. The unaltered dental charts proved that the corpse found at Le Sepey was indeed the body of Betty Belshaw.

Strong suspicion centered on Professor Belshaw. Swiss detectives arrived in Vancouver to question him. He refused to return to Switzerland, but on November 1, 1979, was arrested in Paris, where he had flown to attend a United Nations conference. The Swiss immediately instituted extradition proceedings in order to transfer Belshaw to Switzerland and charge him with his wife's murder.

On December 3, 1980, Cyril Belshaw, then editor-in-chief of *Current Ethnological Sciences*, author, former member of the Academic Board of British Columbia, and adviser to the U.N. Bureau of Social Affairs, stood trial for the murder of his wife.

At Belshaw's trial the prosecution claimed that the falsification of the dental records was the action of a guilty man. They further stated that the motive for the murder was Belshaw's involvement with Elida Harris of Vancouver, a married graduate student at the university. It was proven that Mrs. Harris had visited with the professor alone in his chalet in Montana, Switzerland, for a week before the Belshaws took occupancy. (Mrs. Belshaw was still at home when Professor Belshaw went to Switzerland.) Upon returning to Canada, Belshaw saw Harris about once a month.

The prosecution contended that Betty Belshaw was murdered because she found out about the couple's prolonged affair. They further claimed Mrs. Belshaw never reached Paris but was killed either in Montana or on the way to Le Sepey where her body was found. Hotel employees where Belshaw stopped over on his way to Paris, and in Paris itself, could not recall ever having seen Mrs. Belshaw.

In his defence, Professor Belshaw admitted falsifying the dental records and having an affair with Mrs. Harris, but vehemently denied murdering his wife. He claimed that if his wife had found out about his affair, she would have admonished him, but the incident would not have broken up their marriage.

A panel of three judges and a six-member jury acquitted Cyril Belshaw of the murder of his wife. He walked out of court a free man.

The murder of Betty Belshaw remains unsolved to this day.

– PAUL BERNARDO AND KARLA HOMOLKA –

THERE HAVE BEEN MANY notorious couples throughout the history of crime. One is reminded of Myra Hindley and Ian Brady, a despicable British pair who, in 1964–65, murdered children and buried them on desolate Saddleworth Moor in northern England. More recently the infamous husband-and-wife team of Rosemary and Fred West killed their roomers and buried their bodies in and around their home in Gloucester, England. We in Canada have not been cursed with deadly duos whose crimes are so horrible they boggle the imagination. These unspeakable crimes always seemed to take place somewhere else. Then along came Paul Bernardo and Karla Homolka and changed all that forever.

He was a handsome University of Toronto graduate. She was a high school student who worked part-time at a pet store in St. Catharines, Ontario. They met quite by accident. Paul Bernardo had time on his hands on the evening of October 17, 1987, when it all began. He and his best buddy, Van Smirnis, dropped into Howard Johnson's on Markham Road in the Toronto suburb of Scarborough for a bite to eat. The popular orange-roofed motel often hosted trade shows and conventions. As luck would have it, 17-year-old Karla Homolka and a friend, Debbie Purdie, were in Toronto attending a pet show.

The two young men were veterans in the art of picking up girls. When they spotted Karla and Debbie in the restaurant, they wasted little time in introducing themselves and joining the girls at their table. Paul sidled up to Karla. She did nothing to discourage his all-too-obvious advances.

As the guys flirted with the girls, they learned that the young women were in the city for a pet show. In fact, they were staying right there at Howard Johnson's. It didn't take long before Paul and Van were in the girls' room. Van and Debbie didn't hit it off. Paul and Karla were another kettle of fish altogether. They took to each other as if a magnetic force was at play. Karla fell hard for the slim charmer, who she found out was an accountant with the prestigious firm of Price Waterhouse. The couple had vigorous and satisfying sex on the first night.

Karla was smitten. Apparently, so was Paul. After their first sexual encounter, Paul spent most weekends in St. Catharines. Eventually he met Karla's friends, whose opinion of him was split. Some thought he was a hunk. Others felt he dressed too well, acted like a know-it-all. Generally, though, they felt he really liked Karla. For sure he treated her better than the locals who attended Sir Winston Churchill High School and dated Karla's friends.

Paul did have a distinct advantage over the high school students of St. Catharines. After all, he was a junior accountant with a well-known accounting firm. He was earning an excellent salary and could well afford to take Karla out to the best restaurants. Often, he gifted her with flowers.

Paul was spending so many weekends in St. Catharines, about an hour-and-a-half drive from his Scarborough home, that Karla's parents, Dorothy and Karel Homolka, invited him to stay weekends at their home. They quickly accepted Paul as if he were a member of the family. On rare occasions, Karla would visit with the Bernardos in Scarborough. It was obvious to everyone that the young, clean-cut couple were totally enamoured with each other.

However, Paul was seeing other girls on the side. Sometimes he grew annoyed when Karla, by her very presence, interfered with his extracurricular activities. For her part, Karla was totally devoted to her true love. She constantly spoke to her guy on the phone and talked incessantly to her friends about how wonderful he was.

Certainly, Paul had idiosyncrasies. He disliked Karla discussing her previous boyfriends. Sometimes, he told her she was unattractive and didn't know how to behave properly. But what the heck, he was her guy and someday she hoped to become Mrs. Paul Bernardo.

Toward the end of 1988, Paul leased a gold 1989 two-door Nissan, the better to impress Karla and her family when he drove up to their front door on weekends. Karla was flying high. She had a good-looking, six-foot-one-inch boyfriend who was very serious about their relationship. Careerwise, Paul would rise to the top. Of that she had no doubt. As for herself, she loved animals and planned to become a veterinarian one day. The future looked brighter than bright.

No one knew that Paul Bernardo was leading a double life. Back in Scarborough he was raping young women. In May, two girls were attacked in separate incidents as they got off a bus. Toward the end of July, another attack took place. Later in the year, on December 16, a fourth rape occurred. Two days before Christmas, the Scarborough Rapist, as he was now called, struck again. The 19-year-old victim was made to repeat over and over that she loved her attacker and wished him a merry Christmas. She was made to endure unspeakable indignities under the threat of the rapist's ever-present knife. All of the rapes followed a distinct pattern. The rapist talked a lot. He approached his quarry from behind after they disembarked from a bus and all the attacks took place in Scarborough. Paul Bernardo lived in Scarborough at 21 Sir Raymond Drive.

The rapes continued through 1988 and 1989. On May 26, 1990, a young woman walking along Midland Avenue was raped on the campus of Agincourt Collegiate. She was able to give police an extremely detailed and accurate description of her attacker. A composite drawing was made from the description.

I remember well the day the picture appeared on the front page of the *Toronto Sun* beside the heading "Have You Seen This Man?" Van Smirnis recognized the drawing of his good buddy Paul Bernardo. He told his brother, who in turn told his wife. Much later, she informed police of her suspicions. Still later, Paul was contacted by police who took DNA samples from him. Paul was polite and obliging. He laughingly told his friends he had been tested and cleared. Everyone got a chuckle out of the incident. Their friend Paul a vicious rapist? Preposterous. Their friend Paul with the sexy girlfriend? Unbelievable. Their friend Paul who could pick up a different chick every night of the week? Tell us another one. It was nothing more than a coincidence. Paul's DNA samples were filed away with hundreds of others to be checked.

Life goes on.

Karla decided not to further her education. Instead she went to work full time at the Martindale Animal Clinic. Paul left Price Waterhouse and caught on with the Toronto firm of Goldfarb Shulman Patel and Co. He came highly recommended. The year 1991 would be a banner year. Paul and Karla planned to marry.

By now the couple had experienced every conceivable

type of sex that can be indulged in by two consenting partners. Karla was a compliant partner to every depravity. At any time she could have broken off their relationship, but she didn't. She loved her man, despite his peculiar desires.

The lovers and the entire Homolka family had been devastated by a traumatic and tragic death the Christmas before. There were six occupants in the Homolka home on the snowy night of December 23, 1990. Karla's father, Karel, was watching TV. Her mother, Dorothy, was working in the kitchen. Paul, Karla and her two younger sisters, Lori and Tammy, were watching television in the family room. Paul was horsing around with his latest toy, a Sony video camera. If it moved, Paul shot it. Only two people in the house knew that Karla had promised Paul a unique Christmas present. She would arrange and assist in Paul's rape of her 15-year-old sister, Tammy.

Preparations for the rape had been meticulous and lengthy. Paul had expressed his interest in having sex with Tammy some months earlier. Initially, Karla had opposed the idea, but eventually she agreed. Anything for Paul.

That night, two days before Christmas, booze flowed like water in the Homolka household. Paul, Karla and Tammy drank through most of the evening. In time, Lori grew tired of watching television and went to bed. Tammy was feeling no pain. Dorothy and Karel retired after saying goodnight to Paul and their two daughters.

According to Paul, he and Karla dozed off while watching TV, but awoke with a start to find Tammy choking and vomiting. He moved her from the couch she had been sitting on to the floor and attempted to revive her by mouth-to-mouth resuscitation. While he tried to move her into Karla's bedroom, Karla dialed 911.

A short time later, ambulance attendants and police were at the scene. Tammy, in serious distress, was rushed to hospital. Constable David Weeks couldn't help noticing the red blotches around Tammy's mouth and nostrils. He found it most unusual. The Homolka household was understandably in a turmoil. Their worst fears were realized when, shortly after 2 a.m., they were informed that their daughter was dead. Paul Bernardo was heartbroken. Karla too was devastated by her sister's untimely death.

An autopsy confirmed that Tammy had suffered cardiac arrest after choking on her own vomit. Standard drug tests indicated that no drugs had been present in the girl's body (Note: Halcion is not on the list of standard drugs.) Authorities decided that the vomiting had been caused by the combination of her dinner that night and the variety of alcoholic beverages she had consumed. It was just one of those weird and tragic accidents that occur from time to time. No one was to blame and no one delved into the mystery of the red blotches on Tammy's face.

The subject of delaying Karla and Paul's wedding scheduled for that June was discussed. Karla wouldn't hear of it. The wedding would take place as planned and that was that.

The devoted couple moved into a rented house at 57 Bayview Drive in Port Dalhousie, just outside St. Catharines. Paul had left his accounting position and was now making a fine living smuggling cigarettes into Canada from the United States, only a few miles away. Paul and his buddy Van converted the back of Paul's Nissan into a virtual secret compartment to hold the cigarettes. The partnership flourished, grossing roughly $2,000 a week.

Wedding plans, mostly under Paul's direction, were

proceeding nicely, although there were a couple of glitches. Karla's friends noticed that she seemed to be bruised much of the time. Karla always had a ready explanation. She had fallen, one of the animals at the clinic had become rough, that sort of thing. No one paid too much attention.

The bruising wasn't everything. There was something else—the dark secret shared by Paul and Karla. They well knew that Tammy's death was far from accidental. Karla, intent on giving her sister to her fiancé as a Christmas gift, had had no problem obtaining the necessary drugs from the clinic where she was employed. She picked up several Halcion pills, which Paul ground into a powder. The sleeping pills should do the job, but just to make sure, Karla stole a quantity of halothane, an anaesthetic that was often used at the clinic on animals before and during an operation. She knew she didn't have the proper equipment to administer the halothane, but felt that she could give it to her sister by simply soaking some on a cloth and holding it over Tammy's face.

After consuming several drinks laced with Halcion, Tammy fell asleep. Karla placed the halothane-soaked cloth over her sister's mouth. Paul undressed the hapless girl and raped her. He performed other sex acts on the unconscious teenager, while Karla joined in the sex games, sometimes under Paul's direction. The entire assault was videotaped. When the camera was turned off, Tammy started vomiting and stopped breathing. Paul attempted mouth-to-mouth while Karla dialed 911.

Later, Karla would relate that together they dressed Tammy and got rid of the incriminating evidence. They hid the video camera in Karla's room. It wasn't long before ambulance attendants and Constable Weeks were at the scene.

The wedding date was fast approaching. Karla played grotesque sex games with her partner in crime. She was told to refer to him as the king or big-shot businessman. She displayed more and more bruising. Friends were given the same old excuses. Sometimes Karla said she'd had a mishap in her garden. On one occasion she told them she had bumped her head on the dashboard of the car. After Tammy's death the beatings seemed to escalate. Paul often had Karla dress in Tammy's clothing and had sex with her, pretending that she was her dead sister.

The heavy drinking, weird sex and beatings continued. The team of Paul and Karla was on a rampage, but only they knew the extent of their monstrous lifestyle. By day they were that attractive young couple who lived in the comfortable home in Port Dalhousie. By night they were something else.

Paul wasn't satisfied. He often talked to Karla about capturing his very own sex slave. Karla thought it was a great idea. That's why she wasn't that surprised when, on the night of June 14, 1991, Paul brought a young girl into their home. It was 14-year-old Leslie Mahaffy's misfortune to be standing in front of her Burlington, Ontario, home when Paul Bernardo was on the prowl.

Leslie was in a bit of a bind. Her folks had locked her out because she had missed her curfew and she was hesitant about waking them up. Paul made the youngster's acquaintance and convinced her that there would be no harm in joining him for a cigarette in his Nissan. Once Leslie was in the vehicle, Paul pulled out his knife and blindfolded the terrified girl.

In the wee hours of the morning Paul was back in Port Dalhousie, explaining to his wife that he had captured a sex slave. Karla wasn't that upset. She went back to sleep. Paul had sex with his captive. Eventually, the diabolical pair had three-way sex with Leslie. All that weekend, Leslie was sexually attacked while the scenes were videotaped. Early Sunday morning, Paul decided that Leslie could identify him and would have to be killed. Karla would later describe how Leslie fell asleep, after which Paul tied an electric cord around his victim's neck and strangled her to death. To this day, Paul claims he didn't kill Leslie.

The teenager's body was wrapped in a blanket and lugged downstairs to a root cellar. Next day, Karla and Paul had her folks over for a Father's Day dinner at their home. Dorothy and Karel were unaware that they were a few feet from the corpse of the young girl from Burlington.

Next day Karla went to work after Paul discussed what he would do with the body in the root cellar. He had a great idea. He would dismember the body, encase it in cement and throw it in a lake. Using a chainsaw, Paul dissected Leslie's body and encased it in cement blocks, which were formed in cardboard boxes. Paul insists that Karla assisted throughout the operation, while she claims that the entire undertaking was performed while she was at work. The cement blocks were lugged out to the Nissan. It took a few trips to Lake Gibson to dispose of the mortal remains of Leslie Mahaffy. Karla helped carry the heavier blocks. That night Paul meticulously cleaned the house.

The big wedding was less than two weeks away. Both the prospective bride and groom were hyper as the day approached. Their efforts were rewarded. By any standards the Bernardo-Homolka nuptials were spectacular. The bride and groom were transported from St. Mark's Anglican Church in Niagara-on-the-Lake in a horse-drawn white carriage. The reception was held at the historic little town's most luxurious facility, the Queen's Landing Hotel. The Bernardos made a handsome couple indeed.

That same day, Bill Grekul and his wife, Mary, were busy putting their canoe in the waters of Lake Gibson when they came across a block of cement. The Grekuls had stumbled across a portion of the cement-encased body of Leslie Mahaffy.

The Bernardos honeymooned in Hawaii. Karla endured terrible beatings and came home looking a mess. Still, she was the envy of many, with her quaint suburban home and handsome husband.

From time to time, Karla's injuries were severe enough for her to visit local doctors. She complained of a bad back. Once she had a broken finger; on another occasion a cracked rib. Karla always had a convenient excuse to explain away her injuries.

Soon, Paul had the urge to capture another sex slave. Sometimes he took Karla with him when he went on the prowl, feeling that it would be easier to pick up a young girl with another woman present. Besides, Karla could help with the actual abduction. His wife enthusiastically agreed.

On Thursday, April 16, 1992, the pair of stalkers trolled the streets of St. Catharines for a young girl. The expedition had been well planned. Paul felt that the best time to pluck a victim off the streets would be when the unsuspecting youngsters were coming home from school.

There she was—just the type Paul wanted. He pulled the Nissan into the Grace Lutheran Church parking lot.

Karla leaned out the window and asked Kristen French for directions. As the girl attempted to be helpful, Karla produced a map, which Kristen studied. In an instant, Paul was behind her, wielding a knife. He pushed Kristen into the car. Karla jumped into the back seat and held Kristen's head back by clutching her hair. Paul drove home to Port Dalhousie. There was one concern. During the brief struggle to get Kristen into the car, she had dropped one of her shoes, but there were other things on Paul's mind.

He give Kristen explicit instructions. She was to call him master and king. Simply put, she was to do exactly as he commanded. Most of the indignities Kristen was forced to endure were videotaped. Karla, as usual, appeared to be a willing accomplice who enjoyed herself to the fullest. Sometimes Karla and Kristen were the main performers in Paul's warped movie-making exploits.

Karla and Paul knew that Kristen could identify them and so all through her captivity the schoolgirl's fate was sealed. After Kristen had suffered through Paul and Karla's every sexual whim for 13 days, Paul approached her from behind and wrapped a black electrical cord around her throat. He held it tight until Kristen breathed no more.

That night the Bernardos untied Kristen's ankles and undid her handcuffs. The body was stripped and washed in a Jacuzzi. Paul instructed Karla to cut off Kristen's hair because it might have picked up fibres from the carpet. They burned their victim's clothing in the fireplace. Finally they drove the body to Burlington, where Paul and Karla carried it into some bushes.

Within 24 hours Kristen French's body was found by a man searching for scrap metal only a few miles from Lake Gibson, where Leslie's body had been discovered in the cement blocks. The two murders were linked. Some madman in southern Ontario was abducting young girls off the streets. A monster was loose among us.

Police had some clues. Kristen's shoe established the point from which she had been kidnapped. Several witnesses reported that a cream-coloured, late 1970s Camaro was seen in the area around the time Kristen was observed walking home from school. A massive search was conducted for the Camaro but, like all the other clues, nothing led the investigators to the killer or killers.

Paul enjoyed watching the TV and newspaper coverage of his latest crime. He firmly believed he would never be caught. Meanwhile Paul's verbal and physical abuse of Karla escalated. He would strike his wife with little or no provocation. Karla was finding it increasingly difficult to hide her bruises from colleagues at the clinic. After a brief trip to Montreal, Paul returned and severely beat his wife about the head with a flashlight. The resulting swelling and discolouration to her face was so pronounced that a co-worker, Wendy Lutczyn, anonymously called Karla's mother, telling her something had to be done about Karla's condition.

Dorothy Homolka drove to the Martindale Clinic and was aghast at the bruising around her daughter's eyes. Despite her condition, Karla went to work that afternoon, but her family was not to be dissuaded. That evening, her father, mother and sister showed up at her Port Dalhousie home. The house was in darkness. The family reluctantly returned to St. Catharines.

Next day, Karla's mother again visited her daughter at the animal clinic. Karla was in worse shape than she had been the day before. Now both her eyes were nothing more than black sockets. Her entire face was horribly swollen. Karla attempted to lie to her mother, saying that she had been in a car accident. This time, her excuses weren't believed. Eventually Karla confessed to her mother that Paul had viciously beaten her with a flashlight. She had been over the border on a cigarette-smuggling junket the night before. Paul had continually beaten her all the way home.

That night, while Paul was out of the house, the Homolkas removed their daughter from her Port Dalhousie home and for a short time hid her with one of Lori's friends. The police were called and Karla was transported to the St. Catharines General Hospital, where bruises were found all over her body. She remained in hospital for three days, after which her family thought it best for her to stay with relatives in Brampton, an hour's drive from St. Catharines. There was grave fear that Paul would come looking for his wife.

Meanwhile, DNA testing continued on samples that had been gathered two years earlier from victims of the Scarborough Rapist. The results were compared with specimens taken from suspects. The Ontario Centre of Forensic Sciences came up with a match—Paul Bernardo. Bernardo was placed under surveillance while investigators looked into any connection he might have with the deaths of Leslie Mahaffy and Kristen French. They learned that a month earlier, his wife, Karla, had filed assault charges against him. In addition, he was connected to another death, that of his wife's sister, Tammy Homolka, who had died under unusual circumstances. The report indicated that there were mysterious red blotches around the girl's nostrils and mouth. No one knew with any degree of certainty what had caused the strange red stains.

Unknown to the authorities, Karla had told her aunt, with whom she was staying in Brampton, about the life she had led while living with Paul Bernardo, including the taking of human life. Her aunt advised her to hire a lawyer and suggested George Walker of Niagara Falls.

For the past several days, Detectives Ron Whitefield and Mary Lee Metcalfe had been questioning Karla about her husband's involvement in the Scarborough rapes. When her uncle was unable to drive Karla to Niagara Falls to see her lawyer, he asked detectives if they would give her a lift. They agreed and drove Karla to Niagara Falls, where she told Walker her unbelievable story. Walker accepted Karla as a client and advised her to talk to absolutely no one other than himself.

On Wednesday, February 17, 1993, detectives drove up to the front door of what was to become the most notorious house in Canada and arrested Paul Bernardo. Once he was transported to an interrogation facility, Bernardo was advised that his wife had pulled the plug. Investigators knew about Leslie Mahaffy, Kristen French and his activities as the Scarborough Rapist. At this point, Paul Bernardo had been charged with rape. He had not been charged with any murder. In fact, the evidence against him was primarily his battered wife's statements pointing to him as the killer. He retained lawyer Barry Fox, but they soon had a falling-out and Fox withdrew from the Bernardo affair.

The infamous home in Port Dalhousie was searched for 10 weeks. Several items were found—a hunting knife, traces of the sleeping medication Halcion, cardboard boxes similar to those used in the boxes that held Leslie Mahaffy's body parts. Above all, police recovered hundreds of videotapes.

Most were of popular television shows. Among the tapes was one of less than two minutes, depicting Karla having sex in a variety of ways with another, unidentified woman. She appeared to be thoroughly enjoying herself.

Of the fingerprints found in the house, not one belonged to Leslie Mahaffy or Kristen French. Short of taking the house apart, all agreed it was a meticulous search.

On April 30, 1993, police left the Bernardo residence, convinced that they had found everything the house had to offer. They were wrong.

By this time, Bernardo had a new lawyer, Ken Murray. Murray received permission to remove some of Paul's belongings from the house. It was a reasonable request. The lawyer took a television set and other items. Unknown to all, under Paul's instructions, he removed a tape hidden behind a built-in light fixture. The lawyer told no one of its existence.

Karla's lawyer, George Walker, was contacted by the St. Catharines prosecutor's office. A deal was in the offing. They desperately needed more information to guarantee a conviction of murder as it applied to Bernardo. Walker met with regional prosecutor Ray Houlahan. The deal was simple enough. Walker knew Bernardo had killed Leslie and Kristen. According to him, Karla had been forced to take part in the sexual attacks. She was a battered, abused wife. The pair had taped the indignities inflicted on the two girls, but not the actual killings.

For her eyewitness testimony, Karla sought immunity from prosecution. The deal was passed along to the director of the Crown law office, Murray Segal. After two weeks of meetings, Walker and Segal came to an agreement.

Karla would plead guilty to two manslaughter charges in return for two ten-year prison sentences to run concurrently. With time off for good behaviour, she would be eligible for parole in three years and four months. She would be arrested, but released on $100,000 bail, which her parents had raised on their St. Catharines home. Any false statement by Karla would immediately make the arrangement invalid.

All in all, not a bad deal for Karla, considering that she assisted in the kidnapping of Kristen French and had several opportunities to release the girl when Paul was out of the house. Walker saw to it that Karla was confined to Northwestern General Hospital for a battery of tests. While there, she told several doctors how her sister Tammy had met her death. In addition, she wrote a letter to her parents, explaining in detail how her sister had really died.

Under these rather strange circumstances, Crown prosecutor Murray Segal now felt that to conclude the deal, Karla must spend additional time in prison for her involvement in Tammy's death. He and Walker agreed that for Karla's complete testimony, including the circumstances surrounding her sister's death, she should receive two twelve-year sentences to run concurrently, making her eligible for parole in four years and four months. In other words, she would face no further charges, but would have two years tacked on to the previously agreed-on ten-year sentence. The deal was struck.

Karla gave a complete statement on her life with Paul Bernardo, including details of the deaths of three young girls. She described their agonies while they were subjugated to hideous indignities and their horrible deaths.

While she didn't confess to the actual killings, she revealed her depraved role as an assistant in all the girls' torments. The statement, in question-and-answer form, took three days to complete. Karla concluded her session May 17, 1993. As a result, Paul Bernardo was charged with two counts of first-degree murder, two counts of unlawful confinement, two counts of aggravated sexual assault, two counts of kidnapping and one count of causing indignity to a human body.

Karla was the first of the pair to make a court appearance. The press was banned from reporting the proceedings. She pleaded guilty to the two counts of manslaughter and was then hustled off to spend her first night in Kingston's Prison for Women.

With Karla safely tucked away in prison, investigators concentrated on gathering evidence against Bernardo. His lawyer, Ken Murray, constantly complained that the Crown was tardy in sharing information with him. When he and his junior, Carolyn MacDonald, questioned Karla in Kingston, he had Karla repeat that another woman, who has remained anonymous and was later referred to in court as Jane Doe, was also subjected to the Halcion/halothane treatment. On that occasion, Jane had stopped breathing, but before 911 had been called, she came around. Murray and MacDonald questioned Karla for almost a week.

On August 15, 1994, Ken Murray had an appointment with well-known, respected defence lawyer John Rosen at the latter's office. Murray was on a mission. He wanted to drop Bernardo as a client and ask Rosen to take on his defence. Murray claimed he simply didn't have the staff or the facilities to follow through in what had become one of the most publicized cases ever to be tried in Canada. After thinking it over for a few days, Rosen consented to take over the defence of Paul Bernardo. He met his client in jail. Bernardo was pleased with his new lawyer.

Unknown to Rosen, Ken Murray had retained another icon of the Canadian bar, Austin Cooper, to represent him. It was Cooper who informed Rosen that Ken Murray had in his possession important incriminating videotapes. Murray had procured them under Bernardo's instructions when he went to the Port Dalhousie home to pick up his client's personal items after the extensive police search. In due course, the six 8mm tapes were turned over to John Rosen, who immediately shared them with the Crown.

The tapes told it all. There was Karla, administering halothane to her helpless sister, as well as to Jane Doe. There were Leslie Mahaffy and Kristen French being forced to engage in sex acts and indignities while being threatened with death. The tapes did not show the murders of the two school girls. Throughout the tapes, Karla appeared to be enjoying herself immensely. The impression of a battered woman forced to participate was fading. There was little doubt in anyone's mind that had the tapes been available to the Crown when Ken Murray picked them up, Karla would have been charged with murder along with Paul Bernardo. Her evidence would not have been needed to put Bernardo away, but an ironclad deal had been struck and Karla was immune from further prosecution.

On May 1, 1994, Paul Bernardo pleaded not guilty to the nine serious charges against him. Karla, who had obtained a divorce while in prison, was the star witness against him. John Rosen did the best he could with an unwinnable case. Karla's testimony and the tapes were unassailable. Bernardo was found guilty of all nine charges and sentenced to the maximum term of life imprisonment with no possibility of parole for 25 years.

As this book goes to press, both Karla and Paul are in prison, but there has been fallout over the case which lingers still.

Lawyer Ken Murray has been charged with obstruction of justice for holding on to those incriminating tapes for 16 months before revealing their existence. Paul Bernardo is appealing his conviction. Beyond that, the Canadian public has not forgotten the "deal with the devil" which will allow Karla Homolka the possibility of gaining her freedom after spending a little over four years in confinement.

Homolka was eligible for parole in 1997, but didn't apply. In 2001, she will be eligible for statutory release, which means Homolka will have served two-thirds of her sentence.

One is left with the sickening feeling that justice has not been served.

− SAUL BETESH −

IT IS OVER 20 YEARS since Crown attorney Peter Rickaby asked Werner Gruener, standing on trial for Emanuel Jaques's murder, to read from the Holy Bible—Matthew, Chapter 18. The accused man, an avid reader of the Bible, had little trouble finding the specific chapter. "But whoso shall offend one of these little ones which believe in me, it were better for him that a millstone were hanged about his neck, and that he were drowned in the depth of the sea." Dramatic moments in court, which awakened Toronto's social conscience as no other murder trial has before or since.

The horror which was to become 12-year-old Emanuel Jaques's last day on earth began innocently enough. On a pleasant day in July 1977, Emanuel, his brother Luciano, 13, and a friend, Shane McLean, 12, spent the day shining shoes on the corner of Yonge and Dundas Streets. At 5:30 p.m., a customer asked Luciano if he was interested in making $35 an hour helping to move photographic equipment. As Luciano explained at the time, "I said no, but my brother, who had only made a dollar during the afternoon, said he'd like to go." Luciano and Shane ran off to phone Maria Jaques for permission. Mrs. Jaques forbade any of the boys to go with the stranger, but by the time the two lads returned to the corner, Emanuel and the stranger were gone.

Luciano ran home and told his parents that Emanuel had gone off with a stranger. Maria and Valdemiro Jaques had been living in Toronto for only three years at the time of their son's disappearance. Relatively recent immigrants from Portugal, they were stunned with the terrible fears every parent feels when one of their brood is exposed to danger.

Valdemiro spent all that night unsuccessfully searching the area around the Yonge Street strip for his son. Next morning he reported Emanuel missing to the police.

Three days later, on a Sunday night, Saul David Betesh, 27, walked into the Regent Street Police Station and told Sergeant Stan Shillington that he had picked up Emanuel on the previous Thursday evening, but had last seen the 12-year-old boy walking up Yonge Street. Many hours after arriving at the police station Saul Betesh told all. What he confessed to that night, every detail of which was to become public knowledge later at his trial, shocked Torontonians as no other murder ever has.

Betesh's confession also revealed the hideous subculture that exists just below the city's facade of respectability; a subculture where pornography, male prostitution and sadomasochism are a way of life.

Who was Saul David Betesh? Adopted when he was six days old, Saul had every opportunity in life. His parents were loving, caring people, who became aware early in their son's life that he was not normal. Later his mother would testify in tears that as a baby Saul had banged his head against his crib to gain attention. When he was only three, he poured nail polish down a sleeping maid's ear. He attended four schools and was thrown out of each one, including kindergarten.

While Saul was a live-in student at private Crescent School in Toronto, his mother noticed bruises on his body. Her complaints to the school authorities brought about the dismissal of one of the teachers at the school. Saul had been molested by a male teacher.

At the age of 15 he was sent to a private training school in Pennsylvania. On his return to Toronto, he wired the Betesh home and threatened to electrocute his parents. Terrified by their own son, the Beteshes placed a lock on their bedroom door and enrolled Saul in Browndale, a home for emotionally disturbed children. By the time he was 19, Saul's family and friends knew he was a homosexual. He moved out of his parents' home and lived in a succession of filthy rooms for the next eight years.

Betesh's confession led police to 245 Yonge Street, to an apartment above Charlie's Angels Body Rub Parlor. There, on the roof of the building, wrapped in green garbage bags, detectives found the body of Emanuel Jaques. From information garnered from Betesh, as well as evidence found in the apartment, detectives realized that the three occupants of the apartment, Albert Wayne Kribs, 29, Josef Wood, 26, and Werner Greuner, 28, were on a transcontinental train headed for Vancouver. Detectives wired the Ontario Provincial Police, who intercepted the train at Sioux Lookout. The three men were picked up and returned to Toronto, to face first-degree murder charges with their pal Saul Betesh.

In February 1978, Betesh, Kribs, Wood and Gruener stood trial for the murder of Emanuel Jaques. On the opening day of the trial, Kribs pleaded guilty, and so had only to wait until the end of the trial to have sentence passed upon him.

Betesh, who had craved attention all his life, found himself in the limelight as the major figure in a meticulously reported murder trial. He listened impassively as Metro Police Sergeant Paton Weir read from the notes he took on the night Betesh confessed. Saul admitted he was the man who had offered Emanuel $35 an hour to move nonexistent photographic equipment. It was he who had lured Emanuel to the sleazy apartment above the body-rub parlour, and to his night of horror and eventual death.

For 12 hours Emanuel was held captive, continually raped and forced to perform other sex acts with the men. Their orgy at an end, the men discussed what to do with the boy. Betesh's statement reveals, "By mutual agreement, we decided to kill him." He goes on, "I tried to strangle him with a stretch cord, the kind you wrap suitcases with. I tried for two or three minutes, but I couldn't finish it." Joe Wood suggested smothering the boy with a pillow. Finally Kribs and Betesh carried Emanuel to a sink, and while Kribs held the boy's feet, Betesh held his head underwater until Emanuel was dead. Later the official cause of death was attributed to drowning.

In an attempt to illustrate that Emanuel's ordeal was not an isolated incident, the Crown paraded several young boys to the witness box. All testified that they'd been held captive by the accused men and forced into performing perverse sex acts with them. They lived, but Emanuel died.

Betesh, Wood and Kribs all admitted to their involvement in the murder. Gruener claimed that although he was in the apartment all through the orgy, he was either watching television or sleeping and did not take an active part in the murder. Evidence presented at the trial indicated that he helped dispose of the body. Gruener stated that he only learned that a murder had been committed when he was taken off the train at Sioux Lookout.

Saul Betesh was found guilty of murder in the first degree and sentenced to life imprisonment. He is eligible for parole after he has served 25 years. Kribs received a similar sentence. Josef Wood was found guilty of second-degree murder and sentenced to life imprisonment with no possibility of parole for 18 years. Gruener was found not guilty and walked out of court a free man.

The Crown appealed the Gruener acquittal, arguing that the trial judge had erred in instructing the jury. However, the appeal was dismissed. Wood's lawyers appealed the severity of their client's 18-year minimum sentence. This appeal was also dismissed.

The three convicted killers of Emanuel Jaques were shipped off to prison.

I T IS NOW MORE THAN 100 years since the murder took place. The railway station in Eastwood, Ontario, where the two educated Englishmen disembarked for their walk with death has long since disappeared. Dark, foreboding Blenheim swamp is still there, its floor oozing muck and strewn with decayed vegetation deposited over the centuries.

You can still enter Ross Anderson's General Store in the tiny hamlet of Princeton and, within two minutes, the genial owner will tell you that his grandfather arrived in Princeton in 1890, the very same year the crime was committed. He and everyone in the store are only too willing to direct you to the reminders of murder which remain after all these years.

The names Reginald Birchall and Frederick Benwell may mean little to us now, but back in 1890 they were household words. The drama that unfolded in a Woodstock, Ontario, courtroom was covered by reporters from England, Italy, France, Germany, Spain and the United States. Indeed, a direct line ran from the courtroom in Woodstock to London, England.

Although he was the son of a respected English clergyman, Reginald Birchall was a ne'er-do-well. While still a young lad he developed expensive tastes which he could ill afford. As a result, he was always in trouble. Petty theft, rubber cheques and chronic lying kept young Birchall in one jam after another. The one constant in his life was the fact that he was always in debt. Even while attending Oxford University he insisted on maintaining a string of horses, which did nothing to alleviate his already precarious financial condition. This added burden, plus the other sundry debts that accompany high living, necessitated Birchall's terminating his education. He left Oxford.

Birchall was a fine-looking man. With the air of aristocracy about him, coupled with his Oxford accent, he could charm the birds out of the trees. The bird he charmed was Londoner Florence Stevenson, whom he married. Florence's father was not enthralled with his new son-in-law, and it is believed that Birchall was less than thrilled with the financial remuneration that resulted from his marriage.

In 1888, the Birchalls arrived in Canada and settled in Woodstock. Birchall did nothing to change his lifestyle. He and his wife passed themselves off as Lord and Lady Somerset. The self-styled lord soon was well known to southern Ontario social bigwigs and, of course, his creditors. With the wolf at the door, Birchall and his wife returned to England dead broke. They stayed with Florence's father, but Reg's creditors traced him and gave him no peace. He became desperate for funds. There had to be some way for him to get his hands on some hard cash. That's when he got his great idea.

Birchall received a hot tip on a horse race, the Epsom Derby of 1890. A long shot, Sanefain was a sure thing. As Birchall saw it, all he had to do was raise enough money to place a substantial bet—but how?

He hatched a diabolical but extremely plausible scheme for the times. The colonies were thought to be the land of opportunity, where young Englishmen could seek fame and fortune. Realizing this, Birchall placed an ad in the *Daily Telegram*: Canada—University man—having farm— wishes to meet gentleman's son to live with him and learn the business with a view to partnership; must invest £500 to extend stock; board, lodging and 5% interest till partnership arranged."

Lieuenant Cololnel Frederick Benwell of Cheltenham saw the ad, and thought it presented a great opportunity for his 25-year-old son, Frederick. In due time Colonel Benwell, Frederick and Birchall met. Cololnel Benwell was impressed. He signed an agreement to pay £500, but before any money changed hands, Fred was to visit the farm in Canada. Birchall seemed satisfied with this agreement. Unknown to Fred Benwell or his father, another lad from a good family had answered Birchall's ad. Douglas Pelly, an Oxford graduate, also fell for the scheme, advancing Birchall £170, but he, too, wanted to see his investment.

On February 5, 1890, when Reginald Birchall and his wife, Florence, boarded the *Britannic* at Liverpool, they were accompanied by two young, excited Englishmen just itching to set foot in the New World. They had no idea that Reg Birchall planned to kill them both.

Once aboard the ship, Birchall went about poisoning the minds of his two companions. He set up a situation in which Pelly and Benwell became antagonistic toward one another. They quarrelled openly in front of other passengers. Birchall wanted everyone to remember the bickering. Later, if both men disappeared, the natural assumption would be that one had killed the other, with the killer taking off. No suspicion would fall on Lord Somerset.

The *Britannic* docked in the United States. The four principal players in the drama which was soon to unfold made their way to Buffalo. It was decided that Pelly and Mrs. Birchall would remain in Buffalo while Birchall and Benwell went on ahead to Ontario to inspect the farm. On

February 17, the two men set out by train for Birchall's nonexistent farm. Later the men were well remembered by fellow passengers on the train, and at the Eastwood Station near Woodstock, where they got off. They walked into Blenheim swamp.

Birchall assured his companion that the farm lay on the other side of the swamp. By walking over the frozen terrain, Benwell would get the true feel of the area. Once in the swamp, Birchall pulled out a revolver and shot his companion twice in the head. He cut away all labels from Benwell's clothing and dragged the body farther into the swamp. That same night he returned to Buffalo alone. He accounted for Benwell's absence with the not-too-convincing story that Benwell had become disenchanted with the entire adventure, pulled out of the agreement and left.

The day after Birchall's murderous excursion to Canada, he and Pelly visited the Canadian side of Niagara Falls. Pelly would later relate that on two occasions while they were viewing the falls from precarious positions, Birchall almost seemed to be preparing to make a move, as if to shove him into the churning water. Both times, strangers happened by, which apparently had the effect of changing Birchall's mind. In the light of future events, young Pelly owed his life to the chance passing of the strangers.

Back in England, Colonel Benwell received a letter from Birchall stating that young Fred was doing well on the farm. He added that he would appreciate the £500.

Meanwhile, on February 21, two brothers, George and Joseph Eldridge, were cutting wood in Blenheim swamp. They found Benwell's body. The one-in-a-million discovery, only four days after the murder, spelled doom for Birchall. News of the unidentified murder victim was in all the newspapers. Pelly read about the body found near Woodstock, the same location as Birchall's "farm." He immediately suspected that the body was that of Benwell. He confronted Birchall, who must have been stunned at the news of the body being found so soon. He decided to bluff it out.

Birchall told Doug Pelly that he was wrong, but to satisfy him, he and his wife would travel to Woodstock to view the body and identify it, if possible. This they did, and Birchall had the unnerving experience of gazing on the countenance of a man he had so recently killed and had never dreamed of ever seeing again. He identified the dead man as Frederick Benwell, but made light of their relationship, saying that Benwell had been a chance shipboard acquaintance.

The police, headed by Canada's famed detective, John Wilson Murray, were satisfied with the identification. A cigar case initialled F.C.B. had been found near the body. However, Murray was far from satisfied with our friend Birchall. The detective let his suspect run free, but had the Niagara Falls police follow his every move. In the meantime, he checked out his quarry. He found out about the letter written to Colonel Benwell dated after the murder. Then he travelled to Niagara Falls and found Doug Pelly living with the Birchalls. After Pelly told his story, both Mr. and Mrs. Birchall were arrested and charged with murder. Mrs. Birchall was released after the inquest.

In September, Birchall's trial for the murder of Frederick Benwell opened in Woodstock's town hall. In that year of 1890, ballads were sung and poems were written about Reg Birchall and his scheme to become financially secure by means of murder. While there was never any doubt of his guilt, Birchall's trial caught the imagination of the world. Foreign reporters flocked to Woodstock to hear of Oxford-educated men in the wilds of Canada, imaginary farms, hot-tip horses and murder.

It took the jury only 90 minutes to find Birchall guilty. On November 14, 1890, his face white as a ghost, dressed in evening clothes at his insistence, he walked steadily up the gallows steps. He shook hands with the hangman and plunged to eternity. Reg Birchall was buried beside a wall of the Woodstock jail.

What happened to the rest of the cast in the Birchall drama?

Fred Benwell, the colonel's son, who arrived in Canada with such high hopes, is buried in Princeton, Ontario. The inscription on his stone reads: Frederick Cornwallis Benwell, Born 15th September 1865, Murdered in the township of Blenheim February 17, 1890.

Florence Birchall returned to England and later remarried.

Douglas Pelly, the young man who came so very close to being a victim, returned to England to a hero's welcome. A torchlight parade accompanied him to his home. Forever after he was known as the man who was almost murdered.

We mustn't forget Sanefain, the horse that gave Birchall the germ of the idea from which he hatched his diabolical plot. Ironically, in 1890, Sanefain did win the Epsom Derby.

– EDWIN ALONZO BOYD –

THE RATHER CHECKERED history of crime in the United States features many famous gangs of bank robbers. Such names as Pretty Boy Floyd, Dillinger, and Bonnie and Clyde conjure up visions of daring raids, high-speed chases and big money.

Canada boasts only one bona fide gang of bank robbers—the Boyd Gang.

Edwin Alonzo Boyd was born in Toronto. His father was a retired police officer, but young Edwin had a natural inclination to wander. By the time he was 16 he had quit high school and travelled to western Canada. Although he was intelligent and presentable, he could never get a good-paying job. The menial tasks he was able to obtain bored him. In 1936, he was making his living by breaking and entering. He was caught and convicted on 21 individual charges, and received three years in prison.

For approximately 10 years, which included a stint in the army, it appears Boyd did nothing that brought him to the attention of the police.

Then, on October 16, 1951, the Dominion Bank on the corner of Toronto's Yonge Street and Lawrence Avenue was held up and robbed by two men. An alert employee spotted the men and pressed the alarm button. The robbers completed their work, stuffing $12,234 into a shopping bag. Howard Gault was caught outside the bank with the money. The other robber got away from the scene in a stolen automobile which had been parked for the purpose of escape. Within hours, a small delivery truck driving on the outskirts of the city caught the attention of the police. They forced the truck to stop. They searched the vehicle and found a fully loaded 9-mm Luger automatic pistol and a full make-up kit.

The Toronto police got their first introduction to the driver of the truck—Edwin Boyd. Subsequent investigation of Boyd's activities resulted in his being charged with several robberies. From September 9, 1949, to September 1, 1951, he was connected to six bank robberies in the Toronto area.

While in jail awaiting trial on these charges, Boyd met Leonard Jackson and William R. Jackson (not related). Both were awaiting transfer to Kingston Penitentiary after having been convicted of armed robbery.

On November 4, Boyd and the two Jacksons sawed their way through their cell doors and made a dramatic escape from jail. Leonard Jackson took off for Montreal and Boyd and Willie Jackson hid out at the home of the parents of a friend, Valent J. Lesso, who was better known by his alias of Steve Suchan. Boyd and Willie stayed in hiding until November 20, when they successfully held up the Boustead Avenue and Roncesvalles Avenue branch of the Bank of Toronto. They got away with $4,300. Ten days later, another bank was hit, the Royal Bank of Canada, in Leaside. It was relieved of $42,000.

Willie Jackson and Boyd took off for Montreal and moved in with Steve Suchan. Police subsequently picked up Willie in a restaurant. Once his identity was established, he was sent back to Toronto, and ended up in the Kingston Pen.

On January 25, 1952, the Bank of Toronto on Kingston Road in Scarborough was robbed of $10,000. Then on March 4, the Bank of Montreal on College Street had an unscheduled withdrawal of $24,496. Through witnesses it was established that Boyd was the leader of the gang.

On March 6, 1952, Sergeant of Detectives Edmund Tong and Detective Sergeant Roy Perry became suspicious of a 1951 Monarch occupied by two men. They drove alongside. Tong called out, "Pull over, boys."

The car stopped. Tong got out and walked to the suspicious vehicle. As he did so, he was shot down. Perry tried to get to the lefthand side of the car. He could hear the whine of bullets flying past. In an instinctive reaction, he thrust his arm up to protect his head, and took two slugs in the arm. Perry raised the alarm over the police radio. Tong was seriously wounded, but before he lost consciousness he told the first detective at the scene that the person who had shot him was Steve Suchan.

Suchan and Lenny Jackson got away, but police later discovered their hideout in Montreal. Suchan elected to shoot it out, and was wounded. The gun he was holding when captured was the gun that had been used to shoot Detective Tong. Lenny Jackson was located in another apartment a couple of blocks away. He too fired at the police, and was wounded during the capture.

On March 23, Sergeant of Detectives Tong died of his wounds, and the two fugitives were returned to Toronto to face murder charges.

In the meantime, the police were trying to trace Boyd through his brother, Norman. They became convinced that Boyd was hiding out in a house on Heath Street. The police rushed Boyd in the middle of the night. He was asleep in bed with his wife when taken by surprise.

Willie Jackson, who had missed some of the action because he was apprehended earlier, was brought from Kingston to Toronto due to his previous involvement in other robberies.

Now that the police had the four main members of the Boyd gang under lock and key, they continued their investigation. It included implicating other gang members who may have been in on one or two of the robberies. Also investigated and charged were relatives and friends who helped the four bandits while they were free.

Then, on September 8, 1952, with a flair for the dramatic, the four members of the Boyd Gang, using a key they'd made themselves, opened their cell doors. They sawed their way through some bars on a window and dropped themselves onto a low roof below. For the next eight days these most wanted men in the country were sighted from Newfoundland to British Columbia. Every day, newspapers featured every detail of their past lives. Across the country, radio newscasts started with "The Boyd Gang is still at large."

On September 16, the North York Police Department received a call that men were seen coming and going at an old barn north of Sheppard Avenue, east of Yonge Street The four heavily armed men were taken by surprise. The Boyd Gang was recaptured.

Leonard Jackson and Steve Suchan were tried, found guilty and hanged back to back for the murder of Sergeant of Detectives Edmund Tong.

Boyd and Willie Jackson were never directly involved in the detective's murder. Boyd received a life sentence, while Jackson received 20 years' imprisonment, in addition to the nine years he was already serving.

Whatever happened to the two surviving members of the Boyd Gang?

Willie Jackson spent 14 years in Kingston Penitentiary. He was paroled in the mid 1960s and worked as the janitor of a Toronto church. Not many people knew about his past, and those who did considered him a completely reformed individual. When he talked of days gone by, it was as if he were talking about another person. Willie left

Toronto several years ago to work in another church in Vancouver.

Boyd was paroled in 1962. He received a great deal of publicity and became hostile toward the close watch parole authorities held over him. Four months after his release he was returned to prison as a parole violator. In 1966, Boyd was paroled for the second time. This time he made it.

Somewhere in a small town in Canada, a grey-haired old man is employed as a social worker. He is a devoted member of a well-known religious organization and spends most of his time assisting the physically challenged. The parole authorities claim he is a living example of a reformed gangster. He was once Canada's most wanted fugitive—Edwin Alonzo Boyd.

– PHOEBE CAMPBELL –

THERE IS A MISTAKEN belief that, during Canada's formative years, violence was committed at high noon by louts who strolled down Main Street, six-shooters ablaze. Admittedly, there were a few isolated shoot-outs, but, never fear, many of our early settlers planned and implemented murder scenarios that would rival Agatha at her best.

Let's go back 135 years to 1863 and visit the tiny village of Thorndale, Ontario, located about 20 miles northeast of London. Phoebe McWain was the most sought-after young woman of the area. Nary an evening would pass without some young swain of the district hitching up old Dobbin and going out to court Phoebe.

Twenty-year-old Phoebe apparently had everything in

the right places. She was pretty in an apple-pie sort of way, and had a figure that enticed farmhands to lean on their pitchforks and take a second look.

As if Phoebe's physical attributes weren't enough to attract virile lads like bees to honey, her daddy was rich. He was one of the wealthiest farmers in the district, owned a prosperous lumber mill and held title to choice land north of London. Phoebe, an only child, was given pretty well everything a young girl could desire. Fact is, she was a spoiled brat. A few of her many suitors would later state that Phoebe seemed to enjoy keeping them on a string before discarding them.

One suitor, George Campbell, didn't appear to be doing any better or worse than the others. It came as something of a surprise to everyone when Phoebe announced to one and all that after two years of trying, George had succeeded in winning her hand.

There was a minor complication to be cleared up. George was engaged to marry Laura Hughes. But what the heck, the path of true love is never an easy one to follow. George jettisoned Laura and married Phoebe. The marriage went off without a hitch. Joe McWain gave his only daughter and his new son-in-law a well-stocked farm as a wedding present.

And what happened to Laura? Well, I'll tell you, that girl never did have any luck. Laura, heartbroken at losing George, never married. She turned prematurely grey and a few years after being jilted, lost her father, her only living parent. Laura was left the family home in Burford, Ontario, where she lived in relative solitude with an aunt. They say Laura never looked at another man from the moment George bid her adieu.

Six rather peaceful years passed, but one particular idio-syncrasy of Phoebe's caused some little gossip. Every three or four months she would pack a suitcase and spend a week in London alone. Tongues wagged, but Phoebe laughed off any suggestion of intrigue. She reminded nosy parkers that she used to visit London all the time before she was married.

One thing was obvious. Phoebe was a good wife and, lest we forget, a good mother. By 1871, she had two chil-dren, a daughter, 5, and a son, 1. No hint of scandal had ever been directed toward Phoebe Campbell.

One fine day in July, George Campbell confided to fellow farmer John Wiseman that a strange thing had hap-pened at his farm the previous evening when he was absent. Two big bruisers had visited his home. They forced them-selves into the house past Phoebe and proceeded to wreck the kitchen, overturning food and dishes and leaving the place in a mess. When Phoebe attempted to intervene, one of the men had slapped her face. Phoebe felt the two men must be crazy. She had never seen them before and believed they were transients.

While George was relating this story to his friend, Eddy Scanlon, a part-time worker on Wiseman's farm, volun-teered that he had seen two burly men walking toward the Campbell place the day before.

George was furious and, at the same time, puzzled. Who would want to wreck his kitchen and slap his wife? He would be prepared if the men ever showed up again.

The men did show up again the next afternoon when George was busy working at a gravel pit some miles away with John Wiseman. When George returned home, he found his wife bound and gagged on a sofa. Her head was bruised and she was mumbling incoherently. The house was a shambles. Cupboards were overturned, tables and chairs tossed about. Pictures had been torn from the walls. In a state of shock, Phoebe blurted out that the same two men had returned, demanding money. When she turned over the few dollars she had, they demanded more and proceeded to beat her and wreck the house searching for the nonexistent cash.

Then Phoebe, her deep blue eyes filled with tears, told her husband how the two men had raped her. George returned to the gravel pit and told Wiseman of the outrage. Both men were thunderstruck. They contacted Thorndale's only police officer, a man named Gardiner, who proceeded immediately to the Campbell farm. He was met by an angry throng of farmers. News of a vulnerable woman alone on a farm being violated spread through the district like wildfire. Gardiner questioned Phoebe. She informed the constable that one of the men had said that they had completed only half their job. They wouldn't get paid until they killed George.

This was no wanton attack, but a well-thought-out scheme, possibly with revenge as the motive. To rape a man's wife and then plan on killing him was an outrage. Who hated George Campbell enough to hatch such a diabolic plot?

All that night, weary men lugging lanterns scoured the countryside. Scores more joined the hunt at daybreak, but no trace of the two men was uncovered.

The following morning, at 2 a.m., the Campbells' closest neighbour, John Wiseman, was awakened by someone pounding on his door. He scrambled to the door and was amazed to find Phoebe Campbell, clad only in her nightgown, screaming hysterically while tears poured down her cheeks, mixing with the blood which smeared her face. Phoebe shrieked, "They came again! Those devils returned! Once more they forced me to submit to them. Poor George. They hacked him to bits."

Phoebe was not one to overstate the facts. Her husband had indeed been chopped to death. She explained that she had been awakened by the same two men who had raped her. They were in her bedroom. George jumped up and grappled with the two men, all the while shouting to her to bring him something with which to fight off the attackers.

Phoebe ran to the kitchen and picked up a butcher knife and an axe from a chopping block behind the house. The intruders wrested both weapons from her before she was able to give them to her husband. They then turned the knife and axe on George, hacking and slashing the helpless man until he was dead. Not content with their night's work, the two men proceeded to rape the hysterical Phoebe before leaving the house and disappearing into the dark countryside.

Rape and murder in pioneer Canada! The crimes perpetrated on the Campbells now ranked as the vilest ever committed in the young country. Informal search parties were formed. They could be seen poking into haymows, searching barns and tramping through fields. Why would anyone want to harm a husband and wife who had no apparent enemies? Constable Gardiner firmly believed that should the killers be found by one of the search parties, they would be lynched before they could be taken into custody. He decided to seek assistance.

The day after the murder, Detective John Phair arrived from London, Ontario, to head the investigation. Within half a day he had interviewed Phoebe and taken her statement of the horrendous murder and rape. He also was made well aware of the Campbells' fine reputation and the series of attacks by the two strangers, which had culminated in George Campbell's murder.

Detective Phair was convinced that the two killers would have been found had they not been receiving assistance from someone in the district. He felt that there was a villain out there who had hired the transients to rape Phoebe Campbell and kill her husband.

He was dead wrong.

Detective Phair questioned neighbours and acquaintances, trying to find a motive for the vicious murder of George Campbell. In due course he was told that before George married Phoebe, he had been engaged to Laura Hughes. When George broke the engagement to marry Phoebe, Laura had been heartbroken.

The dectective travelled to Burford to question Laura Hughes. Her aunt informed the detective that she wasn't home, but could be found at the local cemetery tending to her parents' graves.

Phair found Laura in the country graveyard. She was a tiny woman, only 33 years old, but looked much older. Laura held nothing back, and even indicated that she had expected the detective to interview her as she realized that someone or other would mention her engagement to George so many years earlier. Laura admitted that she was crushed when George broke their engagement. In fact, Laura informed the startled detective, her love had never waned. She still loved George and was devastated that he had been murdered.

Phair believed Laura and assured her that he would do everything in his power to bring the killers to justice. A wry smile crossed Laura's countenance as she told the detective, "You are never going to find them."

How could this little grey-haired spinster make such a statement when the whole countryside was out searching for the killers? the detective wondered. Laura confided, "George Campbell, the man I loved and the husband of another is slain. Two strangers are said to be the killers and the search goes on. Yet I know—call it intuition if you want—I know that a hundred years of searching will never find them. Those two men are figments of an imagination that exists only in the mind of Phoebe Campbell."

John Phair went to work. Now, with his sights aimed in a different direction, he sought a reason for Phoebe to want her husband dead. He learned of her eight-year-long habit of visiting London alone three or four times a year. He also learned that Phoebe's cousin, Charles Bisham, a 40-year-old ne'er-do-well bachelor from St. Marys, had exactly the same habit. There was definitely smoke. Phair decided to find out if there was fire.

He visited Bisham and bluntly asked, "How long have you been Phoebe Campbell's lover?" Bisham denied the connection, but when Phair, who had done his homework, informed his quarry that he had even located the hotel where the lovers met, Bisham decided to tell all. Yes, he and Phoebe had been lovers for eight years. It had started when she was only 18 years old, two years before her marriage. Her daddy had found out about the affair and attempted to break them up. Phoebe had promised never to see Bisham, but she had lied and continued the romance.

Strangely, Phoebe, who had rejected many lovers and was thought of as cold and aloof, was a positive firecracker between the sheets with Bisham. In desperation, Daddy promised Phoebe a well-stocked farm as a wedding present if she would break off with Bisham and marry George. Phoebe married George, but didn't break off with her lover.

Bisham told the detective about his love affair with the married Phoebe, but insisted that none of it had anything to do with the murder. He emphasized that John Wiseman's farmhand, Eddie Scanlon, had seen two men heading for the Campbell farm. Phair warned Bisham not to leave the area. He then checked out Bisham's activities, and found out that Bisham was at home drinking with five companions on the night of the murder. He could not be the actual killer.

Phair questioned young Scanlon. Specifically, he wanted to know why Scanlon had lied when he said that he had seen two strangers approaching the Campbell farm. Terrified, Scanlon, in awe of the well-known detective, immediately admitted to lying. He had a lot more to tell. Phoebe had instructed him to lie about seeing the two men. For the first time, Scanlon gave some hint as to the true motive for the murder.

A month earlier, he told Phair, Phoebe had confided to Scanlon that she hated life on the farm. She wanted to frighten George to such an extent that he would sell the farm and move to the city. She promised Scanlon $100 if he would help her. When Scanlon was reluctant, Phoebe promised him something more physical than money. The young farmhand only took a moment to agree.

Scanlon and Phoebe were the ones who had wrecked the kitchen that first time. Phoebe made up the story of the two transients and Scanlon had confirmed her story when he stated that he had seen the men walking toward the Campbell farm.

The second visit Scanlon made to the Campbells' home was more exciting than the first. After wrecking the house, he and Phoebe were intimate. So much for clearing up old debts. Then Phoebe had Scanlon tie her up and strike her several times to make it appear she had been attacked by the two mysterious strangers. Scanlon swore he never once thought he was inadvertently assisting Phoebe in a diabolic murder plot. He honestly believed he was helping her to convince her husband that they should sell the farm and move to the city.

Detective Phair proceeded to the Campbell farm. Phoebe wasn't at home. He was greeted by a neighbour who was taking care of the Campbell children while their mother was attending to some business in London. While waiting for Phoebe, the neighbour slaughtered a chicken in the time-honoured way—by cutting the animal's head off with an axe. The Campbell's five-year-old daughter, witnessing the event, screamed, "That's what Momma did to Poppa."

On April 1, 1872, Phoebe Campbell stood trial in London, Ontario, for the murder of her husband. She claimed to be innocent throughout, first attempting to implicate Charles Bisham and then Eddie Scanlon.

Scanlon came under grave suspicion and stood trial for Campbell's murder. He was found not guilty.

Phoebe Campbell was found guilty and sentenced to death. She maintained her innocence until the night before her execution. With all hope gone, she confessed. She had planned to sell the farm after George's death, move to the city and, after a decent period of time, marry Charles Bisham. She admitted both Bisham and Scanlon knew nothing of her intention to kill her husband.

Phoebe woke up on that fateful night, fetched the axe

from an outside shed and attacked her sleeping husband. The first blow stunned George. He rose out of bed, only to be cut down by his wife. The Campbells' five-year-old daughter was awakened by the din and witnessed the crime. She was sworn to secrecy and told what to say if she was asked. The little girl had blurted out her secret when she saw the blood-smeared axe in the farmyard after the neighbour killed the chicken.

Phoebe Campbell was hanged on June 20, 1872, in London, Ontario.

– ROBERT RAE COOK –

WAS ROBERT RAE COOK guilty of murder? That was the burning question put before the jury in 1960 when he stood trial with his life in the balance.

Bobby was born in Hanna, Alberta, on July 15, 1937. When he was only nine years old, his mother died while undergoing minor surgery. Within two years, his father married schoolteacher Daisy Gaspar and the family moved to Stettler, a small town about 200 kilometres southeast of Edmonton.

In the following 10 years, Daisy Cook gave birth to five children. Who knows what impact this rapid expansion of the family had on Bobby? We do know that, at the age of 13, he stole a car. It was a criminal act he was to repeat time and time again. A year later, he stole another vehicle and ended up in the Bowden Correctional Centre. Bobby continued his career as a car thief, as well as an inept break-and-enter artist. In all, between the ages of 13 and 21, he was convicted 19 times.

In 1959, Queen Elizabeth visited Canada. Bobby Cook was one of the nonviolent offenders who received amnesty in honour of her visit. On June 23, he and other released prisoners drank the day away in Saskatoon. Next day, he stole a car and drove to Bowden to retrieve $4,300 he had buried before his incarceration.

Now well-fixed for cash, Bobby made his way to Edmonton, where once again he spent freely, buying drinks for several ex-cons. On Thursday, June 25, according to Bobby, he got a lift to Stettler, met his father and drank some beer with him. During their father-son chat, Bobby learned that his mechanic father was planning to purchase a garage in British Columbia. Bobby later claimed that he turned over about $4,000 to his father. He planned to move to B.C. with his family. His father urged him to relocate in an attempt to straighten out his life. Bobby agreed.

Rae Cook gave his son the family station wagon, with instructions to trade it in on a new car. Again, according to Bobby, his father gave him his driver's licence, insurance policy and registration.

Father and son parted. Later that night, around 9:30 p.m., Bobby entered the Cook residence. He gave his father his prison-issued blue suit. An hour later, at 10:30 p.m., he left Stettler for Edmonton.

At 1 a.m., Bobby ran into ex-con Sonny Wilson in Edmonton. Together they broke into a dry-cleaning establishment, absconding with the paltry sum of $30. Bobby slept until 9 a.m., when he showed up at Hood Motors, where he traded the station wagon for a 1959 white Chev Impala convertible. He used his father's credentials to purchase the vehicle and made up a history of steady employment. The salesman accepted Bobby at face value, but later that same day, an official at the garage recognized the fraudulent transaction and called the police.

Bobby took a spin in the convertible. He drove to Camrose, then on to Whitecourt and back to Camrose. On Saturday, June 27, he was given a ticket for having open liquor in his car and sent on his way. Bobby claims he then drove to Stettler, but found that his parents had left. He assumed they had started off for B.C. Bobby noticed two suitcases and a metal box containing the family's personal documents. He threw them in the car with the intention of taking them to British Columbia.

Not long after leaving his home that Saturday evening, Bobby was stopped by RCMP Constable Braden. He was told to report to the local RCMP detachment. Bobby proceeded to the detachment office, where Sergeant Thomas Roach advised him that he had used his father's ID to fraudulently purchase the new convertible. Bobby admitted using the ID, but claimed it was with his father's permission. Bobby went on to give an account of his movements, much as I have related here. He never deviated from his story in any detail in the months to follow.

Sergeant Roach visited the Cook residence, but found no one at home. The convertible was searched. Police found the suitcases and metal box. Inside the suitcases were the family's nightclothes. The box contained Mr. Cook's bank book, the children's birth certificates and a marriage licence. Sergeant Roach visited the Cooks' house for the second time. The front door was unlocked. Roach went inside, using a flashlight, and found nothing amiss.

The next day, Sunday, the RCMP visited the Cook residence for the third time. In an attached garage, under floorboards that covered a grease pit, they found the bodies of the entire Cook family.

Rae Cook's body was riddled with bullets. His wife, Daisy, lay beside him. A shotgun blast had blown away half her face. Underneath their bodies lay those of the children: Gerald, 9, Patrick, 8, Christopher, 6, Cathy, 4, and Linda Mae, 3. Their heads had been beaten with the stock of a single-barrel shotgun. Someone had washed blood off the walls inside the house, but traces of the blood were still discernible. Inside the master bedroom, police found Bobby's prison-issued blue suit under a mattress. It was blood-stained.

Bobby had a ready answer for all questions put to him. He had given his father the suit to make the trip to British Columbia. He and his dad were the same size, Bobby said, and it seemed the right thing to do. He had come back to Stettler to wait for his parents' call, telling him where to meet them.

Bobby was charged with the murder of his father and lodged in the Ponoka Mental Institution. He asked permission to attend his family's funeral. When permission was denied, he smashed through a wire-mesh window and escaped. Four days later, a bedraggled, half-starved Bobby Cook was apprehended hiding in a barn not far from Stettler.

Meanwhile, the investigation into the mass murder focused solely on Bobby Cook. Medical examination of the bodies indicated that the murders had taken place at least 24 hours before they were found, but not more than 72 hours. This time frame proved to be ticklish. It put the time of the murders between 11 a.m. on Thursday, June 25, and 11 a.m. on Saturday morning, June 27. During much of this time span, Bobby could prove he was nowhere near Stettler.

Police believed that the murders took place sometime between 9:30 p.m. on Thursday, June 25, and 5 a.m. on Friday, June 26. For Bobby to have committed the crimes at any other time would have been virtually impossible. Reliable witnesses placed him far away from the murder scene.

Unsavoury witnesses, such as admitted thief Sonny Wilson, placed Bobby in Edmonton at 1 a.m., Friday. If these witnesses were to be believed, Bobby would have had to have left Stettler, a two-and-a-half-hour drive, at 10:30 p.m. Thursday, leaving him less than an hour to shoot two adults, bludgeon five children to death, carry bodies to the garage grease pit, replace floorboards, wash bloodstains off walls and get out of town.

The $4,000 Bobby claimed to have given his father was never found. Police believed it never existed. However, several prison inmates were well aware that Bobby had a cache of more than $4,000 buried somewhere on the outside.

Did Bobby Cook, a 21-year-old petty criminal who had never committed a violent act in his life, systematically slaughter his entire family? Is it possible that after Bobby left that Thursday night, someone else committed those murders for the $4,000 in Rae Cook's possession?

In November 1959, Bobby's murder trial opened at Red Deer. It took 10 days to present, but the jury took only an hour and a half to bring in a guilty verdict. Bobby was sentenced to hang. His lawyers appealed the conviction and won a new trial. The results were the same. This time the jury took only 25 minutes to bring in their guilty verdict.

On Monday, November 14, 1960, Robert Rae Cook was hanged at the Fort Saskatchewan Correctional Institute.

— MICHAEL CROWLEY —

THE DAY I DROVE TO the portable emergency command post of the McMaster University campus, Staff Sergeant John Reid of the Hamilton-Wentworth Regional Police was a harassed man, shouting directions, answering phones and deploying officers.

It was a few days before Christmas of 1983. Dr. Edith Wightman had been murdered in her Chester New Hall office on campus. The crime was unusual in many ways. Dr. Wightman had no known enemies, nor was she sexually attacked. Who would murder a university professor in broad daylight in her office?

Later, a much more relaxed Sergeant Reid recalled every detail of his most intriguing murder investigation. "There is no doubt about it, it was my most interesting investigation in 24 years as a police officer. There were many reasons: the status of the victim, the international aspects of the case and the wide publicity given to the investigation. Besides, initially there was a real possibility that the crime had been committed by a student or a colleague."

The call came in on December 17, 1983. A murder had been committed on the McMaster campus. Sergeant Mike Driscoll and Sergeant John Reid would become partners in heading the investigative team attempting to track down the killer. It would take them 24 days.

A security officer had opened Dr. Wightman's fourth-floor office. It was he who had called police. Edith Wightman was found face down on the office floor. Her hands were handcuffed behind her back, her eyes and lips taped shut. One of the professor's boots had been removed and her slacks had been pulled down.

All around the campus, there were signs of the impending holiday season. The city of Hamilton was bedecked in green and red for Christmas. Around McMaster, young people were dashing about, preparing to travel home for Christmas break. It was the time and place of fellowship and good cheer. Inside Edith Wightman's office it was the time and place of death.

Who was the professor whose life was so ignominiously snuffed out while she was working in her office? Edith Wightman was born in Edinburgh, Scotland. Early on, she showed extreme promise as an intellectual and as a musician. She became a member of the National Youth Orchestra of Great Britain, playing the cello. Later, she attended St. Andrews University, where she developed an interest in archaeology and ancient history. Edith graduated from St. Andrews with the highest of honours and enrolled in postgraduate studies at Oxford University. She received a diploma in archaeology and a Ph.D. in Roman history.

In 1969, at the age of 31, Edith obtained the position of assistant professor in McMaster's history department. She quickly fit into university life. Edith Wightman was no shrinking violet. She had opinions and expressed them at university functions. Those who knew her recognized and respected her brilliance. During her first few years at the university, she wrote the book *Roman Trier and Treveri*.

It was somewhat of a shock to Edith's acquaintances when she dated Gregoire Brown. Edith should have known better. Brown, a native of New Zealand, was an unstable, erratic musician, who immigrated to Hamilton to enroll in McMaster's music program. His instrument was the cello. Eventually, he played with the McMaster Symphony Orchestra, where he met Edith Wightman. Ninety days after they met, Gregoire moved in with Edith.

In one fell swoop, Gregoire Brown had a home, a car, enough money to indulge his passion for antiques and, at the same time, an attentive, intelligent companion. Edith appeared to be in love. She was 36, Gregoire 23, when they married.

It didn't take long for cracks of disharmony to appear in the relationship. Gregoire's well-known temper tantrums became more frequent. Perhaps in his eyes, his mediocre career paled by comparison with that of his brilliant wife. Edith's book was now acclaimed internationally. She was a bona fide rising star on the academic horizon, while Gregoire's musical career sputtered and fizzled.

To alleviate the situation, Gregoire suggested he continue his studies in Europe. Surprisingly, Edith agreed to finance the venture. Off Gregoire went to London, England, where he soon took a homosexual lover. Two years later, Edith filed for divorce.

Another man, far more in keeping with Edith's intellectual ability and social status, was to enter her life. Archaeologist John Hayes, associated with the Royal Ontario Museum, became Edith's good friend and co-worker on several projects connected with the Roman Empire.

It was John Hayes who had an appointment with Edith on the day she was killed. He had just arrived from

Toronto. It was 11 a.m. He tried the door to Edith's office and then knocked without getting a response. It wasn't like Edith not to keep an appointment. A few hours later, he tried phoning. Still no response. Finally, around 3 p.m. he called the university security office. The guard opened the door, and so began the most sensational murder case in Hamilton since pieces of John Dick's body were found scattered over Hamilton Mountain in 1946.

Sergeants Reid and Driscoll and their team of investigators had little difficulty tracing the last known actions of the victim. After she'd completed normal Saturday morning activities, Edith went to her office a little after 10:30 a.m. John Hayes pounded on her door around 11 a.m. In that short space of time, someone had entered Edith's office, placed handcuffs on her wrists, taped her eyes and mouth shut, removed one of her boots and pulled down her slacks.

While Edith Wightman shopped and made her way to her office in anticipation of John Hayes's visit, another individual was preparing for his activities that Saturday.

Michael Crowley was a quiet, 27-year-old chemical technician employed at Welmet Industries in Welland, Ontario. Although a bit of a loner, Crowley, a big man standing over six feet and weighing 230 pounds, was well liked by fellow employees. What his colleagues didn't know was that Michael Crowley was a transvestite. He had a particular penchant for university campuses and had often roamed the grounds of Brock University in nearby St. Catharines. On this Saturday, he would visit McMaster University in Hamilton.

Crowley left his Welland apartment and headed for Hamilton in his brown van. En route he stopped, crawled into the back of the van and began his weird transformation from husky man to grotesque woman, as he had done so many times before.

Crowley disrobed. He tugged on his pantyhose, put on a blouse and skirt. Boots and a winter overcoat completed the clothing, but not the illusion. The dark beard had to be covered. Out came the make-up kit. Blush was carefully applied. A touch of eyeshadow and lipstick and the job was done. In the strange world of Michael Crowley, he was now a woman. To those who observed him, he was a large caricature of something either to be laughed at or pitied.

Michael Crowley was prepared. He carried with him the paraphernalia of robbery, if not murder. His equipment that day included handcuffs, tape and a chloroform-soaked rag in a bottle. Crowley parked his van and walked to Chester New Hall. He walked to the top floor. Two floors below, Edith Wightman, unaware of the terror stalking the halls above, worked at her desk. Crowley found every office door on the top floor locked. Disappointed, he walked downstairs to the fourth floor. He saw only one person, Edith Wightman, sitting at her desk with her back to him.

Silently, he approached the unsuspecting woman. Another step and he could reach out and touch her. Suddenly, Edith turned and recoiled at the sight facing her. According to Crowley, she said, "What do you want?" before he was on her cramming the chloroform rag into her mouth. In moments, Edith was unconscious. Crowley locked the office door from inside. He handcuffed Edith's wrists and applied tape to her eyes and mouth.

Crowley pulled down his victim's slacks, but her boots made the task difficult. He decided to remove the boots.

He managed to wrench one boot free, but then the unexpected happened. There was a knock on the door.

Just like infamous English mass murderer Reginald Christie, Michael Crowley was confronted with the fearful possibility of being discovered in the very act of murder. Crowley, couching over the still form of Edith Wightman, didn't move a muscle. Another knock, louder. Then nothing. On the other side of the door, John Hayes thought to himself that it wasn't like Edith not to keep an appointment. No use to keep knocking. He walked away.

Whatever thoughts may have been in Michael Crowley's mind before the knock on the door were now gone. Frantically, he rummaged through Edith's purse. He pulled out a driver's licence and credit cards, opened the office door and left Chester New Hall without being seen.

The strange-looking man dressed as a woman went shopping. Using Wightman's stolen credit cards, he made purchases at a Canadian Tire store and a Towers store. In St. Catharines he stopped at the Penn Centre, where he picked up tools at a Canadian Tire store and a TV converter at Robinsons. At the latter store, he had an anxious moment. He was asked to give a home phone number. Crowley had to think fast. He blurted out a number. Later, it was discovered that the first three digits corresponded with his phone number in Welland. No one bothered to check if the signatures written by the strange-looking woman were similar to the ones on the credit cards. In fact, there was no similarity whatsoever.

Michael Crowley made his way to his Welland apartment. That Monday, he reported to work at the Welmet Industries plant as usual. There was one great difference, though. Michael Crowley read in the newspaper that

Edith Wightman was dead. Police were searching for her murderer.

Sergeants Reid and Driscoll believed that someone who knew Wightman might be the killer, maybe a disgruntled student or a shunned lover. However, as time passed, they homed in on the theory that the murder was the result of a robbery gone awry. They decided that it was unusual for Professor Wightman not to have a driver's licence or credit cards in her purse.

The day after the Wightman murder, Reid found himself, together with Sergeant Rae Greenwood, meticulously sifting through every item in the Wightman home. They found the first solid clues, which were to assist in leading them to the killer—credit card receipts, but no cards.

These clues reinforced the robbery theory. The killer had stolen Wightman's credit cards. A small army of policemen was dispatched to stores in an effort to find out if the killer had used the stolen cards. They struck pay dirt. Cashiers who had handled Crowley's transactions remembered the strange looking man disguised as a woman. They gave descriptions to police, enabling the authorities to make a composite drawing of the suspect.

Lending credence to the suspicion that the culprit was a transvestite, police immediately received reports that a transvestite had often been seen roaming the grounds of the McMaster campus.

At this stage in the investigation, Reid felt that an arrest might be imminent. "We had a lot to go on, although it was a huge puzzle that had to be brought together. We believed the killer was a transvestite. We had a sample of his handwriting. We had his description. We knew he had chloroformed Dr. Wightman and that she had choked to

death on the rag stuffed in her mouth. We had a fingerprint believed to be the killer's, which we had lifted off a
file cabinet in Professor Wightman's office. We even
thought he might be from Welland, because he gave the
Welland exchange when (a clerk) asked for his phone
number. What we didn't know was the identity of the man
we sought."

Transvestites were questioned throughout the Niagara
Peninsula. Samples of their handwriting were sent to the
Toronto Centre for Forensic Sciences to be compared with
that of the suspected killer. All came back negative. Reid
and Driscoll worked around the clock. New Year's came
and went. The killer remained at large.

Following reports that a transvestite had been seen on
the Brock University campus, police set up an investigative
office at the university. Sergeants Grant Scobie and David
McCulloch of the St. Catharines office felt that publicity
might help. It was now 20 days since Dr. Wightman's
murder. They asked the editor of the Welland–Port
Colbourne *Tribune* to review the murder in the newspaper,
appealing to the public for information.

Sure enough, a citizen reported knowing a transvestite
who resembled the composite drawing. This call in itself
was not unusual, but when the caller added that this particular transvestite had been seen carrying handcuffs, the
detectives believed they had their man. His name was
Michael Crowley.

Crowley was picked up leaving work. His handwriting
was matched against that of the man who had used Dr.
Wightman's credit cards. Even to the inexperienced eye,
the writing was identical. The hunt was over. A search of
Crowley's apartment yielded leather harnesses, whips, rope

and handcuffs. He also had stacks of pornographic magazines, most featuring bondage.

When taken into custody, Crowley implored the officers to believe him. "It was an accident!" he sobbed, over and over. He handed over a capsule containing potassium cyanide to Sergeant McCulloch. Crowley had planned to commit suicide rather than be taken into custody, but had changed his mind.

Michael Crowley wrote out a full confession in longhand, detailing the attack on Dr. Wightman. He pleaded guilty to first-degree murder and was sentenced to 25 years with no possibility of parole for 15 years.

What was the killer's motive when he stalked the offices of Chester New Hall? Because Dr. Wightman's boot was removed and her slacks pulled down, many believed that the motive was sexual. Others believed that the prime motive was robbery. Did Crowley intend to kill his victim, or was it all an accident as he maintained?

It matters little. The Criminal Code of Canada is clear. When death is caused during an act of criminal confinement, the charge is first-degree murder.

Michael Crowley is presently serving his sentence at Kingston Penitentiary. Staff Sergeants Reid and Driscoll have long since moved on to other cases. Future generations of McMaster students will walk past Chester New Hall oblivious to the terrible crime that took place there, when a brilliant professor turned in her chair and exclaimed in fear, "What do you want?"

– BRUCE CURTIS –

ANY PARENT WOULD BE proud of a well-behaved, studious son like Bruce Curtis. Bruce attended prestigious King's College School in Windsor, Nova Scotia, the oldest private school in Canada. He was a member of the debating team and led his class academically in his graduating year. In that summer of 1982, Bruce, 18, had been accepted by Dalhousie University in Halifax, where he planned to study astrophysics.

He had no way of knowing that soon he would be incarcerated in the Bordentown Youth Correctional Institution in New Jersey, serving a 20-year sentence for manslaughter. Something went wrong, drastically wrong.

During that summer, Bruce received several long-distance phone calls from a school chum, Scott Franz. Scott had graduated with Bruce and was planning to attend Mount Allison University in New Brunswick. In the meantime, he invited Bruce to visit him at his home in the village of Loch Arbor, New Jersey. Scott painted an extremely attractive picture of life in Loch Arbor, alluding to cars, servants and a large home overlooking the ocean.

Bruce succumbed to Scott's verbal picture of a fantastic visit. It would be Bruce's first trip out of Nova Scotia by himself. His parents consented to the visit. The boy deserved some kind of break before embarking on his university career. Bruce left his family's 750-acre property in Mount Hanley, near Middleton, Nova Scotia, for New Jersey.

From the moment Bruce's plane landed at Newark Airport on June 29, everything went wrong. The plane was late. Scott's stepfather, Alfred Podgis, had come to pick him up and was irritable. He was an avid collector of baseball cards and evidently had missed an appointment with a dealer in order to meet the plane.

The Podgis home at 401 Euclid Avenue was far from a happy one. Bruce, who had been raised by loving, caring parents, found himself in the midst of intense family arguments between stepfather and son. Al Podgis and his wife, Rosemary, also argued incessantly. Police had been called to the Podgis home more than 100 times in the previous 14 years.

On the evening of July 3, Al Podgis was in such a state the boys decided to stay outdoors. The two friends spent some time that night walking to pass the time. When they returned, Al and Rosemary Podgis were still up and about, arguing. The boys ducked under the front porch and listened to the argument. Finally, Al went to bed. Mrs. Podgis came outside and suggested that the boys sleep on couches in the living room.

According to Scott, the next morning, Independence Day, he ventured upstairs to fetch Bruce's traveller's cheques and suitcase. He fled the house when his stepfather fired at him. The two boys spent the day away from 401 Euclid Avenue, but still had the practical problem of getting their belongings out of the house. Bruce had only purchased a one-way ticket to New Jersey. He and Scott had planned to drive back to Nova Scotia together.

That evening, the two boys watched fireworks before returning to Euclid Avenue. Scott knew his stepfather had hidden firearms in the family's International Harvester Scout van. He took out two Winchester 30-30s and entered the house. The boys went to sleep on the downstairs couch with the weapons at their side.

Early on Monday morning, shots reverberated throughout the house and Al lay dead in an upstairs bedroom. His son admits shooting him. According to Scott, he killed his stepfather as Al was reaching for a .22 rifle.

Downstairs, Mrs. Podgis was preparing French toast for breakfast. Startled at the shots, Bruce grabbed the 30-30. At the same time, Mrs. Podgis heard the shots and dashed around the corner, colliding with Bruce. The gun went off and Rosemary Podgis lay dead at Bruce's feet. In the exact words quoted in Bruce's original statement to police, "I don't know whether when I jumped back, my hand moved too and I pulled the trigger or if it just went off. It was just a blur."

Scott ran downstairs and was confronted with the sight of his mother's body. He could only ask, "What happened?" Bruce replied, "I shot your mother."

The two boys cleaned the house of blood. They lifted the bodies of Al and Rosemary Podgis into the family van and made their way to Pennsylvania's Ravenburg State Park, where they unceremoniously dumped the bodies over an embankment. When they drove back to Loch Arbor, they observed police cars on Euclid Avenue and decided to keep going.

The two boys disposed of the rifles down a storm drain, and threw their ammunition out of the van window as the vehicle sped down the highway to Atlantic City. They stayed overnight at Harrahs, the famous gambling casino. Next day, they arrived in Washington, where they did some sightseeing. Then they moved on to Knoxville, Tennessee. Scott had some vague notion that his sister, Rosie, who lived in Texas, would be sympathetic to their predicament.

On Tuesday evening two men walking along a path in

Ravenburg State Park found the bodies at the base of the embankment. Al Podgis's nude body had been stuffed into a trunk. Rosemary Podgis's body was wrapped in a sleeping bag.

Meanwhile, back on Euclid Avenue, the Podgises' married daughter, Barbara Czacherski, couldn't locate her parents. She called police, who investigated the now-deserted home. When they found bloodstained bedclothes and weapons, they assumed that murder had taken place in the home. Their suspicions were confirmed with the discovery of the two bodies and the information that Scott, Bruce and the Scout van were missing. Scott and Bruce were picked up in Texas and returned to New Jersey.

In the months between apprehension and trial, several events took place that played havoc with Bruce Curtis's story of accidentally shooting Rosemary Podgis.

On the advice of his attorney, Scott was persuaded to plead guilty to the murder of his stepfather. It was pointed out to him that the physical evidence and expert testimony indicated that his father was not killed from across the room while sitting up reaching for a weapon, but was killed at close range while lying on his back with his head on the pillow.

Scott agreed to plead guilty and testify against Bruce in return for a reduced sentence. Gradually, he added small but pertinent changes to his story. He claimed it was Bruce who wanted to bring weapons into the house. It was Bruce who wouldn't let him call police after the shootings. It was Bruce who suggested getting rid of the bodies.

On March 14, 1983, Bruce Curtis stood trial for the murder of Rosemary Podgis in Monmouth County Courthouse in Freehold, New Jersey. Scott Franz was the chief witness for the prosecution. He admitted that there was extreme animosity between himself and his stepfather, but insinuated that Bruce enjoyed the murders. According to Scott, Bruce smiled and joked as he cleaned up the blood after the killings. Bruce cleaned off the weapons before discarding them.

After more than 11 hours of deliberation, the New Jersey jury found Bruce Curtis not guilty of murder but guilty of aggravated manslaughter.

Scott Franz pleaded guilty to the murder of his stepfather and was given the minimum sentence of 20 years' imprisonment with eligibility for parole in 10 years. He was placed in a medium-security institution, but because of disciplinary problems has been transferred to Rahway Prison, in New Jersey, one of the toughest in the United States, where he is presently serving his sentence.

A month after his trial, Bruce Curtis was sentenced to 20 years' imprisonment with eligibility for parole in 10 years. This is the maximum sentence for aggravated manslaughter.

The relative sentences of the two boys outraged many who had followed the case. Put simply, one boy who admitted shooting his stepfather in the head while the man lay in bed, received exactly the same sentence as the boy who professed that he had killed accidentally and was found guilty of a far less serious crime.

For five years the Curtis family exhausted every legal avenue open to them to gain some semblance of justice for their son. Governor Thomas Kean of New Jersey rejected Bruce's plea for clemency, after a year's consideration.

The Curtis family then concentrated on efforts to have Bruce serve his time in a Canadian institution. It was a frustrating process. Although the United States ratified an agreement in 1978 whereby prisoners may be transferred to Canada, each state had the choice of ratifying the agreement individually. New Jersey took eight years to ratify this agreement.

Eventually Bruce Curtis was transferred to a Canadian prison. He has since been paroled.

– FATHER ADELARD DELORME –

OVER THE YEARS, MONTREAL has been the scene of many notorious murders. One of the most sensational centred on the Father Adelard Delorme murder case. This particular crime has the dubious distinction of being Montreal's, and quite possibly Canada's, most sensational murder.

It happened long ago, but is still recalled by old-timers who remember the headlines and speculation that kept the good citizens of La Belle Province talking about little else for almost three years. You see, the principal character, and the man who eventually stood trial for murder, not once, but three times, was a Roman Catholic priest. To my knowledge, Father Adelard Delorme is the only priest who has ever stood trial for murder in Canada.

Early on Saturday morning, January 7, 1922, James Higginbotham and Elric Larin trudged through the crisp Montreal snow toward a shack on the corner of Coolbrook and Snowdon Streets. Both men worked for the city, and the shack contained their tools. As they walked, they caught sight of the crumpled form of a man lying in the snow in a nearby field. There was no doubt that he was dead. The man's overcoat was saturated with blood, as was the quilt-like material wrapped around his head.

The two city employees summoned the police, who were at the scene in a matter of minutes. Investigating officers noted that the snow under the body had not melted, indicating that the victim was probably dead before he was placed where he had been found. Upon searching the body, the officers discovered letters addressed to Raoul Delorme, 190 St. Hubert Street, Montreal.

The body was removed to the city morgue. The quilt-like material was unwrapped from the corpse's head, revealing six bullet wounds. The victim's hands were securely tied together with cord. There were no bullet holes in his overcoat.

When officers called at 190 St. Hubert Street, they encountered a Roman Catholic priest, Father Adelard Delorme. Police accompanied him to the morgue to view the body. Father Delorme tearfully and regretfully identified the victim as his half-brother Raoul.

Father Delorme explained that his half-brother was a commerce student at the University of Ottawa, and was home on vacation. The priest became enraged when he was informed that someone had bound his brother's hands and poured six bullets into his head at close range. Then the murderer must have pinned the overcoat over the man's head and transported the body to the field where it was found. What cold-blooded madman would do such a thing to a 24-year-old student?

On Monday, January 9, a coroner's inquest was conducted into the death of Raoul Delorme. Father Delorme was the principal witness. He explained his family's history.

Adelard Delorme's father had been a wealthy contractor

who died leaving an estate of over $160,000. The estate, which consisted mainly of several properties located in Montreal's east end, was left to six relatives. The largest portion by far had been left to Raoul, who received an annual income in excess of $10,000 from the properties.

Father Delorme administered his late father's estate, and took care of Raoul's income as well. In fact, Raoul was attending the University of Ottawa solely to become equipped in the ways of finance in order to handle his own affairs upon graduation.

At the inquest, some curiosity was expressed as to why Father Delorme did not have a regular parish. He readily disclosed the details. Delorme was born in Ste. Anne des Plaines, Quebec. After attending the village school, he entered Ste. Therese College, and then studied theology at Montreal's Grand Seminary on Sherbrooke Street. At the time of the murder, he was 37 years old, and had been ordained for some years.

Father Delorme had been appointed vicar of the Ste. Anne des Plaines Church in 1915, and later was transferred, as vicar, to the church at Tetreaultville, near Montreal. This latter move had been made at his own request, as his father's death and his position as sole executor of the estate made it imperative that he be located near Montreal.

Father Delorme explained that after a year he found he could not properly attend to the affairs of the parish as well as his father's estate. He requested a special dispensation to change positions once more. Permission was granted, and he became chaplain of L'Assistance Publique. This enabled him to administer his father's estate.

On the evening of January 6, Raoul phoned his brother

from downtown Montreal. He informed Father Delorme that he was staying downtown for supper, and planned on going to the theatre with friends. Raoul also mentioned that if he didn't return by 11:30 he would not be coming home that night. When, and if, he made that phone call, Raoul didn't realize that he only had hours to live.

Father Delorme stated that later that night he received several strange phone calls, with no one at the other end of the line. Once he thought he heard loud moaning. He claimed to have reported the incident to the phone company. Later, phone company officials stated that they had no record of his complaint.

Two days into the inquest, with detectives working around the clock checking out every possible clue, Father Delorme turned over a .25-calibre Bayard automatic revolver. He stated that he kept it in his car for protection. Normally he used his late father's gun but, by coincidence, a few days before the murder he had traded in his old weapon for his present one. Raoul had been shot with a .25-calibre weapon.

On Wednesday, January 11, funeral services for Raoul Delorme were conducted at St. James Church in downtown Montreal. Father Delorme celebrated the requiem mass.

The coroner's inquest was delayed several times in order to examine new evidence which was constantly being uncovered by the police. In the meantime, Father Delorme issued statements which were conscientiously reported in the daily press.

A few days after the funeral, Father Delorme announced that he was posting a $10,000 reward for the arrest and conviction of his half-brother's murderer. He duly deposited this amount in the Bank of Hochelaga.

Father Delorme was full of announcements. He also stated that once the murderer was convicted, he should be publicly executed at a local outdoor skating rink. Such proclamations were not becoming to a man of the cloth.

When it was learned that Father Delorme was the main beneficiary of Raoul's will, suspicion openly fell upon the priest. It seemed impossible, but as the days wore on, more and more circumstantial evidence pointed to Father Delorme as a murderer. It couldn't be. Nothing like this had ever happened in Montreal. Saving souls, yes. Saving lives, yes. But a priest a murderer! There had to be some other explanation.

Father Delorme kept spewing quotable quotes. He likened himself to his saviour, and compared the slanderous remarks made about him to those hurled at Jesus Christ during his last days on earth.

At precisely 7 p.m. on February 14, 1922, Father Delorme was arrested and charged with the murder of his half-brother, Raoul Delorme.

The thought of a Roman Catholic priest standing trial for murder was so against the grain of the average Quebecker in 1922 that many thought it was all an English plot to undermine the Church.

Those who remember the murder recall the unbelievable aspects of the case. The fact that the victim was bound and shot six times almost precluded the possibility that a priest had been the perpetrator of such a horrendous act. Rumours of every kind spread throughout Montreal. Everyone had a pet theory. Newspaper circulation soared as the news spread through the province of Quebec and across the land. Word of a priest being tried for murder was reported in the press of Europe and even Asia.

Father Delorme's legal counsel pleaded that his client was insane, and therefore unfit to stand trial. For a while it appeared that this tactic would be successful, for on June 30 a special jury did find Father Delorme insane. He was committed to the Beauport Asylum. Almost a year later, in May 1923, Father Delorme was released from the asylum on the grounds that he was now sane. The month following his release he was committed to trial for the murder of his brother. The trial began on June 20, 1923.

A tremendous amount of circumstantial evidence was presented in an effort to prove the priest guilty of murder. Motive was established when Monsignor Louis Rhéaume of Ottawa took the witness stand. He told of a day in February 1921, when Raoul was to undergo a minor operation in Ottawa. On that occasion, Father Delorme and Raoul composed Raoul's will in longhand in the hospital. The Monsignor had signed it as a witness. Under the terms of the will, Father Delorme was to receive the bulk of his half-brother's estate upon Raoul's death.

To add fuel to the fire, it was established that only seven days before the murder a $25,000 insurance policy had been issued on Raoul's life. Father Delorme was the sole beneficiary and had paid the first premium.

Because there were no bullet holes in the victim's overcoat, it had been theorized that Raoul had been shot indoors. Dr. Wilfred Derome, who performed the autopsy, lent credence to this theory when he testified that the piece of quilt wrapped around the dead man's head corresponded to quilting found in Father Delorme's home. Dr. Derome, who achieved star status during the trial, also testified that he had found bloodstains in the priest's car. Father Delorme claimed these stains were the result of the scratches to his knuckles received when he had changed a flat tire.

A gunsmith, Cesar Haynes, testified that he had sold Father Delorme a .25-calibre revolver only 10 days before the murder. Upon comparing a bullet extracted from Raoul's head with one fired from the priest's gun, the gunsmith was willing to state that both bullets had most probably come from the same gun.

Raoul's rubbers and overshoes were found at home. The Crown believed that he had been killed in the cellar of Father Delorme's home. They claimed it was quite possible that Father Delorme had planned to kill his brother with one shot at close range. Upon testing, it was discovered that the priest's revolver was constructed in such a way that the sight was off by one and three-quarter inches. The initial bullet had travelled through the side of Raoul's face, rather than directly into his temple. They further claimed that once Father Delorme wounded his brother, he had no choice but to keep shooting.

Every minute of the night of the murder came under close scrutiny. The house at 190 St. Hubert was home to Father Delorme, his three sisters, Lily, Rosa and Florence, and, of course, Raoul, home from Ottawa on vacation.

All the occupants gave evidence that Raoul left the house after lunch, stating that he might not be back for supper. Lily and Florence had supper with Father Delorme. All three sisters left the house to attend the theatre about eight o'clock that evening, and didn't return until 11:20 p.m.

At eight o'clock Father Delorme went outdoors, where he was observed by several witnesses. He returned at 9:30 p.m. If Raoul was killed at home, Father Delorme was the only one there, and could have committed the crime between 9:30 p.m. and 11:30 p.m., when his sisters returned home. Neighbours swore they heard Father Delorme's car at about eleven o'clock that night in the lane beside his garage. They heard the garage door open and close, but were unable to state if he was coming in or going out.

The victim's pocket watch had been torn from his body. A piece of watch chain was found hanging from Raoul's pocket. Strangely, the watch itself was anonymously sent by mail to Chief of Provincial Detectives Dieudonné Lorraine. The writing on the parcel containing the watch was carefully examined. Experts compared the handwriting on the parcel to that of Father Delorme. Three experts swore the writing matched Father Delorme's, while a fourth refused to swear to it.

The Crown claimed that the priest had sent the watch as an erratic method of getting rid of it. The defence countered with the claim that someone had probably stumbled across the body and had stolen the watch. Later a guilty conscience may have forced the individual to mail the watch to the police.

Father Delorme stated simply that all the evidence against him was circumstantial. No one saw him kill his brother. He was in his cellar from about ten o'clock that night until one in the morning repairing a furnace, until one of his sisters called out to him to come to bed.

The jury retired to reach a verdict. On July 21, they reported that they were hopelessly deadlocked. Sent back to continue their deliberations, they reported two days later that they stood at ten for conviction and two for acquittal. The jury was dismissed.

The jury, made up of French and English citizens, was

criticized for not bringing in a guilty verdict. It was believed that no one of the Catholic faith would find a priest guilty of murder. We must remember that in 1923 a guilty verdict was tantamount to death on the gallows.

In February 1924, Delorme's second trial for the murder of his half-brother again resulted in a deadlocked jury. It all had to be done a third time.

Father Delorme's third and last murder trial began on October 6, 1924, almost three years after his brother's body was found with six bullets in his head. On October 31, the jury retired to reach a decision. Thousands stood outside the old courthouse awaiting the results of their deliberations. Three hours and forty-five minutes later they returned with their verdict. Not guilty.

Father Delorme made a brief statement: "I knew I would be freed, because I am innocent. I hold no grudge against any person who worked against me in the case. I forgive all."

With that magnanimous statement he walked out of the courtroom a free man after spending more than two years and nine months in jail and asylums. The verdict was received outside the province of Quebec as a travesty of justice.

Father Delorme died of natural causes in 1942.

– PETER DEMETER –

ON DECEMBER 4, 1974, intelligent, wealthy real estate developer Peter Demeter was sentenced to life imprisonment for procuring the murder of his wife, Christine.

Christine's body was found on the garage floor of the Demeter home in Mississauga, Ontario. She had been bludgeoned to death.

The gates of Millhaven Penitentiary closed behind the tall, debonair builder as they have closed behind hundreds of convicted murderers who preceded him.

Most are never heard of again.

But Peter Demeter was different. He was not an average man, or more precisely, he was not an average prisoner. European-born, university-educated, he was poles apart from the three-time losers and impulsive killers with whom he now found himself in close quarters.

After Demeter commenced serving his sentence, word drifted back to the law enforcement community that he harboured a grudge against the Peel Regional Police, who had gathered the evidence that had convicted him of his wife's murder. In particular, he had a passionate hatred for Deputy Chief William Teggart.

In Millhaven, Demeter made a friend, some say a friend who received payment for his services, for Demeter had entered Millhaven with a net worth in excess of one million dollars.

Mike Hodgson, better known as "The Butcher," was Demeter's bodyguard. To harm Demeter was to cross the Butcher's path. Hodgson, serving time for manslaughter, cast a long shadow. Few dared mess with Peter Demeter at Millhaven.

After Demeter had served four and a half years at Millhaven, Hodgson was transferred to the medium-security facility at Warkworth. Three days later, Peter Demeter, now without his bodyguard, was attacked by a fellow inmate in his cell. Demeter let it be known that without protection he was a dead man. As if by magic, within 72 hours, he was transferred to Warkworth.

During the intervening years and, in fact, from the day of Christine Demeter's murder in 1973, the couple's daughter, three-year-old Andrea, lived with Peter's cousin, Dr. Steven Demeter, and his family. Peter gave Dr. Demeter power of attorney, enabling him to act on Peter's behalf in financial matters.

By 1981, the over one million dollars' insurance on Christine's life had accumulated to more than three million dollars, including interest. Peter initiated legal action against the three insurance companies who held the policies in order to lay his hands on the money. He also instructed Steven Demeter to initiate an action on Andrea's behalf against the same companies. The Demeters lost the lawsuits. Both appeals were dismissed.

Dr. Demeter approached Peter with $30,000 in legal fees, which the insurance fight had cost him. Peter refused to pay, and the two had a falling-out. Steven Demeter was secretly placed on Peter Demeter's hate list, along with the Peel Regional Police and Deputy Chief William Teggart.

Dr. Demeter didn't have long to wait to hear from his cousin. In April 1982, he received a threatening letter from Peter. He travelled to the prison and informed Peter that the letter would be turned over to the authorities should anything happen to him. Dr. Demeter also expressed his concern to parole authorities, as well as to Deputy Chief Teggart. From that day to this, there has been no communication between the two cousins.

Initially, Andrea Demeter had been told that her father was on a prolonged business trip in Europe. As the years passed, this pretence was dropped and the little girl was told the truth about her father. In 1979, at the age of nine, Andrea started visiting her father at Warkworth. She had difficulty coping with the visits. At times, her father was rude and abusive. Finally, she stopped visiting.

Meanwhile, Mike Hodgson was paroled from prison, and had become involved in a fraud-related matter in Hamilton. He skipped to England, where he stayed a short time before returning to Canada. Once back in Hamilton, he lived with Anthony Preston, 48, a former prison inmate, who had spent eight years behind bars.

By the summer of 1983, Peter Demeter had himself spent more than eight years in prison. His status had greatly changed since his Millhaven days. He was domiciled at Edmison House, a halfway house in Peterborough. He was required to spend from 12 a.m. to 7 a.m. each day at the house. He also had to return to Warkworth each weekend.

Demeter, with an IQ of 146, considered to be in the genius category, had no difficulty ingratiating himself with the prison officials who controlled his destiny. He had the key to the parole officer's home and often attended family barbecues there. Demeter spent many pleasant evenings at the official's home. Occasionally, he took the man's two children swimming.

Demeter visited his living-unit officer's cottage in the Muskokas, and has admitted giving gifts such as liquor to the families of other correctional facility officials. He gave his classification officer's son a gift of designer jeans. On one occasion, charming Peter took the boy to Toronto and lined him up with a prostitute.

Correctional authorities maintain a Life Skills office at 331 Rubige Street in Peterborough, where six inmates counsel institutionalized inmates on how to cope with life on the outside. Peter Demeter ran the office.

That summer of 1983, Demeter arranged a meeting with Anthony Preston and Mike Hodgson at the Holiday Inn in Peterborough. Shortly after the meeting, Hodgson returned to Hamilton and turned himself in to the police. Two months later, Demeter set up another meeting with Preston at the House of Chan on Eglinton Avenue in Toronto. For the first time, Peter Demeter told someone in an ambiguous manner that he had a job he needed done. Preston listened and was interested. He returned to Hamilton, but was once more summoned by Demeter, this time to Peterborough. Coincidentally, they met a mutual friend, Mike Lane, an ex-convict on parole from a life sentence for manslaughter. Lane left the meeting. Demeter and Preston sat around a picnic table in the park.

According to Preston's later testimony, Demeter said, "My cousin's been cheating me out of my money." Demeter went on to accuse Stephen Demeter of stripping his house in Mississauga of valuable paintings and of turning his daughter against him. At this time, Peter Demeter was well aware that Stephen Demeter had applied to the public trustee to be appointed Andrea's legal guardian.

The meeting continued. Preston claims Peter said, "While in jail I have worked out a three-part plan. I spent an awful lot of time working it out."

In essence, Peter wanted his home in Mississauga burned to the ground in order to collect the insurance of $138,000 to finance the rest of his scheme. The second phase of the plan involved the kidnapping of his cousin's son, Stuart Demeter, 19, a computer science student. He was to be lured to a parked van on the pretext of obtaining summer employment. Preston would want a van for this purpose.

When the unsuspecting boy opened the door of the van, Peter Demeter, secreted inside, would shoot him dead. Preston later testified, "Demeter said Stuart was going to have to be sacrificed, because Dr. and Mrs. Demeter had to pay for what they had done to him." After the murder, the boy's teeth were to be removed and his fingers amputated to deter identification. The body was to be placed in a body bag and burned.

The third phase of the scheme was the kidnapping of a Progressive Conservative fund-raiser living in Rose-dale. The kidnappers were to appoint Peter Demeter as mediator. The goodwill generated by Demeter in return-ing the politician to his family would go a long way with the parole board.

Preston agreed to the razing of Demeter's house, but was leery of murder and mutilation. The sum of $8,000 was agreed upon for the torch job. Demeter passed over a down payment of $500 to Preston. Preston returned to Hamilton, and made up his mind to go through with the arson job, but to have nothing to do with the murder and kidnapping.

In subsequent meetings between the two men at Hy's Restaurant on Richmond Avenue, Hemingway's on Cumberland Avenue and the Long Bar in the Sheraton Centre, Preston received a further $3,500 in cash and a ransom note to be read over the phone to Dr. Demeter after the job was done.

On August 15, 1983, the Mississauga fire department extinguished a blaze at Demeter's vacant house at 1437 Dundas Crescent. Seven days later, on August 22, the house again mysteriously caught fire, but the fire burned itself out. The very next night, the luxurious home burned to the ground.

Anthony Preston had done his job well, but wanted nothing more to do with Demeter, who made several attempts to contact him. Preston feared for his life. He gave a copy of the ransom note to his girlfriend, instructing her to go to the police with it if anything ever happened to him.

On September 3, 1983, Police Chief D.K. Burrows and Deputy Chief William Teggart of the Peel Regional Police met with Inspector Noel Catney, a veteran of 18 years' police work and 46 murder investigations. They advised him that they felt that Peter Demeter was behind the suspected arson of his own home. Inspector Catney was given the green light to consider the arson a major project. He hand-picked his team of investigators.

Five days later, Catney was advised that Peter Demeter would be at the site of his burned-out house. Catney made a point of being there. The two men met. The master manipulator gazed at the ruins of the home which he hadn't seen for nine years. Catney, the professional cop, asked Demeter if he had any idea how the house had burned down. Demeter replied that he didn't know. Catney promised Demeter he would find out who set the fire. At the time, he had no idea that he would live and breathe the Peter Demeter saga for the next two years.

Three weeks later, the arson was to take a back seat when Inspector Catney received a phone call from Inspector Bob Lewis of the Peterborough Police Deptartment. Lewis had a strange story to tell. The night before, Mike Lane, 32, the parolee who had a reputation as a strongman, had flagged down a police cruiser. Lane reported that Peter Demeter had approached him with a proposition to lure a 19-year-old boy to a van in a parking lot, where Demeter would shoot the boy. He went on to relate many of the same details that Preston would later reveal to the police. Mike Lane wanted no part of Demeter's murderous scheme.

Inspector Catney had questioned the Demeter family during the arson investigation and knew that the intended murder victim was Stephen Demeter's son, Stuart. Catney travelled to Peterborough and received Mike Lane's promise of co-operation. Meetings were set up between Demeter and Lane at the Holiday Inn in Peterborough. Unknown to Demeter, video- and audiotapes were made of these conversations.

Demeter went through his entire plan to kidnap and murder Stuart Demeter. He had purchased a house at 426 Donegal Street in Peterborough. The old home had a crawl space with a dirt floor. Part of Lane's job, for which he would receive $10,000, was to dig a hole in the crawl space. Demeter wanted the hole to be six feet four inches long. Stuart Demeter's exact height. The hole was to be Stuart Demeter's grave.

On October 19, 1983, Inspector Catney arrested Peter Demeter. He was charged with two counts of counselling to commit murder, three counts of arson and one count of conspiring to commit arson. At the same time, Anthony Preston was taken into custody and charged with arson. He would later be found guilty, and sentenced to nine months' imprisonment. Preston also told police of Demeter's plan to murder Stuart Demeter. He even turned over a ransom note complete with Peter Demeter's fingerprints.

Noel Catney's two-year odyssey was over. Today, Catney says, "Peter Demeter is probably the most dangerous individual I have ever been involved with during my police career. He should never be considered for parole."

On July 8, 1985, Peter Demeter, 54, was found guilty of two counts of counselling to commit murder and received two life terms. Demeter remained active while serving his time. In 1988, he was given an additional life sentence for conspiring to kidnap his lawyer's daughter.

– EVELYN DICK –

W E'VE FOUND A DEAD MAN! Part of a dead man!" shouted Bob Weaver, 10, and his brother, Fred, 9, to their friends.

From the moment these words were spoken on March 16, 1946, the Evelyn Dick case captured the imagination of the Canadian public. From Antigonish, Nova Scotia, to Port Alberni, British Columbia, everyone followed the exploits of a handful of characters who told unbelievable and horrible stories of what took place in the days and months before the youngsters' gruesome discovery on Hamilton Mountain.

The body was without arms, legs and head. Two days after it was found, Alexander Kammerer reported that a roomer of his, John Dick, had been missing since March 6. Dick, who worked for the Hamilton Street Railway Co. as a conductor, had not shown up for work that day. The police located his wife, Evelyn, who lived at 32 Carrick Avenue. She could throw no light on her husband's disappearance, except to volunteer that she and Mr. Dick were living apart. They had been married only five months. The next day, two brothers of John Dick positively identified the body as that of their missing brother. Mrs. Dick was now questioned more closely. She gave the first of her many statements.

Evelyn said she married John Dick using the name Evelyn White. She told John Dick that she was a widow whose husband, a navy man, had passed away. She told him that she had a retarded daughter, Heather, 4, who had been fathered by White. Evelyn admitted to having affairs with other men while married to Dick, but claimed that he saw other women as well. Then she told the most fantastic tale of all. She related how she had received a phone call instructing her to borrow a car. The caller told her that he was a member of a hired gang who had been retained to kill her husband. The mysterious caller said the reason her husband must die was that he had been seeing another man's wife. The caller made an appointment to meet her on Claremont Drive on March 6. She borrowed a Packard and when she arrived at the appointed spot, the man was there with a heavy sack. After placing the sack in the back seat, he got into the Packard and the two drove away. The stranger told Evelyn that the sack contained a part of John Dick.

Finally they arrived at Hamilton Mountain and the stranger dumped the contents of the sack on the ground. Evelyn said she became sick. The man tossed the body parts over the edge of a bank. She let her mysterious passenger off at the Royal Connaught Hotel and returned the Packard to its owner. To account for the blood in the vehicle, Evelyn wrote a note to the owner of the car saying that her little girl had cut her finger. The police proceeded to check 32 Carrick Avenue. Here they found pictures of handsome Bill Bohozuk. They also found bank books containing large balances and a bloodstained skirt of Evelyn's.

Evelyn was detained by the police. In the meantime, the authorities started to uncover the tumultuous life led by the main characters in our cast. First and foremost there was beautiful Evelyn, with long black hair and a natural flirtatious look that oozed charisma. She lived on Carrick Avenue with her mother, Mrs. Donald MacLean, and her 4-year-old daughter, Heather. Her father lived at 214 Rosslyn Avenue. He, too, was living apart from his wife. When his home was searched, police found a revolver and ammunition, as well as an axe, saws and a butcher knife. The house also contained enough incriminating evidence to charge him with theft from his employer, the Hamilton Street Railway Co.

Bill Bohozuk, the handsome other man in Evelyn's life, was found to own a revolver as well.

The more the police poked around, the more suspect everyone became. The police even found a bloody necktie in the back seat of the Packard that Evelyn had borrowed.

Mrs. Dick now changed her story and claimed that she witnessed the shooting of her husband by one Anthony Romanelli. That story was still news when she gave out a statement that it, too, was false. A more thorough search of the now-infamous house at 32 Carrick Avenue uncovered a bushel basket of ashes. Later, these ashes were found to contain bits of bone and teeth. The missing parts of John Dick had been cremated in the furnace. It seems that every time a search was instituted at the house new evidence was uncovered.

On Friday, March 22, the whole affair blew wide open.

The police found a ladies' beige travelling case in the house. When the lock was broken, it was discovered that the case contained a cardboard carton filled with cement. Under the supervision of a pathologist, Dr. W.J. Deadman, the cement was chipped away to reveal the body of a newborn baby boy. There was a cord fastened around the infant's neck.

Evelyn was quick to give her third statement. This time she told of bad feelings between her husband and Bill Bohozuk. She was having sexual relations with Bohozuk, and her husband was strongly suspicious. John Dick kept telling everyone about the affair, but other than drive Bohozuk half-crazy, he didn't do anything about it. She stated that Bohozuk told her he had killed her husband. She claimed that he even brought some of the pieces of John Dick's body to her home and put them in the little garage beside the house, to be later burned in the furnace.

While Evelyn continued to make statements, the investigation was grinding out more grisly facts. The baby in the cement was the child of Evelyn and Bill Bohozuk. She had given birth to a boy, in September 1944, at the Mount Hamilton Hospital. The very day she was discharged from the hospital, she claimed that Bill Bohozuk placed a cord around the baby's neck and strangled it. She made further statements incriminating her father, saying he and her husband argued bitterly.

In the end, Evelyn Dick stood trial for the murder of her husband. She was found guilty on October 16, 1946, and was sentenced to hang. Her counsel immediately advised the court that there would be an appeal for a new trial. The following day, October 17, Bill Bohozuk and Evelyn's father, Donald MacLean, stood trial for the same murder. One of the main witnesses to be called at their trial was none other than Evelyn. When this occurred, she refused to give evidence. Presumably, she refused because she was appealing her case and did not want to prejudice her chances. The judge was compelled to discharge the jury and delay the proceedings.

Evelyn's lawyer, J.J. Robinette, won the appeal for a new trial. It started on February 24, 1947, and Robinette leaned heavily toward her father being the actual murderer. This time the jury brought in a verdict of not guilty. While everyone realized she had guilty knowledge of the crime, there was a reasonable doubt as to whether she'd actually killed her husband.

Only four days later, she was back in court facing a new charge, that of murdering her own child. This time the prosecution proved that Evelyn left her home with a live baby and returned with a locked travelling case. The jury brought in a verdict of not guilty of murder, but guilty of manslaughter. She was sentenced to life imprisonment.

The next trial was that of Bill Bohozuk for the murder of the baby. He claimed he was not the father of the child, and had never killed the baby. Another field day for the press occurred when Mrs. Bill Bohozuk showed up. No one was aware that he was married. She had been living in the United States for months. Mrs. Bohozuk stated that she was with her husband all day on the date Evelyn claimed he had strangled the child. The jury obviously believed her. They took only ten minutes to find him not guilty.

Both Donald MacLean and Bill Bohozuk then stood trial for the murder of John Dick. When Mrs. Dick again refused to testify, the judge instructed the jury to bring in a verdict of not guilty pertaining to Bohozuk. This they did without leaving the jury box. Donald MacLean heard all the same evidence one more time. He was finally acquitted of murder, but was convicted of being an accessory after the fact of murder. MacLean received a sentence of five years in prison.

No one was ever convicted of murdering John Dick and cutting off his arms, legs and head.

Whatever happened to all the characters in this tangled, fascinating case?

Mrs. Donald MacLean took little Heather and moved away from Hamilton.

Donald MacLean spent four years in Kingston Penitentiary and was released in 1951. He worked for some time as a parking-lot attendant, and died in 1955.

Bill Bohozuk's whereabouts are unknown.

Evelyn Dick served 11 years in prison, and was paroled in 1958. She has disappeared from view.

– DONNELLY FAMILY –

THEY CAME FROM County Tipperary in the mid–19th century to settle in a new land. Most of the immigrants made their way to Lucan, Ontario, about 14 miles north of London, to be with their compatriots and to carve small farms out of the wilderness. It was a tempting proposition. Land could be purchased for a mere 13 shillings an acre. The new immigrants worked hard and they played hard.

One of their number was Jim Donnelly, a small, handsome man, who preceded his wife, Johannah, and son,

James, to this new country. Two years after Jim's arrival, Johannah and her little son joined him in Lucan. A year later, Johannah gave birth to a second son, William, who was born with a club foot. Five more boys, John, Patrick, Michael, Robert, Thomas and a lone girl, Jenny, would bless the union.

Whatever reputation Jim Donnelly later attained, no one has ever claimed that he was a lazy or unambitious man. He settled on a piece of vacant land along the Roman Line, so called for the large number of Roman Catholics whose farms faced the road. The lot that Jim settled on belonged to John Grace. In 1855, Grace sold half the site to Michael Maher, who, in turn, leased it to Patrick Farrell.

Patrick Farrell wanted his land and therein lies the crunch. One must take sides when studying the saga of Jim Donnelly and his family. At every turn he can be seen either as a moody bully or as a man justified in fighting for his rights and maintaining his principles. It is for the reader to decide.

The Irish had brought with them to the new world all the superstitions and feuds that had been passed down through generations back in Tipperary. Alliances were soon formed along the Roman Line. Neighbour fought neighbour. Disputes about land boundaries, livestock and rights of way were sometimes settled in court. More often, they were settled with fists outside Keefes Tavern, one of 12 watering holes that prospered in the small town.

Now, Patrick Farrell wanted the land which he legally owned. Then there was Jim Donnelly. He and his wife, with the help of their small boys, had worked year after year, from dawn to dusk, clearing the land until it was a functioning farm. By all that was holy, it was his property.

After all, others had squatted on land with little regard for legal formalities.

Farrell rode up to the Donnelly homestead. Jim came out of the barn, which still stands, 111 years later, as a grim witness to the events that were to follow. Farrell gave Jim an hour to get off his property. Words were exchanged. Blows were struck. Farrell towered over Jim and outweighed him by at least 40 pounds. Despite these inequalities, Jim is reported to have given Farrell a severe beating, as Johannah and the boys cheered him on.

Farrell took his case to court. The results of the court action didn't sit well with Jim Donnelly. Farrell was awarded the south 50 acres, while Jim was given legal title to the north 50.

The two men became mortal enemies. Donnelly is said to have taken a potshot at Farrell, who lived close by his farm. The shot missed, but Farrell was convinced that his enemy had attempted to kill him. He formally charged Jim with "felonious shooting." Just before New Year's, 1856, Jim stood in the Goderich Courthouse and swore to keep the peace for one year and not to molest Patrick Farrell.

For the next two years, Farrell blamed Jim for the string of misfortunes that befell his farm. Cows took ill and suddenly died. Farrell's barn mysteriously caught fire. Indeed, legend has it that it was Farrell who first coined the phrase "Black Donnellys." As things turned out, he had good reason to be the originator of the derogatory description.

The second confrontation between Jim Donnelly and Patrick Farrell took place on June 27, 1857.

In pioneer days it was the custom to hold bees to clear land or raise a barn. The menfolk of the community donated their labour and animals to complete the work in record time. On that fateful hot day in June, several men were engaged at a logging bee on the small property of William Maloney. Some of the men brought jugs of whisky. Others relied on Maloney to provide the sauce for the day's efforts. Big Pat Farrell was there. So was Jim Donnelly.

Oxen grunted and chains were pulled taut. Sweat-stained men stripped to the waist. It was hard work, conducive to taking long deep slugs of whisky from Maloney's liberal supply.

According to reports, it is certain that both Farrell and Donnelly were drinking that day. Most likely, Farrell was intoxicated. Each time the two men were in proximity, a nasty remark would pass between them. Jim and Pat teed off against each other, but were separated before any harm was done. Jim is reported to have taunted Pat into continuing the fight. Big Pat grabbed the nearest weapon, a big hand spike. The hand spike, a three-foot-long piece of hardwood, was used as a lever to move large logs. It made a formidable weapon.

Within minutes, Pat faced Jim, who had also picked up a hand spike. Once again, cooler heads prevailed. The two adversaries were separated. It is reported that Pat fell to his knees, either from a push or from the effects of Maloney's whisky. At that precise moment, Jim raised his hand spike and brought it down full force on Farrell's head. A few moments later, Patrick Farrell died. The logging bee came to an abrupt halt. Ashen-faced men looked at Jim Donnelly. Jim slowly left the scene and walked home.

Two days later, an inquest was held into Farrell's death. Jim Donnelly didn't show up, but the inquest jury managed just fine without his presence. They came to the conclusion that Jim had murdered Pat Farrell and a warrant was issued for his arrest.

Jim was nowhere to be found. He had fled, but not far. Tough Jim was hiding out in the woods that skirted the rear of all the farms along the Roman Line. Jim's older boys, James, 15, Will, 12, and John, 10, brought their father provisions. Sometimes Jim donned women's clothing and managed to work his distant fields while being sought by the law.

With the coming of winter and the severe windswept snows that swirled along the Roman Line, Jim had much more difficulty staying at large. He frequently spent the cold nights in a farmer's barn. There is some evidence that friends of the Donnellys allowed him to stay in their homes for short periods of time.

Still, life in hiding was no life at all. Johannah needed her man. Jim's children needed a father. On May 7, 1858, after being at large for a year, Jim Donnelly turned himself in to the local sheriff. Jim was tried, found guilty of murder and sentenced to hang.

Johannah Donnelly couldn't sit back and do nothing while her husband's life was in jeopardy. She went about getting signatures on a petition for clemency. Some of the citizens' hatred of Jim Donnelly was overcome by their sense of fairness. The death had taken place during a drunken brawl. Had Pat Farrell's wild swings connected with Jim's head, they rationalized, it would be Farrell standing in the shadow of the hangman's noose.

Johannah wandered far afield to London and Goderich in search of men who knew her husband and regarded him quite differently than his enemies in Lucan. No less a personage than Attorney-General John A. Macdonald, who would later become prime minister of Canada, commuted Jim's sentence from death to seven years' imprisonment.

The cold iron gates of Kingston Penitentiary closed behind Jim Donnelly. Two months later, Johannah gave birth to Jenny, her only daughter.

One can only imagine the plight of Johannah Donnelly, with seven boys and a baby daughter to care for and a farm to run, living amongst many who hated the Donnelly clan with a passion. It is a tribute to this remarkable woman's resolve that she was successful in running and improving the farm during her husband's absence.

Seven years passed. Despite petitions, Jim served every day of his prison term. Now 48 years old, he returned to his family. His oldest son, Jim, was a young man of 23.

Jim Donnelly was back in town, and life in Lucan would never be the same.

After Jim's return, every mishap that befell those who had testified at his trial seven years earlier was laid at the feet of the Donnelly family. The Donnelly boys could scrap like hellions and there is no record of them ever losing a fight.

The Donnellys prospered. In the 1860s, they went into the stagecoach business. Will and young Jim discovered they had a knack for business. From all reports, their small line was the cleanest, most efficient of any in service in the area. Their competition, old Bob Hawkshaw, planned to retire. Will and Jim offered to purchase his line, but Hawkshaw sold out to John Flannigan. John was well liked and was confident that customers would patronize his stagecoach line rather than that of the Donnellys. He was right.

Then, as if willed by the devil himself, strange and

unusual misfortunes befell Flannigan's stagecoach line. One day an axle broke, shaking up the passengers, severely damaging the coach and injuring a horse. Accident, maybe. Sabotage, possibly. One of Flannigan's barns burned to the ground. Five days later, another Flannigan barn inexplicably caught fire. A stagecoach was burned beyond repair, but eight horses were rescued from the blazing building. It is even reported that on one occasion Flannigan found his horses with their tongues cut out.

Flannigan was understandably incensed at the Donnellys. Together with 17 men, who believed that the Donnellys had gone too far, he advanced on the Donnelly farm. Will and James were preparing the stagecoach for the run to London. The unruly mob stopped in front of the Donnelly barn. Jim, Sr., and all seven sons looked at the mob and rolled up their sleeves. Jim, Sr., spoke first, "You gentlemen seem to be looking for trouble. If so, the boys and I will be pleased to oblige you."

Flannigan hesitated at the cockiness of Jim Donnelly. That hesitation was to cost him dearly. The eight Donnellys tore into the 18-member mob. Several witnesses observed the Donnelly boys as they clubbed and punched until their enemies lay prostrate on the ground or took flight. It was all over in 10 minutes, but the scene of the fearless family fighting against better than two-to-one odds remained indelibly etched in the minds of the witnesses, who never tired of telling the story of the epic battle.

To gain some perspective into the terror that was the Donnelly family, one has only to scan the charges against them in the first three months of 1876. It is an impressive list of 33 charges, including assault, arson, wounding, robbing and shooting with intent.

As with all pioneer families, the Donnellys had their share of personal tragedies. Jim, Jr., is reported to have died of pneumonia. Like everything about the Donnellys, his death is shrouded in mystery. Some say he was shot to death and the shooting was kept secret by the family. Whatever the truth, he lies today in the country graveyard beside St. Patrick's Church. Later, brother Michael was stabbed to death in a bar-room brawl. He is buried beside his older brother.

The feuds continued, fiercer and crueller than before. Word of the acts of terrorism and the law's inability to cope with the Black Donnellys slowly trickled to the outside world. Inside the tight pocket of pioneer Canada, desperate men had had enough. If the law couldn't tame the Donnellys, they would mete out their own brand of justice.

Jim Carroll was the catalyst required to ignite the locals to action. Jim was born in the area, but had moved to the United States, returning in 1878, at age 26. He was quickly made aware of the scourge known as the Black Donnellys. Big Jim let it be known that he had no fear of the Donnellys.

Robert Donnelly was hustled off to Kingston Penitentiary for taking a pot-shot at Constable Sam Everett. Everett was given a severe thrashing soon after Robert's conviction. He couldn't or wouldn't identify his attackers and, soon after, resigned his position.

Jim Carroll became a Lucan constable with the promise, "I will drive the Donnellys out of Lucan." In a way, he did just that.

On the night of February 3, 1880, grim-faced men met at the Cedar Swamp Schoolhouse. They called themselves the Biddulph Vigilance Committee. The stone schoolhouse had been the gathering place for socials and political meetings, but this was different. By lantern light, jugs of whisky were passed from man to man. Although the weather was not overly cold, the whisky was necessary for the task at hand.

Some say there were 31 men in attendance, some say over 40. It matters little. They walked down the road toward the home of Jim Donnelly. Other men joined them en route. Into the Donnelly home they marched. Patrick "Grouchy" Ryder was among their number. Grouchy's barn had been burned. After many postponements, Johannah and Jim, Sr., were to appear in Granton to answer to the charge of arson the next day.

Farming is a demanding occupation. Chores must be carried out and farm animals must be fed. To that end, the Donnellys had a neighbouring youngster, 11-year-old Johnny O'Connor, sleeping over that night. Johnny was to take care of the animals the next day, while the Donnellys drove to Granton to appear in court. A niece, Bridget, was visiting from Ireland. Tom was at home with his parents.

Constable Jim Carroll led the group. He sighted Tom Donnelly asleep in a tiny bedroom off the kitchen. Jim snapped handcuffs on his wrist. Tom awoke with a start and cried out, "What the hell!" Carroll responded, "You're under arrest."

The noise woke up Johannah, who in turn woke up her niece, Bridget. Jim, Sr., was sleeping with Johnny O'Connor. He pulled on his trousers and joined the rest in the kitchen. He saw his son in handcuffs. "What? Tom, are you handcuffed?" he asked.

"Yes," Tom replied. "He thinks he is smart." By candle-light, Jim, Sr., went back to the bedroom for his coat. Johnny O'Connor had been using the elder Donnelly's coat for a pillow. Now he held it out for Jim, who returned to the kitchen.

There, in the eerie glow of the candle, Johnny O'Connor's eyes met Jim Carroll's. Later, Johnny would state there was no way Carroll was unaware of his presence. In light of future events, it is a minor mystery that Johnny O'Connor's life was spared.

Did the men intend only to beat up the Donnelly clan? Bill Ryder, a great-great-great-nephew of Grouchy Ryder, says, "I believe the intent was to rough up the Donnellys, but something went wrong and, once started, the mob got out of hand."

All but one of the inhabitants of the house that night were beaten and clubbed to death. Tom Donnelly fell. So did his parents and so did his cousin, Bridget. Johnny O'Connor, trembling with fear, hid under a bed, where he could see a shovel being brought down time after time on a Donnelly skull.

The house was set ablaze and in moments the mob was gone. Johnny escaped from the burning house and ran barefoot to a neighbouring farm. But the mob hadn't finished their work. Down the road they marched to the home of Will Donnelly. It was his brother John who answered the door. Silhouetted in the light of the doorway, he was an easy target. John died moments after being shot. The mob thought it had killed the hated Will. Now the carnage came to an end. The men dispersed, leaving five members of the one family dead in their wake.

Next day, word of the tragedy spread. Initially, 13 men were held on suspicion. Of these, six were charged with murder—James Carroll, John Kennedy, Martin McLaughlin, Thomas Ryder, James Ryder and John Purtell. The six men were lodged in the jail behind the London court-house. Only Carroll stood trial, but the local jury failed to reach a verdict.

On January 24, 1881, Jim Carroll stood trial for the murder of Johannah Donnelly for the second time. This time, he was found not guilty. Because the case against Carroll had been so strong, it was felt that it would be futile to try any of the remaining men. They were all released from custody. No one has ever been convicted of the five murders that took place in the wee hours of the morning of February 4, 1880.

In the years that followed the massacre of the Donnelly family, members of the Biddulph Vigilance Committee were buried in the little graveyard beside St. Patrick's Church. Ironically, they rest forever beside the Donnelly family.

– LEONARD EDE –

CANADIANS DO NOT regularly ship sundry bodies across our fair land in assorted trunks and suitcases. But one must not rush to the conclusion that Canada's criminal history is devoid of that certain élan associated with a body speeding over land and sea. Nothing could be further from the truth.

Why, back in 1960, all of Canada spent the quiet summer months enthralled with fast-breaking develop-ments concerning the case of the c.o.d. corpse.

Down in Argentia, Newfoundland, CNR station agent Thomas Donovan has just polished off a heaping plate of salt cod and boiled potatoes before returning to his job at the station. Tommy was more than a little bit perturbed. An unclaimed trunk addressed to a Mrs. Williams was hanging around the station. No one had claimed the trunk, no one had paid the c.o.d. charges of $17.68. Above all, there was the distressing matter of the odor. It was getting a tad worse every day.

Tommy decided to take a peek. He was relieved to discover that the beat-up old trunk was full of nothing worse than some used clothing and blankets. Tommy removed a blanket. Whoops. There, staring vacantly up at the grey, overcast Newfoundland sky were the unseeing eyes of a dead woman. Tommy let out a yell that could be heard all the way to Joe Batts Arm.

RCMP Inspector D.O. Bartram took over the investigation. He found 60 individual pieces of clothing in the trunk and, of course, the unidentified dead woman. No discernible marks were found on the body to indicate how the poor lady had met her death.

Within two days, Inspector Bartram was helped by a Newfoundland woman who positively identified the partially decomposed body as that of her long-lost daughter, Frances Elaine Haines. Frances had married a sailor and moved away 10 years earlier. Was someone playing a sadistic joke by returning Frances from whence she came? No, not really. Frances was found in the United States, alive and well. Mother had simply been mistaken.

After dispensing with this red herring, the Mounties, in conjunction with Metro detectives, concentrated their efforts in Toronto where the c.o.d. corpse had originated. Detectives found that CNR express agent William Squires had handled the death trunk. He vaguely remembered helping someone unload the trunk on May 4, a little over a month before Tommy Donovan took his famous peek in Argentia. Squires could give no description of the man who turned the trunk over to him.

An autopsy on the unidentified woman revealed no signs of violence. A week after the body was discovered, a routine fingerprint check in Ottawa positively identified the victim as Mrs. Marjorie Scott. Marjorie had a police record. She had been a hard-drinking, hard-living woman who, while she had no future, had quite a past.

Marjorie was born Marjorie Sagar in 1923 in Napanee, Ontario. Folks there remembered her as being a wild teenager. When she was 17 she married ex-con Clement Scott in Kingston. It didn't work out. Clement hanged himself in New Westminster, British Columbia, in 1958.

At the age of 20, Marjorie had her first rather serious brush with the law. She was convicted of theft from a farm-house near her home in Napanee and received a suspended sentence. In 1944, she looted a Whitby home, was apprehended and sentenced to three months in the Mercer Reformatory.

Marjorie apparently favoured gentlemen who had spent some time behind bars. She met hard-drinking ex-convict Leonard Ede when she was a young but extremely experienced 21-year-old. Although legally married to the still-living Clement Scott, she bigamously married Ede on December 5, 1946. Their turbulent relationship continued off and on for the next 14 years until Marjorie ended up in that battered old trunk.

Lennie drank heavily. No, that's an understatement. Would you believe that some days he killed six bottles of the very cheapest wine money could buy? Marjorie joined him on his binges whenever possible, which was pretty well all the time. They fought incessantly. Sometimes the police were called to break up the combatants. On other occasions one or the other would leave for months at a time, but for better or worse, they always returned to live together.

On May 3, 1960, the odd couple was living in a double room with kitchen on Granby Street in Toronto. They commenced drinking in the afternoon. Soon they were arguing. According to Lennie, Marjorie came at him with a kitchen knife. He disarmed her. Incensed, Marjorie picked up a broom and swung at Lennie. He ducked and punched Marjorie hard across the mouth. She went down, but got up fighting mad. Lennie then grabbed her by the throat and shook her. Marjorie quieted down. Later she asked Lennie for a drink of water. Lennie gave her the water. Marjorie lay down and fell fast asleep.

Next morning Lennie woke up. Marjorie didn't. She was dead. What to do? Lennie picked up the phone to call police, but thought better of it. In the past, the police had often been to Granby Street to quell fights. No one would believe that he hadn't killed Marjorie. There had to be another solution.

Lennie solved his immediate problem by picking up six bottles of wine. After serious meditation, he remembered a friend who had an old steamer trunk. Lennie picked up the trunk, explaining to his friend that he had to move. Returning to Granby Street, he placed Marjorie's clothing in the trunk and ever so gently deposited Marjorie. He then covered the clothing and the deceased with blankets. It was an unsettling experience. Lennie dropped over to the Avonmore Hotel to have a few beers.

On the way home, he met one-armed truck driver

Rollie Tremblay, who innocently agreed to help deliver the trunk to Union Station. Lennie and Rollie drove over to Granby Street where, with the help of unsuspecting fellow roomer Pete Campbell, they loaded Marjorie aboard the truck. The trunk weighed 172 pounds.

When Lennie arrived at the train station, he was asked to give the trunk's destination. It was a trick question, but Lennie rose to the occasion. Years before, while in the navy, he had been stationed in Argentia, Newfoundland. It was the farthest place he could think of, and so, by chance, Marjorie began her 1,500-mile journey across land and sea.

Rollie Tremblay and Lennie became so friendly that Rollie invited Lennie to join him at his home for an impromptu wine-and-cheese party. Lennie picked up four bottles of wine. There is no record that he purchased any cheese.

Next day, Lennie took a bus to Cleveland, knowing that sooner or later someone would open that trunk in Argentia, Newfoundland. He obtained part-time work and stayed sloshed. Each day he purchased the Toronto papers, looking for the inevitable. One night, while drunk, he called Pete Campbell in Toronto fishing for news, but there was none.

Once Marjorie's body was identified and Lennie's relationship to the dead woman established, the police were actively hunting for Leonard Ede. They located Rollie Tremblay, who told them of taking the trunk to Union Station. Pete Campbell related how he helped place the trunk onto Tremblay's truck. He also told police about the phone call he received from Ede in Cleveland. Circulars, complete with pictures, were widely distributed to Cleveland police.

Sure enough, a Cleveland police officer spotted Lennie on the street and took him into custody. Lennie seemed relieved that the whole thing was coming to an end. He co-operated with police officers, waived the extradition and was returned to Toronto.

Initially, Lennie was charged with murder, but this charge was dropped. While medical evidence indicated that Marjorie had died of asphyxiation, doctors were unable to determine what caused the asphyxiation. There was no evidence of foul play, either internally or externally, on the body.

However, Lennie wasn't completely out of the woods. He was immediately charged with public mischief and causing indignities to a human body. Leonard Ede pleaded guilty and was sentenced to 15 months in Burwash Reformatory.

– ALBERT GUAY –

THREE TIMES A WEEK, a Quebec Airways flight left Montreal for Seven Islands, with stops at Quebec City and Baie Comeau. It was so punctual and reliable that people along the route used to set their watches by the roar of the engines.

On September 9, 1949, Patrick Simard was fishing for eels near his home at Sault-au-Cochon, Quebec. He glanced up, idly following the flight of the Douglas DC-3 as it approached Cap Tourmente. Then he heard a loud explosion, and as he watched in horror the plane veered crazily to the left and went into a power dive, heading straight for the peak of Cap Tourmente.

Simard ran through thick bush toward the crash; it took him an hour to get to the scene. Scattered among the wreckage of the aircraft were the remains of the passengers and their luggage. Surprisingly, there was no fire, but the ominous smell of leaking gasoline hung over the entire area. The propellers had been turning when the plane smashed vertically into the ground. There was no swath of torn trees, only the aircraft with its wings ripped off and its horribly mangled nose sticking into the earth.

The plane had held four crew members and 19 passengers. Simard checked the wreckage for survivors. Finding none, he started down the mountain for help. He met some men who were working on railway tracks nearby, and they took the news to St. Joachim, where it was relayed to Quebec City. Within hours, Canadian Pacific Airlines, the parent company of Quebec Airways, had their investigation officials at the scene of the crash.

The left front luggage compartment showed signs of an explosion, and it was this explosion that had destroyed the control system of the aircraft, causing the disaster. The investigators examined everything aboard the aircraft that could have caused an explosion. Items such as fire extinguishers and storage batteries were checked, but none of these was found to be the cause of the crash. The four crew members and 19 passengers had been killed instantly upon impact, but the lack of fire made identifying the bodies relatively easy, and the next of kin were quickly notified.

Because of the explosion in the baggage compartment, the authorities concluded that they were dealing with a criminal case and not an accident. On September 12, the entire matter was turned over to the RCMP. The Mounties were to be assisted by the Quebec Provincial Police and the Quebec City Police Force.

The left front luggage compartment had been loaded in Montreal with cargo destined for Quebec City. It was completely emptied in Quebec City and reloaded with cargo destined for Baie Comeau. This was routine practice, meant to reduce unnecessary delay during the flight's many stops. The authorities realized that the explosive material must have been put into the left front baggage compartment at Ancienne Lorette Airport in Quebec City.

The passenger list of the ill-fated aircraft was closely scrutinized, as was the list of insurance policies taken out on passengers' lives. A cursory check turned up nothing unusual, and the police decided to place all relatives of victims who boarded the plane in Quebec City under observation and investigate their private lives.

Undertaking the investigation from another direction, the police started with the plane on the ground in Quebec City and the left front baggage compartment empty. They questioned Willie Lamonde, the freight clerk who had been on duty on September 9, but he could recall nothing significant except that several pieces of freight had been placed on the aircraft, in addition to the passengers' regular luggage.

From company records the police were able to obtain the names of the senders and prospective receivers of all the air freight shipments, and they set about checking every name on the list. This approach bore fruit with the discovery of a 28-pound parcel sent by Delphis Bouchard of St. Simeon, Quebec, to Alfred Plouffe, 180 Laval Street, Baie Comeau. Neither sender nor addressee existed, so it seemed reasonable to assume that someone had walked up to Willie Lamonde with a bomb and shipped it air freight to Baie Comeau.

The police begged Willie to try to remember who had given him the parcel. Willie's memory was now jarred by names and addresses he could relate to, and he came up with a mental picture of the person who had given him the bomb. He said it was a fat woman who had come to the airport by cab. He remembered this because the cabbie had carried the parcel to the scale for her. The cost of shipping the 28-pound parcel to Baie Comeau was $2.72, which she paid to Willie, who gave her a receipt. The police started the tedious task of questioning every cabbie in Quebec City, and almost immediately they found the right man.

Paul Pelletier, who worked for the Yellow Cab Co., had picked up the fat lady on September 9 at the Palais Railroad Station. He described her as middle-aged and overweight, with dark hair and dark eyes. She didn't say one word to him on the trip to the airport, but because she was returning to the city with him, he had carried the parcel to the freight clerk. When they returned to the city, she got out of his cab at the rear of the Château Frontenac Hotel, and Pelletier recalled seeing her walking toward Lower Town or the older section of the city.

Then, upon checking the relatives of the victims, the police for the first time heard the name of Albert Guay, whose wife, Rita, had died in the crash. Albert had been fined $25 for causing a scene some months previously in a restaurant, where he had brandished a revolver at a waitress named Marie-Ange Robitaille. It was a small and relatively insignificant incident, but one that couldn't be overlooked by the authorities. The girl still worked at the restaurant and the police decided to question her about her relationship with Guay. Detectives confronted an attractive, shapely young girl who would have caused heads to turn anywhere.

Marie-Ange openly admitted knowing Albert Guay, and when asked if Guay had anything to do with a fat middle-aged woman, she immediately gave the police the name of Marguerite Pitre, who lived at 49 Monseigneur Gauvreau Street. The police stationed the cab driver outside Marguerite Pitre's house, so that when she came out he would be able to identify her. On September 20, a taxi drove up and Pelletier had a good look at Marguerite as she got in. He positively identified her as the lady he had driven to the airport on September 9. Marguerite had taken an overdose of sleeping pills, and the taxi had been summoned to rush her to Infant Jesus Hospital. The police decided to arrest her as soon as she was released.

Who was this strange woman? What circumstances tied her to the young waitress, Marie-Ange Robitaille? How was Albert Guay connected to the two women?

The tangled web started to unravel. Albert Guay was born in 1917 to a working-class family. As a child, he liked games in which he played the part of a ship's captain or commander of great armies, and always had illusions of power and wealth. By the time he was 22, he was working in a defence plant and selling watches as a sideline. During the war he married the former Rita Morel, and when peace came he gravitated to the jewellery business as a full-time occupation, opening up a shop in Seven Islands, Quebec. In 1948, he closed his store and opened a shop on St. Sauveur Street, which he soon owned.

Guay was having a prolonged affair with Marie-Ange. It is almost certain that Rita Guay had knowledge of the affair, but being wise to the ways of men with wandering eyes, she figured Albert would have his fling, tire of the waitress and return to her. Marie-Ange had lived in a room in Marguerite Pitre's house, and it was here that Albert Guay would come to make love to his mistress, with Marguerite's complicity.

The heavy-set Marguerite, who always wore black, and as a result came to be known as the Raven, had met Guay during the war when they both worked in the same munitions plant. Another member of the Raven's family, her crippled brother, Genereux Ruest, worked for Guay as a watch repairman in his jewellery shop. The Raven had come under Guay's influence when she started borrowing small amounts of money from him during the war. This led to more and more loans until finally she was compelled to comply with his every wish.

When questioned, the Raven first denied taking the bomb out to the airport, but when faced with the cab driver, she confessed that she had delivered the explosives. Once started, the Raven continued to sing. She admitted she owed Albert $600. He always demanded favours of her, and when Marie-Ange was only 16, she set up the good-looking young girl in her own apartment at his insistence. The Raven claimed that Guay promised he would forget the debt if she would get him some dynamite, knowing that her neighbour had acquaintances in the construction business who had access to explosives. Guay had told the Raven that he needed the dynamite for a friend who was removing tree stumps. The Raven told her neighbour that if she could get her hands on some dynamite it would be her chance to get out of Albert's clutches once and for all. In the end, the Raven succeeded in obtaining 10 pounds of dynamite and 19 blasting caps.

On September 23, Albert Guay was arrested and taken into custody. He admitted everything except murder. Albert said he knew the Raven very well because she brought him leads for watch sales, and her crippled brother worked for him. He even admitted to having the affair with Marie-Ange, but claimed it was over before the plane crash. Through it all he swore he loved his wife dearly, and that the Raven was a barefaced liar.

The police descended on Genereux Ruest's workshop to search it for any evidence that a bomb had been manufactured there. They found an insignificant piece of corrugated cardboard coated with black deposits. It was the only thing in the shop that looked unusual in any way, and it was rushed to a Montreal laboratory for testing. In the lab, blasting caps were exploded using a piece of corrugated cardboard as a shield.

The explosions left black deposits on the cardboard matching the ones on the cardboard taken from Ruest's workshop. The same tell-tale black deposits appeared on the inside of the left front luggage compartment of the downed aircraft.

Armed with this incriminating evidence, the authorities faced Ruest. Finally he confessed that he had constructed a time mechanism, and that he and Albert had experimented with setting it off. He claimed that Albert had brought him all the materials for the bomb, and insisted that he had no idea that Guay planned to use it for anything other than clearing stumps. He said he was afraid to volunteer the information earlier because he thought the police would believe he knew Guay's intentions.

Meanwhile, Marie-Ange Robitaille added her chapter to the increasingly well-documented life and loves of

Albert Guay. She said she had met Guay at a dance in 1947, when she was 16 years old. She thought he was a glamorous man about town in the jewellery business, and even though she knew he was married, it wasn't long before they were having sexual relations. Rita Guay had even complained to the girl's parents, but Marie-Ange moved out of her parents' home and moved into a spare room that the Raven provided. Several times she tried to break up with Guay, but each time he went after her and brought her back. There is little doubt that Marie-Ange was physically attracted to Guay, but in the end she could see no future with a married man. She had only seen Guay once since the crash. On that occasion he begged her to come back to him, pleading that since his wife was dead, no obstacles stood in their way. She told him their affair was over, and she now told the police that she knew nothing about any bomb.

Despite the incriminating statements of the Raven and her brother, Albert steadfastly maintained his innocence. On February 23, 1950, Albert Guay stood trial for murder. The jury took only 17 minutes to find him guilty. He was sentenced to death by hanging. Once in Bordeaux Jail awaiting death, he made a full confession, implicating the Raven and her brother as willing accomplices. Both had been motivated by the money he had promised them from a small insurance policy he had taken out on his wife's life, and both had been well aware that he planned to blow up the aircraft.

Albert Guay was hanged on January 12, 1951. Genereux Ruest followed him to the gallows in 1952. The Raven was hanged in 1953.

THE MOTIVES THAT generate murder, this most final of all acts, can come from a variety of sources—greed, hate, lust, jealousy; the list is endless. But what of the murders that take place without motive, without reason and without explanation? Nothing can be more tragic. This is the story of one such case.

Shell Lake, Saskatchewan, is a tiny farming community of 250 people, situated about 90 miles north-west of Saskatoon. The closest town of any size is Prince Albert. The huge farms often associated with western Canada are not evident in this area. The farms are small. Hardy men work long, hard hours in the fields to wrest a living from the ground. In addition to their crops, they raise horses, cattle, pigs and chickens.

Jim Peterson had a farm approximately four miles from Shell Lake. His farm was about a mile square, and stood some 300 yards off Highway 3. A plain clapboard farmhouse was home to 47-year-old Jim, his 42-year-old wife, Evelyn, and their eight children, ranging in age from Larry, 1, to Jean, 17. An older daughter, Katherine, had recently married and was living in Chetwynd, British Columbia.

Wildrew Lang owned the farm adjoining the Petersons'. Lang and Peterson often worked together on each other's farms. During haying time they pooled their labour, first doing one farm and then the other.

At eight-thirty on the morning of August 15, 1967, Wildrew Lang started off in his truck for the Peterson farm. Because the men were always giving each other a helping hand, they rarely drove down their long driveways and along Highway 3 to the next farm. Instead, they had worn a sort of path or crude road through a connecting field, in order to go directly from one farm to another.

On this perfect summer day, Lang and Peterson were going to clean out a granary, which was really an old house used for storage. It was located not too far from the Peterson house. Lang made his way across the field and started to load his truck alone. He idly thought that Jim should have joined him. They had discussed loading the grain the night before. Jim planned on hauling it to the elevator, so that he could give his 17-year-old daughter, Jean, a little extra money. Jean was a runner, and slated to participate in a track-and-field meet in Dundurn, Saskatchewan. The whole Peterson family was excited about the prospect of Jean running.

What could be keeping Jim? Lang decided to go to the farmhouse and find out. As he approached the front door, it dawned on him that the place seemed to be so very quiet and still. It was close to nine o'clock. Where was Jim? he wondered again. Eight active kids, and not a sound to be heard.

Lang opened the door and apprehensively called out, "Hello." He peered inside. There, on the kitchen floor, clad only in his shorts, lying face down, was the body of his friend, Jim Peterson. Lang didn't look any further. He drove the few miles to Shell Lake and made contact with the RCMP at Spiritwood.

Corporal B.L. Richards arrived at the Peterson home, and while Lang waited in the car outside, Richards entered the house. He instinctively knew that Jim Peterson was dead. In the living room, on a cot, he found the body of 11-year-old Dorothy. He continued to the children's bedroom.

In the first bed he discovered the bodies of Pearl, 9, and Jean, 17. In another double bed were three bodies—Mary, 13; William, 5; and Colin, 2. All had been shot in the head.

Corporal Richards noticed a slight movement between the bodies of Pearl and Jean. He bent over and discovered tiny 4-year-old Phyllis, her face buried in the mattress. Richards lifted her from the bed and took her outside. The child didn't speak. Richards saw to it that she was taken to a farm across the highway.

Corporal Richards then drove to Shell Lake for help. He returned accompanied by Dr. J.R. Michaud. As he approached the house for the second time, he discovered the bodies of Mrs. Peterson and baby Larry, clad only in his diaper. The bodies were found outside the house. Apparently, Mrs. Peterson had grabbed her infant son and jumped out a window in an attempt to escape. Both had been shot through the head.

Nine human beings had fallen that morning to some madman. Who could hate this God-fearing, hard-working family enough to kill them? Why the Petersons? Why was Phyllis spared?

The RCMP had no murder weapon and no motive, but they did have some clues. The killer had left an identifiable footprint on the Petersons' kitchen floor. It had been made by a rubber boot, which had distinguishable markings. One of these markings were the words "Made in Taiwan." The bullets that had killed the Petersons came from a .22-calibre rifle.

Three days after the murder the RCMP received a call from a farmer. He gave them the name of someone whom he thought they should check out. The name was Victor Hoffman.

Victor was 21 years old. He had been in and out of trouble for the past few years. From 1961 to 1964, he had been charged three times with breaking and entering. Each time it appeared that he was interested in stealing guns. He had received a two-year suspended sentence for these offences. More recently he had behaved strangely around his own home. When he started shooting his rifle in the air, explaining that he was shooting at the devil, his parents had him committed to the Saskatchewan Mental Hospital at North Battleford.

While being treated at the hospital, he confessed to doctors that he had seen the devil many times. From as far back as he could remember, the devil had appeared to him. He described the apparition as being well over six feet tall with a face resembling a pig's. Doctors in the mental institution diagnosed Victor's illness as schizophrenia. They prescribed drugs to suppress his hallucinations, as well as electric-shock treatments.

Victor received a series of 12 shock treatments, and his condition seemed to improve. On July 26 he was released. Although he was still introverted, he was capable of working on the farm and socializing with acquaintances. The doctors who released him felt that drugs would keep his illness under control.

The RCMP visited the Hoffman farm, and confiscated Victor's .22-calibre Browning rifle and his rubber boots. On August 19, four days after the murders, and the day of the Petersons' funeral, the Crime Detection Laboratory in Regina informed the investigating officers that Victor Hoffman's rubber boots had made the track on the Petersons' kitchen floor, and his rifle had fired all the fatal bullets.

Victor Hoffman was taken into custody and questioned. He told the police that on August 15 he got of bed at 4 a.m. and worked on the family car. Then, without warning, Victor blurted out, "O.K., I killed them. I tried to change the rifling on it. I should have burned the house, then you would not have found those cartridges. I stopped at the gate. I don't know what made me do it. I collected 17 cartridges. I didn't want to shoot anymore. The one I left didn't see me."

When Victor's rifle was examined, it showed signs of having been tampered with in order to make ballistic comparisons more difficult. Hoffman was obsessed with changing the characteristics of his rifle so that the fatal bullets could not be traced to him. His statement also revealed why little Phyllis was spared. She had not looked up, and in his warped mind Hoffman ordained that she would live because she could not identify him.

Victor was studied extensively by psychiatrists. His story began to unfold. After working on the car on the day of the murder, the devil told him to go for a drive. The thought entered his mind that he should kill both his parents, but instead he put a box of shells in the glove compartment and placed his loaded .22 on the front seat. Victor took off, and as he passed each house he had an urge to pull into the driveway and kill the occupants. As he drove past each farm the urge grew stronger, until at last he did pull into a driveway. It was the farm of Jim and Evelyn Peterson.

Victor opened the front door. Jim Peterson was sitting on the side of his bed in his shorts and was about to put on his shoes. Jim looked up, saw the rifle and lunged out of the bedroom at Hoffman. Victor emptied his rifle at Jim, whose forward motion brought him almost to Hoffman's feet.

The children screamed. Hoffman went out to his car, reloaded his rifle and systematically went through the house, killing all the children. He killed Mrs. Peterson and the baby in the yard. They had made their way out through a window.

Little Phyllis was purposely left alive. Hoffman says it was because she didn't see him. Psychiatrists feel that the reason she was spared was because his impulse to kill was exhausted. Hoffman had never met nor even seen any member of the Peterson family until the August morning he opened their front door.

Victor Hoffman stood trial for murder and was found not guilty by reason of insanity. He was confined to a mental institution.

– DENNIS MELVYN HOWE –

DENNIS MELVYN HOWE — the infamous name is gradually fading from memory, but back in 1983 it was on everyone's lips. His horrendous crime was publicized across the country. Howe had a nine-day head start, but police had little doubt that the bungling, inept criminal would be apprehended within days. Almost 16 years have come and gone since the terrible murder occurred and neither hide nor hair of Dennis Melvyn Howe has been uncovered.

It was every parent's worst nightmare. On January 23, 1983, Sharin' Morningstar Keenan, a pretty nine-year-old, failed to come home for dinner. She had last been seen playing in Toronto's Jean Sibelius Park, about four blocks from her Dupont Street home. A massive search was conducted for the missing child. Nine days later, Sharin's body was found in a nearby Brunswick Avenue rooming house. She had been sexually assaulted, strangled and stuffed into a functioning refrigerator. The day after Sharin' went missing, the man who had rented the room in which the body was discovered simply disappeared.

Initially the suspect was thought to be Michael Burns, the name he used to gain employment with a Spadina Avenue hosiery firm. Using the social security card of the genuine Michael Burns, who had lost his card four years previously in Estevan, Saskatchewan, the alleged killer of Sharin' Keenan had carved out a new identity for himself in Toronto. It was left to Staff Sergeant David Boothby and Sergeant Wayne Oldham to figure out the suspect's real identity and where he had gone.

The detectives learned that "Burns" had attempted to obtain a birth certificate from Saskatchewan the previous spring. Under the alias of Wayne Edward King, he made the mistake of using genuine bits of his parents' names. He also gave his correct date of birth, September 26, 1940. Nearly a million records of individuals born in Saskatchewan were scanned by hand until the true identity of the suspect was confirmed. He was career criminal Dennis Melvyn Howe.

The hunt was on. Howe was 43 years old, stood five feet nine inches tall, had brown greying hair and weighed about 165 pounds. His criminal record dated back to 1957. In effect, the suspect had spent most of the 17 years from 1965 to 1982 in Prince Albert Penitentiary in Saskatchewan. On February 19, 1982, he was released from prison on parole, but immediately violated his parole by dropping from view.

Before disappearing from Toronto, Howe was able to obtain a $200 advance from his employer, ostensibly to have his teeth fixed. Police believe he used the money to hightail it out of Toronto, probably by bus, his favourite mode of travel. Ticket sellers at all travel facilities were questioned. Understandably, given the number of people leaving Toronto each day, none could remember a man who resembled the photograph investigators now had of Howe.

The massive search for the wanted man gained momentum. A national poster campaign familiarized the public with his likeness. Videotape presentations were given by police. Staff Sergeant Wayne Oldham was Howe's chief hunter. He grew to know every habit and idiosyncrasy of his prey. Howe tends to walk quickly. He dresses sloppily and often calls people and things "turkey," as in, "That movie was a turkey." No detail was too small to overlook. Oldham let it be known that Howe had a small scar under his chin. In the months following his positive identification, Howe was erroneously sighted throughout Canada, the United States and Europe.

I became involved in the case in 1988, when a concerned citizen read a piece I had written on Howe in the *Sun*. It was her custom to tape the "Phil Donahue Show," broadcast out of New York City, for her husband to view later. My article was firmly entrenched in her mind when there before her eyes, sitting in the Donahue audience, was Howe. She made the tape available to me. I took it to Oldham and, for 72 hours, that tape was the best lead police had in the case. All concerned were disappointed that the amazing lookalike turned out not to be Howe.

Howe's photograph appeared in all possible media across the country. His brother and sister in Saskatchewan were questioned. Both revealed that their wayward brother had not kept in contact with them. Investigators learned that Howe never made friends. He was a loner, the toughest type of criminal to trace. A reward of $100,000 initiated hundreds of leads, but all failed to produce concrete results.

From time to time I have featured Howe in my newspaper, the *Toronto Sun*, in an attempt to keep his likeness before the public. Once again, in 1990, I became personally involved when I accompanied Inspector Wayne Oldham to Washington, D.C., where the TV program, "America's Most Wanted," would feature the Howe case. More than 200 sightings of Howe were phoned in from across North America that night. I waited in a hotel room with Inspector Oldham while the FBI checked out the hottest leads. None of these sightings proved to be the elusive Howe. Back in Toronto, the balance of the sightings were routinely checked. Not one was the suspected killer.

Detectives get promoted, leaving others to pick up the old cases. Boothby and Oldham moved on, Boothby to become Metro Toronto's chief of police. Inspector Jim Crowley was in charge of the Howe case in 1991, when I again wrote about Canada's number-one fugitive. As a result, Howe was reported to have been seen in various locations across Canada. One such report from a remote northern lumber camp led investigators all the way to Russia. It too proved to be a false lead.

Now it is time to once more bring Howe to the public's attention. It is amazing that this inept transient has managed to avoid detection for so long. If he is dead, as some believe, it is also unusual that no one has reported or has knowledge of his demise.

A great deal is known about Howe. He has the ability to gain and lose about 30 pounds rather quickly, and has done so over the course of his checkered career. He enjoys country music. His beverage of choice is beer and he prefers to drink in restaurants rather than taverns. He is a heavy smoker who sometimes lines up his unfiltered cigarettes on end at the bar while he lingers over a drink. When on the move, Howe usually travels by bus and stays in hostels. Both his baby fingers are crooked. When in a good mood he laughs loudly in a jovial manner. His complexion is dark and his arms are hairy. Howe has a reputation of being a convincing liar. He has conned many trusting individuals who have crossed his path over the years. For example, he often talked about his Mercury car, although he has never owned one.

Prison officials in Saskatchewan claim Howe is adaptable and learns new skills quickly. On occasion he has been known to grow a moustache. Although he had never left Canada prior to the Keenan murder, he often talked of liking to work in the woods and sometimes mentioned Texas as a preferred place to live.

I firmly believe that someone out there has enough information to lead police to this alleged killer. Maybe an acquaintance will remember the laugh of the man who whiled away his time lining up his cigarettes on the bar. Who knows, perhaps a girlfriend will notice that her beau has two crooked baby fingers.

When Howe left Toronto he was suffering from decaying, blackened teeth. They were in such bad shape that he constantly rubbed his gums with patent medicine to relieve the pain. It is my feeling that one day in the winter of 1983, the scruffily dressed Howe would have been compelled to walk into a dentist's office to have dental work done on his neglected teeth. The records of that work might very well exist in a dentist's office. It could provide the first clue to the direction Howe took when he left Toronto.

An alleged killer is walking among us, seemingly immune from detection. Almost 16 years ago, a nine-year-old little girl wanted nothing more than to go home and have dinner with her family. Sharin' Morningstar Keenan has not been forgotten. Neither has Dennis Melvyn Howe.

– ALBERT JOHNSON –

THERE I WAS AROUND the bend. I got down on one knee, took careful aim with my .303 and squeezed the trigger. The Mad Trapper was trying to scramble up the banks of the frozen creek. My first shot sent him tumbling down, but didn't penetrate his pack. A second shot had the same effect. Then he turned, and without taking real aim, fired his 30-30 Savage. The impact of the bullet sent me sprawling."

I sat across the desk in Barrie, Ontario, facing Earl Hersey, who was relating this tale of long ago, when he was involved in what may have been Canada's greatest manhunt ever. If you are over 75, the story may bring back memories of below-zero temperatures, dog teams and the Arctic Circle. For in 1931–32 the Mad Trapper of Rat River was the main running news story in North America.

It all began innocently enough. At the time, the Royal Canadian Mounted Police were the only real law in the Northwest Territories and the Yukon. A part of the Mounties' normal routine was to periodically check up on trappers and prospectors, during weeks and even months of living in isolation. The Depression had drawn many an inexperienced man to the north country, ill-equipped to withstand the hardships of that cold, barren land. Many of these men owe their lives to the RCMP.

Constable Spike Millen of the Mounties' Arctic Red River detachment first met Albert Johnson by chance in a store at Fort McPherson. He cautioned him that trapping in the area required a licence. Johnson headed north and built a cabin near Rat River for the winter trapping season. Johnson's cabin was close to the trap lines of three native men, William Vittrekwa, William Nerysoo and Jacob Drymeat.

Everyone who came into contact with Johnson described him in the same way: a close-mouthed, rough man, who spoke with a slight Scandinavian accent. At the time of his appearance in the Arctic, he was between 35 and 40 years old, about 5 feet 9 inches tall, and of average build. It should be pointed out that, although living in isolation had an effect on some men, most were a gregarious lot who welcomed strangers. This was not the case with Johnson.

On Christmas Day, 1931, William Nerysoo entered the Mounties' quarters at the Arctic Red River detachment. He told Constable Spike Millen that Johnson had sprung his traps and hung them on trees. It was decided that Constable Alfred "Buns" King and Special Constable Joe Bernard travel to Rat River to question Johnson.

Travelling by dog team through bitter cold, the men made the 25-mile trip in under two days. King approached Johnson's cabin. All seemed in order. Smoke was lazily drifting out of the chimney. King shouted, then pounded on the door of the cabin, but received no response, although he was certain that Albert Johnson was inside.

King decided that rather than force himself upon Johnson, he should report the strange incident to his superior, Inspector Alexander Eames, commander of the Mounties' subdivision at Aklavik. He and Bernard covered the 80 miles to Aklavik in two days hard travelling. Together with Constable R.G. McDowell and Special Constable Lazarus Sittichinli, they headed back to Johnson's cabin. There was some urgency, as all the men wanted to celebrate New Year's Eve at Fort McPherson.

Again King approached the cabin. This time a shot pierced the still Arctic air. King was hit, but managed to crawl to safety. Johnson shot continuously from the cabin while the Mounties returned his fire.

The three Mounties lashed the badly wounded King to a dogsled and set out on the 80-mile return trip. Their dogs had just made the trip to Johnson's cabin and were fatigued. The wind-chill factor was equivalent to 90 degrees below zero. The terrain was rough and dangerous. The Mounties took only 20 hours to cover the 80 miles. The mad dash over the ice and snow certainly saved King's life. Johnson's bullet had gone clean through King's side. He recovered within a month.

Johnson's status had abruptly changed. He was no longer a reticent troublemaker. He had fired at and wounded a member of the RCMP.

Inspector Eames headed a party of nine men to bring in Johnson. Among these men was Constable Millen, the only one who had actually met the wanted man. On January 9, 1932, the posse approached Johnson's cabin. No one expected him to be there, but strangely enough, Johnson had not moved. Inspector Eames coaxed Johnson to give up, explaining that King was going to survive. Johnson responded by opening fire on the Mounties. He had dug a pit within the cabin. It was virtually impossible to hit the fugitive with gunfire.

The Mounties were not in a good position. Their adversary was warm inside the cabin. They were exposed to the elements, and the longer they stayed, the more food their dogs consumed. Further delay would see the party short of dog food.

Eames had brought dynamite along for just such a contingency. Dynamite sticks were tossed at the cabin, but they proved to be ineffective. Finally, one landed on the roof and blew a portion away, but this did not bother Johnson, who continued firing. In desperation, the officers fastened several sticks of dynamite together and tossed them at the cabin. The walls caved in, but still Johnson returned the Mounties' fire. The battle had raged for almost a full 24 hours when Inspector Eames decided to return to Aklavik.

One man had held off a posse of nine well-equipped Mounties and trappers, all experienced men of the North. Word drifted down from the north country. The Mad Trapper of Rat River was still at large. One man against the combined strength of the RCMP and the elements. Everything possible, including dynamite, had been used to bring him in, but all had failed. It was quite a story. The hunt was a welcome diversion from the Depression which gripped the world. Indeed, radio sales throughout North America increased dramatically expressly to hear news of the Mad Trapper of Rat River.

From January 16 to January 29, a large posse headed by

Inspector Eames hunted the wanted man. Often they would pick up his trail, but each time he would manage to elude his hunters. Even his pursuers began to admire his resourcefulness and stamina against impossible odds.

On January 29, a portion of the posse, four men in all, led by Spike Millen, found Johnson's camp. They waited until he was exposed beside a steep incline, but just as they were about to warn the surrounded man, Johnson spotted Millen. In an instant his 30-30 flashed into action. Millen and his companions returned the fire. During a lull in the shooting Millen shouted to the wanted man to surrender. The wind swirled in the still quiet that sometimes accompanies the bitter cold. The Mad Trapper, hunched behind a fallen log, remained silent.

Two hours passed. It was very possible that Johnson was dead. Millen decided to take his man. Exposing himself to danger, he walked forward a few paces. A shot whistled by Millen's ear as he lunged for cover. Johnson was alive. Millen returned his fire. The Mad Trapper shot once more. Millen sprang to his feet and collapsed in the snow. He was dead.

During the night, Johnson scaled a cliff and escaped. Now Albert Johnson, the Mad Trapper of Rat River, was a murderer.

The Mounties brought their dead colleague back to Aklavik. Here Inspector Eames, who had great respect for the cunning of his adversary, regrouped his forces. For the first time in Canada, an airplane was employed in a manhunt. The plane's main function, other than to search for signs of the Mad Trapper, was to supply Eames's dogs with food. Previously, searches had to be terminated as dog food ran low.

On February 5, famed bush pilot Wop May joined the hunt. Inspector Eames and his party, being supplied by May and his Bellanca, could now extend their search area.

In 1930, Staff Sergeant Earl Hersey had been sent to Merschel Island to open and maintain a radio station. In the winter he made his quarters in Aklavik. Hersey was only 18 years old. He and a colleague, Sergeant R.F. Riddell, had been loaned by the Army Signal Corps to the Mounties. Hersey knew more than radio. A crack shot, the tough young sergeant was an expert with dogs and sled.

During the first week in February, Albert Johnson, now a ragtag desperate man, who had lived off the barren land for over a month, made a break for freedom. During a raging blizzard he managed to cross the treacherous Richardson Mountains. He was spotted near Eagle River. On February 13, thirteen men—trappers, army personnel and Mounties—started off through the mountains via Rat Pass. Wop May in his Bellanca picked up Johnson's trail on February 14, about 20 miles up the Eagle River.

Six dog teams followed Johnson's trail. The cunning Johnson was travelling in caribou tracks in an attempt to evade detection. Young Sergeant Hersey, with his top-notch team of dogs, led the hunt.

Years later, the then 66-year-old Hersey described the scene this way: "With six dog teams yelping and barking there was a lot of noise. We were travelling up the bed of a creek when I came to a hairpin turn. Later we all realized what happened. Johnson, out of sight around the bend, heard our noise and thought we were coming from the other direction. We spotted each other at approximately the same time. We were heading toward each other at a distance of about 300 yards. That's when the shooting started."

When the shot tore into Hersey's knee, elbow and side he dropped immediately into the soft snow. Hersey was paralyzed from the waist down, but had full use of his arms. He frantically burrowed in the snow as fast as he could. The Mad Trapper fired three more shots at Hersey, but all missed their target.

By this time the other dog teams appeared on the scene. Johnson ignored the Mounties' warning shout. A fusillade of bullets brought the wanted man down. His body had been hit by 17 bullets. The Mad Trapper of Rat River was dead.

Wop May, who was observing the shootout from the air, brought his Bellanca to rest beside the seriously wounded Hersey. In less than an hour, the wounded man was in a hospital in Aklavik. Throughout his ordeal he remained conscious and has total recall of the entire episode.

"My arm didn't hurt much, nor did the hole in my side, but my knee hurt like hell."

All Hersey's wounds were tended without the use of anesthetic. Later, Hersey noted a wrinkle on his bedsheet. He patted the wrinkle, but it wouldn't go away. A nurse mentioned the incident to a doctor, who examined the area. He found that a bullet had travelled clear through Hersey's side and had lodged about a quarter of an inch under his skin. The doctor cut the skin and presented Hersey with the bullet.

Although there have been many theories about Johnson's life before he came to the Arctic, no one has succeeded in positively identifying him. He simply appeared in the north country as a quiet, gruff man with no past.

Sergeant Hersey stayed in the army until he retired in 1954 with the rank of major. Almost all traces of the great manhunt have slowly disappeared. Hersey's mitts and parka are on display beside Johnson's homemade snowshoes in the RCMP Museum in Regina.

The Mad Trapper of Rat River left one lasting memorial. Picking up a broom handle, Earl Hersey was quick to point out, "That bullet hole through the elbow has affected my golf swing to this day."

– PATRICK KELLY –

ON MARCH 28, 1981, Jeanette Kelly plunged to her death from the seventeenth floor of her luxurious Palace Pier apartment overlooking Lake Ontario.

Two years later, her husband, Patrick, a former RCMP undercover officer, was charged with murder. This is the story of their lives together, culminating with Jeanette's death and with Patrick standing trial for her murder.

When Pat Kelly was still a child, his family moved from Toronto to Victoria, British Columbia. He attended school in Victoria, graduating from Mountain View High School after completing Grade 12.

Patrick Kelly, a clean-cut, bright young man, tried his hand at banking. He obtained employment with the Bank of Montreal in Port Alberni, British Columbia, and was soon transferred to Dawson Creek. It was only a matter of a few months before Pat knew that the life of a banker was not for him. He left the bank and caught on with a logging company, but here too, a restless streak, maybe an adventurous one, made Pat look to greener pastures. What could hold more promise of adventure than the RCMP?

On November 2, 1970, Pat Kelly joined the Mounties

and was assigned to Regina for basic training. Six months later he graduated and was sent to Toronto, where he spent four months on duty at Pearson International Airport. The next step in Pat's law enforcement career found him stationed at the RCMP detachment at Owen Sound. Here he got his first taste of undercover work, becoming involved in narcotics and customs investigations. A year later, he was transferred back to Toronto to enroll in a French course, which lasted 18 months. Pat was then assigned to the drug squad. Soon he was an undercover drug squad operative.

In 1974, Pat's superiors sent him to the University of Javaria in Bogota, Colombia, to take part in a total immersion course in Spanish. Later, while vacationing in Acapulco with fellow RCMP officer Wayne Humby, Pat met his future wife, Jeanette Hanlon.

The daughter of an automobile dealer in Glasgow, Scotland, attractive Jeanette hit it off with Pat right from the start. She was an employee of Avianca, Colombia's national airline, and was stopping over in Acapulco on her way back to Scotland after setting up a computer program for an airline in New Zealand. Jeanette and Pat were seldom apart during the week they spent in Mexico.

Jeanette, who had a full airline pass, returned to Scotland to visit her family. She and Pat kept in constant touch by phone for a few weeks. Then she joined him in Toronto. The lovers discussed marriage. Jeanette was smitten. She returned to Scotland, but three months later emigrated to Canada to live with Pat Kelly. Ten months after her return, on September 20, 1975, Jeanette and Pat were married.

They had become good friends with another couple, Dawn Tabor and John Pinkerton Hastey, better known as

Pinky. Dawn and Pinky had been childhood friends in Maine. A short time after they arrived in Toronto, they married. They lived at 1900 Bloor Street East in Mississauga. Pat and Jeanette lived at Applewood Towers in Mississauga. Dawn Hastey is a name to remember. Sometime later, in the tangled web of the Kellys' life, Dawn would play a starring role.

By 1976, Pat and Jeanette had purchased their first home from Pat's cousin, Jack McKay, at 16 George Street in Cookstown. Jeanette discovered she had a flair for interior decorating. The young couple worked several months renovating their new home.

Once they were nicely settled, Jeanette opened a craft shop specializing in homemade quilts. She named it The Quilt Shop. Farmers' wives around Cookstown brought their handmade quilts to Jeanette, who sold them in the shop. The trendy shop gradually caught on. While it didn't produce a large profit, it did pay its own way. In the summer of 1978, the Kellys sold their shop at a small profit.

The summer of 1978 was a rather stressful time for Pat. He was deeply involved in an RCMP undercover drug operation and had been attempting to sell his home in Cookstown and purchase a condominium in the Palace Pier apartment building in the west end of Toronto. The house in Cookstown had been up for sale with no takers for more than 10 months. This was of some concern, since Pat had put $3,000 down on the new apartment, but required a further $5,700 to close the deal toward the total price of $87,000.

Later, Pat would testify that he had several sources from whom he could have borrowed the balance of his down payment. However, all his problems appeared to evaporate when, in August, the Cookstown house burned to the ground. At the time of the fire, Pat claimed that he was at a lodge in Algonquin Park, while Jeanette was visiting her family in Glasgow. Pat phoned Jeanette, who flew back to Toronto.

Arson was strongly suspected. Jeanette was understandably shocked when Pat was charged with setting fire to the house, along with two counts of attempting to defraud the insurance companies. Their marriage deteriorated into a strained relationship. In Pat's own words, "Basically a platonic relationship took place. I didn't get in her way and she didn't get in mine. We would often socialize together and go to a movie perhaps or go to dinner." It was a remarkably congenial atmosphere, considering the circumstances.

For some time after the fire took place, Pat and Jeanette lived at the Holiday Inn in Don Mills under police protection. The drug probe involving Pat had been finalized in July and the fire had taken place in August. There was a grave suspicion that Pat's life was in danger. To this day, Pat claims that criminals burned down his house shortly after his cover was blown.

Others obviously had a different theory, but things took a turn for the better for the Kellys. Pat was discharged on the arson charges. He collected $60,000 in insurance for the house and $55,000 for the contents, in all $115,000.

Pat and Jeanette took a holiday in Mexico. The Kellys grew much closer now that the terrible possibility of a conviction and prison sentence had been lifted from their shoulders. When they returned to Toronto, there seemed little reason not to move into the Palace Pier.

On October 3, 1978, the Kellys moved into their luxurious new apartment. Although the Kellys' domestic situation improved, there were other women in Pat Kelly's life. Let's start with Dawn Hastey.

Five years after her marriage Dawn had marital difficulties with her husband, Pinky. It was only natural that she discuss her problems with her close friends, the Kellys. Both Pat and Jeanette were sympathetic listeners. They told her that she would be welcome to stay with them should she leave her husband.

The very night this discussion took place, Dawn had a heart-to-heart talk with her husband. The next day, she moved into the Kellys' one-bedroom apartment. Dawn slept on a pullout couch in the den.

A few weeks after Dawn moved in, Jeanette took a trip to Italy. Pat flew to Vancouver on personal business. The arrangement was working out rather well. The Kellys had an old English sheepdog, appropriately named Kelly, a 90-pound animal that took some looking after. Dawn would take care of the dog.

Pat returned from Vancouver unexpectedly at eight o'clock the next morning. Dawn was sleeping in the den. One thing led to another. Dawn had sexual intercourse with her best friend's husband. It didn't stop there. Over a period of time, they made love again and again.

In various statements, Dawn has admitted, "It could have been 10 times." On other occasions, she testified, "From the first time we made love until the last time, I don't know. I mean, I could say 3 times or, say, 13 times." Obviously, it would have been too much to ask Mrs. Hastey to keep a score card. She is even on record as saying, "Probably every night when I was there."

Pat, who denies ever being intimate with Dawn, well recalls arriving at his apartment after an early morning flight from the West Coast: "She was sleeping in the den, and when I came in, I asked her if she wanted a coffee and I was going to make one for myself, and I made a coffee for her and took it into the den. She mentioned she hadn't slept well and asked for a back rub. I started to give her the back rub, and at one point she turned over and reached up to me and pulled me toward her to kiss her, and I said I would make another cup of coffee and got up."

There were other women in Pat Kelly's busy life. In 1978, during the course of an official investigation, Pat met librarian Jan Bradley. Every few months or so thereafter, he dropped into the library and took Jan out for coffee. For reasons of his own, he told her his name was Pat McLean. This rather casual relationship continued until January 1981. Later that month, he and Jan spent a weekend at the Briars, a resort near Sutton, Ontario. They slept together for the first time. Pat informed Jan that his real name was Kelly, not McLean. She didn't take the deception well. The weekend was cut short, but the lovers made up, and Jan Bradley, like Dawn Hastey, would play a large part in the future lives of the Kellys.

Pat had other diversions besides his wife, Dawn and Jan. In the summer of 1980, he met a young lady named Cheryl. Their relationship lasted until the Christmas season that year. Pat claims it was a casual affair—movies, dinner, drinks, that sort of thing. Another lady, Leslie, was being courted in the same manner.

How did Patrick Kelly manage it all: an expensive car, luxurious apartment, European vacations and his constant squiring of a string of women?

In 1980, Pat left the service of the RCMP. During his career as an undercover agent with the Mounties, he'd made many important contacts, particularly in Colombia. Pat acted as courier for wealthy Colombians who wanted to get their money into the United States or Europe due to the instability of the Colombian government. He received healthy commissions for his services and never reported these commissions as income.

Pat, who clearly had a keen eye for turning a fast dollar, also acted in bringing seller and purchaser together for the sale of real estate in Mexico. Sellers desiring only cash for property would be put in touch with buyers who wanted to purchase properties at considerable discounts. Once the deal was consummated, Pat received commissions from both parties. Here again, Pat never declared this income.

Years earlier, Pat had attended junior high school with Victor Simpson in Victoria. The school chums kept in touch. Victor became a lawyer, while Pat became a law enforcement officer.

In 1980, Victor Simpson formed a company known as K&V Enterprises, which acted as a holding company for a variety of financial transactions. In September 1980, Pat became an employee of K&V Enterprises, with the title of executive manager. His main duties, according to Simpson, were "to investigate and locate investment opportunities for the company." Pat received a salary of $1,200 a month from K&V and a monthly car allowance of $225. From time to time Pat also invested large amounts in K&V to facilitate deals that K&V made in French- and Spanish-speaking countries. In essence, almost everything funnelled into K&V came back to Kelly in wages, allowances, or loans from the company.

Apparently, Jeanette Kelly was unaware of just how her husband made his living. She did, however, know that they had collected a tidy sum in insurance after the Cookstown house fire. She also knew that she lived in a luxurious apartment, drove a late-model Porsche and could afford to slip away to Europe whenever the fancy struck her.

In fact, in 1980, Jeanette travelled to Italy, accompanied by Dawn, who was then separated from her husband. Pat not only financed his wife's expenses, he also loaned $4,000 to Dawn so that she could travel with Jeanette.

Jeanette and Dawn separated after their plane landed in Rome. Dawn took a room at the Holiday Inn in St. Peter's Square, while Jeanette had a liaison with a friend, Marchello Rodocachi. According to Dawn's later testimony, Marchello and Jeanette were madly in love. The couple travelled together to Austria.

Dawn claimed that Jeanette had confided that she had to decide whether to return to Pat in Canada or stay with Marchello as his mistress in Europe.

Dawn returned to Toronto in August, a few days before Jeanette. She stayed at the Kelly apartment, but her affair with Pat had waned. When Jeanette returned, Dawn noticed that she and Pat were extremely cool to each other. It was obvious to her that Jeanette was sorry to be back in Toronto. Dawn moved out of the Kellys' apartment and into a friend's home in Burlington.

A few weeks later, Dawn told Pat that Jeanette had mentioned divorce. If there was a divorce, Pat said, Jeanette would end up with nothing. Jeanette was not aware of many of his debts. He had told Jeanette his feelings on the matter. According to Dawn, Jeanette expressed concern about her lifestyle and decided to leave things exactly as they were. Dawn Hastey paid back the $4,000 she owed Pat Kelly for the European holiday, and shortly thereafter moved to the United States. In February 1981, Dawn returned to Toronto.

That winter was a hectic one for all the participants in the Kelly affair. Pat was seeing Jan Bradley on a regular basis. They slipped away to New York for pleasant and expensive weekends at the Park Plaza and Algonquin Hotels. Their relationship intensified right up until March 28, when Jeanette Kelly plunged to her death from the seventeenth floor of the Palace Pier.

Two distinct versions exist as to how Jeanette Kelly met her death. This is the version Pat Kelly told witnesses at the time of the tragedy. It is the version he would relate from the witness stand three years after the events took place.

The Kellys awoke around 9 a.m. that fateful day. They had tea and toast on the balcony. It was going to be a busy day for Jeanette. She was flying to Italy that evening at 6 p.m. and was busy packing. Pat helped. Then he and Jeanette slipped out for brunch at the Magic Pan in Sherway Gardens. They returned at 2 p.m.

Pat went downstairs to a storage area and carried up his wife's Samsonite luggage. They continued to clean up the apartment and pack Jeanette's clothing until around 3:15 p.m. At that time Pat suggested a pot of tea. He went into the kitchen to prepare the tea. Jeanette strolled in, mentioning something about the sound of rattling on the balcony. She picked up a stool and walked out to the balcony.

Pat went back to preparing the tea when he heard his wife cry out. He dashed to the balcony and saw Jeanette falling. He clutched at his wife and managed to get both hands around the upper part of her legs, but as she was still in motion, he couldn't maintain his grasp and Jeanette fell.

Pat phoned the doorman, instructing him to call an ambulance. He then ran to the elevators and was beside his wife's body in minutes. Pat felt Jeanette's pulse. There was none. Pat Kelly closed his wife's eyes. He followed the body in a separate ambulance to St. Joseph's Hospital. Pat was beside himself with grief.

On April 1, the day Jeanette was buried, Pat demonstrated to Sergeant Michael Duchak of the Toronto Metropolitan Police just how the accident had occurred. According to Duchak, he and Kelly stood about three feet apart. Kelly lunged at Duchak and put his arms around the police officer's waist. He put his right cheek to the right side of the police officer's chest and held on. Then Duchak states, Kelly let go and said, "She was already over the balcony, we were face-to-face, I remember looking at her face. I was leaning over the rail. I was too weak to hold on to her and she fell."

Prior to his wife's death, Pat claims he had arrangements to take a trip to Hawaii with Jan Bradley. Now, completely broken up over his wife's tragic death, he decided that the trip might be just what he needed to take his mind off his troubles. On April 6, 1981, eight days after his wife's untimely death, Patrick Kelly flew off to Hawaii for a holiday with Jan Bradley.

When Pat and Jan returned, Pat found it embarrassing to continually have to explain how the accident occurred. Later, witnesses stated that Pat claimed that his wife had fallen while hanging plants on the balcony. Others stated he told them that she was attempting to fix a noisy rattle. Pat moved to Victoria for the summer.

Back in Toronto, Jan was being questioned by police. Pat sent her money and advised her to retain a lawyer. Meanwhile, Pat, who apparently was never one to let grass grow under his feet, kept company with several other women. Three years later, Crown counsel would insinuate that, as a former police officer, Kelly was cunning enough to consort with other women in order to divert suspicion from Jan Bradley. Pat, of course, claimed his involvement with other women was not serious.

Jan couldn't stand the pressure. She left her job and flew to Victoria to discuss matters with Pat. In June, the couple vacationed in Florida. That fall, Pat decided to sell the Palace Pier condo, which held bitter memories, and move to the south of France. He could well afford the move.

In September 1981, Pat collected life insurance from London Life Insurance Co. on three policies totalling $221,813.83. In addition to these policies, he collected $43,324.80 from Confederation Life, which covered the group plan at Canadian Pacific Airline, where Jeanette had been employed. In all, the insurance proceeds on Jeanette Kelly's life amounted to $271,138.83.

In December 1981, Jan Bradley drove with her mother from Toronto to Montreal's Mirabel Airport. Pat arrived on a flight from Victoria. Together, they flew to France. Later, Mrs. Bradley attended her daughter's wedding in the south of France.

Pat and his new wife adjusted nicely to their lifestyle. They often took pleasant junkets to the Bahamas for the weekend. Pat bought new suits by the dozen.

Meanwhile, Toronto police, who had their suspicions from the day of Jeanette Kelly's death, went about gathering evidence. Dr. John Deck, staff neuropathologist at the

Toronto General Hospital had performed an autopsy on Jeanette Kelly's body the day after the fall. From his examination, Dr. Deck indicated that Jeanette Kelly contacted the ground in a sitting position, resulting in severe injuries to the base of the spine as well as the back of both legs. There were no major external injuries above the waist.

Dr. Deck pointed out that abrasions to the left breast, in his opinion, had not been incurred as a result of the fall. He felt the abrasions were consistent with a blow of some kind. The doctor further pointed out small scrape marks near the deceased's nose, injuries to the upper and lower lip and an abrasion over the jaw, which were not consistent with the major injuries connected to the fall. Later, in answer to prosecution counsel's question, "Are those injuries you noted to the face, the nose and the mouth consistent or inconsistent with a punch, one or more punches?," Dr. Deck replied, "I think they are quite possibly consistent with more than one punch."

Paul Malbeuf, a member of Toronto's Metro Police Emergency Task Force, took part in an interesting experiment. An exact duplicate of the pertinent areas of Apt. 1705 was constructed. A female police officer was positioned on the stool allegedly used by Jeanette Kelly. The stool was placed beside the balcony rail. Malbeuf, an all-around athlete, was positioned in the kitchen beside the kettle, where Kelly claimed to have been when his wife cried out.

When the female police officer screamed, Malbeuf, a former 100-yard-dash champion, wearing running shoes, was to race to her aid before she fell over the rail. Malbeuf extended himself, but try as he might, he never once reached the woman in time to grasp her before she fell, as

Kelly claimed had happened with his wife. In fact, the experiment was tried several times, but Malbeuf never came close to making contact with the police officer.

To add substance to the results of Officer Malbeuf's experiments, Eric Krueger of Toronto's Centre of Forensic Sciences, an expert in velocity, stated that Jeanette, 5 feet 3 inches tall and 132 pounds, would have been on the ground in three seconds. The fastest a runner could make it to her side was four seconds. Besides, according to Krueger, if Jeanette accidentally lost her balance, she would not have landed on her spine.

On a visit to Canada in 1982, Patrick Kelly was arrested on three charges of credit card fraud involving $125,000. He was then charged with his wife's murder.

Much of the evidence related here came from expert testimony and from witnesses who observed Pat Kelly's guilty actions. But the Crown's star witness was not an expert. Dawn Tabor/Hastey/Bragg, the Kellys' dear friend, claimed to be an eyewitness to Jeanette Kelly's murder. By the time Pat came to trial, Dawn had married for the second time.

Dawn Bragg stated she was in Apt. 1705 on the day of Jeanette Kelly's death. On March 29, 1981, Dawn drove up to the Palace Pier and entered the building via a back door, using keys given to her by Jeanette some months earlier. Both Pat and Jeanette were in. They were arguing. Dawn offered to give Jeanette a lift to the airport.

Meanwhile, she was asked to take a seat in the den. She could hear her friends arguing about a divorce. Jeanette was adamant about refusing to grant Pat a divorce. The Kellys raised their voices. Suddenly, Jeanette screamed. Dawn walked out of the den to find her friend Jeanette on the floor. Pat picked up the limp form of his wife. He carried her over to the balcony and opened the doors. From the witness stand, Dawn Bragg would state, "He took Jeanette out to the balcony and dropped her over the edge."

Dawn went out to the balcony, looked down and collapsed. In an instant, Pat was at her side, consoling her, telling her everything would be all right, telling her he loved her. Pat hurried Dawn to the elevators. They went up a few floors. All the while, Pat told Dawn to be quiet, to go out the back way and go home. She listened and did as she was told. After all, she and Pat had been lovers.

Dawn remembered well one night at the Palace Pier Club when Pat had discussed killing Jeanette. He said he would take Dawn to France. He told her he was in love. He also told her there was no way anyone could tell how a person fell off a balcony.

According to Dawn, Pat had previously confided to her how he set fire to his home in Cookstown. He took Dawn to the lodge where he'd supposedly stayed when his house burned down. He explained how he went to bed that night, got up and drove to Cookstown. He spread gasoline throughout the house and lit it, then he drove back to the lodge without being seen.

The day after Jeanette fell to her death, Dawn Bragg was in a dilemma. Three years later, as the Crown's star witness in the murder trial of Pat Kelly, she attempted to explain when she was asked, "What were your feelings on March 30?"

"I was afraid," Dawn answered. "Afraid of what I had seen and I was afraid of Pat. I was afraid I knew too much." A couple of days after Jeanette's funeral, Pat called Dawn.

He told her he was going away alone and would call her if he needed her.

Dawn Bragg's story was fascinating. If true, it branded Pat Kelly a cold-blooded killer. Yet, there were doubts concerning her testimony. Why did she wait two years to inform police that she was a witness to Jeanette's death? Quite possibly, Dawn Bragg felt that she could be charged with conspiracy to commit murder. Given the promise by Metro police Sergeant Ed Stewart that any statement she might give would not be used against her, she decided to reveal to police that she was in Apt. 1705 when Jeanette was killed. Sergeant Stewart, who had doggedly gathered evidence for close to three years, would later earn a commendation for his relentless work on the Kelly case.

Defence counsel Earl Levy pleaded that much of the prosecution evidence was theatrical and circumstantial. If Dawn Bragg, an admitted liar, was still lying when she claimed to be an eyewitness to the murder, then the prosecution's case was without merit.

Crown counsel L. Budzinsky contended that even without Dawn Bragg's testimony, the circumstantial evidence against Kelly was overwhelming. If Dawn's evidence was taken at face value, Pat Kelly was guilty of first-degree murder.

The jury agreed with the Crown. Pat Kelly was found guilty of murder in the first degree. He was sentenced to life imprisonment with no possibility of parole for 25 years.

Kelly appealed his conviction. The Ontario Court of Appeals upheld the conviction. Mr. Justice Bert MacKinnon stated on behalf of the three-man court, "There was no miscarriage of justice."

Despite the Court of Appeal's decision, Kelly's legal counsel has appealed to the federal justice minister under the so-called last-resort protocol. As a result, the court heard new and drastically altered testimony from Dawn Bragg. She now professes that she did not witness Kelly in the act of throwing his wife off the balcony.

The appeal court has still to sift through forensic evidence and cross-examine scientific experts before rendering a decision.

– ARTHUR KENDALL –

ARTHUR KENDALL, HIS WIFE, Helen, and their five children, Jimmie, 12, Margaret, 10, Ann, 8, Jean, 5, and Mary, 1, lived on a farm in Elma Township in southern Ontario.

In the spring of 1952, Arthur and a neighbour put in a crop of flax. Arthur looked around for some way to supplement his farm income during the summer months while the flax grew to maturity. He went on a fishing trip to the Bruce Peninsula on May 24, and met Ashford Pedwell, who owned a sawmill. The elderly Pedwell took a liking to the stocky, serious Kendall, and when Arthur volunteered that he was a carpenter as well as a farmer, Pedwell offered him a job running the sawmill. Kendall accepted the job with the proviso that he had to return to his farm in September to harvest his flax. This was agreeable to Pedwell, who told Kendall that he needed more hands for the mill, and asked Arthur to bring help with him when he came back.

The mill was located a few miles to the south of

Tobermory on a side road, known as the Johnston Harbour Road, that led to Lake Huron. On May 26, Arthur started his new job; he had brought Jim Baillie, the son of a neighbour, with him, and the next week he hired two more boys, Gordon Neabel and George Hislop. The four men worked the mill and lived in a shack directly across the road. The shack came with the job, and was to be used as living quarters. It wasn't long before Baillie tired of the work and returned home.

Then Arthur asked his wife and children to join them. Not many women would feel that crowding into a shack measuring 12 by 14 feet with five children and three adult men was much of a vacation, but Helen Kendall didn't see it that way. They could all stand a change from the farm. The children were out of school, and there was a lake close by for swimming. All in all, the whole family liked the idea. Sleeping arrangements were a bit of a problem, but everyone seemed to fit comfortably enough into the shack. There were upper and lower bunks on each side of the single room. Neabel and Hislop slept in the upper bunk on the west side, while Arthur, Helen and 18-month-old Mary slept in the lower bunk on the east side. Jimmie and Jean had the top bunk on the east side, and Margaret and Ann shared the bottom bunk on the west side. They had a small stove and a table that could seat five.

Both hired men were very impressed with Helen Kendall. Despite trying conditions, she managed to serve good meals and always kept the little shack clean and tidy. She was meticulous about her own appearance, and her children were always clean and neatly dressed.

Mrs. Kendall had no way of knowing that before she arrived on the scene, Arthur had met a waitress named

Beatrice Hogue at the Olympia Restaurant in Wiarton. Beatrice was an attractive redhead who had a total of seven children, two of whom were from a previous marriage. When Arthur met her, six of the children were living with her at her home in Wiarton. Thomas Hogue, her husband, was a sailor on the Great Lakes and was away from home a great deal. Kendall saw a lot of Beatrice during the early summer, and it soon became obvious to friends and acquaintances that they were having an affair.

On July 26, Neabel and Hislop finished at the sawmill for the season. Helen served them dinner, after which Arthur gave them a lift down to Elma Township. He went by way of Wiarton and picked up Beatrice and her six children. Then he dropped the two men off and proceeded to his own farm, where he and the Hogue family stayed the night. Next morning he paid a visit to a neighbour, Martin Barker, and inquired if he would like to hire Beatrice to look after his house and children. Barker replied that she had too many children and let it go at that. Kendall then returned the Hogue family to Wiarton and went on to the little shack on Johnston Harbour Road.

The next we hear of Arthur and his family is when he and his children returned to their farm. They arrived back prematurely, as the flax wasn't ready to be harvested and it was still several weeks until school opened. Their appearance surprised the Kendalls' immediate neighbour, James Broughton, and he went over to speak to his friend Art. Instead of greeting him warmly, Kendall was sullen and sharp. The children, who were normally very friendly to Broughton, tried to avoid him. Helen was nowhere to be seen, but Beatrice Hogue and her children were very much in evidence.

FREDERICK CORNWALLIS BENWELL
SEPT. 15, 1865 — FEB. 17, 1890

THE MOST FAMOUS MURDER AND MURDER TRIAL IN CANADIAN
HISTORY TOOK PLACE IN THE PRINCETON AREA.
FREDERICK C. BENWELL OF CHELTENHAM, ENGLAND, CAME TO EASTWO[OD]
[WITH J]OHN REGINALD BIRCHALL OF ACCRINGTON, ENGLAND. BELIEVING
[HE] WAS TO TRAIN AND INVEST WITH BIRCHALL UNDER THE POPULA[R]
[P]UPIL INDUSTRY PROGRAM. SUPPOSEDLY EN ROUTE TO A
[PRO]SPECTIVE FARM, BIRCHALL TOOK BENWELL TO A SWAMP ON THE 2ND
[C]ONC. OF BLENHEIM TWP. LATER, TWO LOCAL WOODCUTTERS FOUND
BENWELL'S BODY, WHICH WAS TAKEN TO J.H. SWARTS FUNERAL HOME I[N]
PRINCETON. AN AUTOPSY SHOWED CAUSE OF DEATH TO BE TWO GUNSH[OT]
WOUNDS TO THE HEAD. THOUGH BURIED UNIDENTIFIED, THE BODY WAS
EXHUMED AND IDENTIFIED BY BIRCHALL.
   DUE TO THE WORK OF ONT. CHIEF GOVERNMENT DETECTIVE JOHN W[ILSON]
MURRAY, BIRCHALL WAS CHARGED WITH MURDER. HIS TRIAL BY JUR[Y]
TOOK PLACE IN WOODSTOCK BEFORE JUSTICE HUGH MACMAHON. THE C[ASE]
BECAME WORLD FAMOUS DUE TO WIDESPREAD INTEREST IN THE FARM
PUPIL INDUSTRY, MURRAY'S UNPRECEDENTED USE OF NEWSPAPERS TO
PUBLISH A PICTURE OF AN AS-YET-UNIDENTIFIED CORPSE; LEGAL USE O[F]
METEROLOGICAL EVIDENCE TO DETERMINE TIME OF DEATH; AND
TRANSMISSION OF THE TRIAL PROCEEDINGS VIA THE NEW
TRANS-ATLANTIC TELEGRAPH CABLE.
   CONVICTED ON CIRCUMSTANTIAL EVIDENCE, BIRCHALL WAS HANGED
NOV. 14, 1890 AND IS BURIED IN THE WOODSTOCK JAIL YARD. BENWEL[L]
IS BURIED HERE IN THE PRINCETON CEMETERY.

*Author at the last resting place of
murder victim Frederick C. Benwell
(photo by Shawn Hudes)*

May Bannister at the time of her conviction for harbouring a stolen child

Bill Newell kissing his wife Elna during happier times

Evelyn Dick

Albert Guay as he appeared in court after being convicted of his wife's murder

Doubts about Robert Rae Cook, shown here accompanied by a Mountie, remain to this day

*Arthur Kendall
being taken
into custody*

*A policeman
accompanies murder
suspect Ronald Turpin
as he leaves the cells
at City Hall*

Dennis Melvyn Howe as he looked when released from a Saskatchewan prison and an age-enhanced photo of Howe as he might look today.

*Doug Worth taken into custody
in May of 1988*

Paul Bernardo and Karla Homolka
on their wedding day

Broughton inquired about Helen. Art explained that his wife had left him. Broughton found this hard to believe, as he was aware of Helen's deep affection for her children. Arthur said that he and his wife had had a fight in the shack. Angry words had been exchanged and Helen had thrown a cup of tea at him. He had then stormed out of the shack with the idea of driving his car off the wharf at Tobermory, but when he got there, there had been too many cars and he couldn't get to the edge of the wharf. He returned to Johnston Harbour early in the morning and young Jimmie told him that his mother had left right after Art had driven away. Kendall claimed he never saw his wife again.

It was now Friday morning. Kendall made breakfast for the children and went to work at the mill. On Saturday night, he dropped his children off at Mrs. Hogue's and went on to his farm. On Sunday night, he said, he slept with young Jimmie in his car outside Wiarton. He hung around Wiarton all day Monday, and on Monday night slept in the shack at Johnston Harbour with his son. On Tuesday, he loaded his car with some belongings and left Johnston Harbour.

Jim Broughton couldn't get Arthur's story or the children's strange behaviour out of his mind. It was as if Arthur was talking about some other person, not Helen, the devoted wife and mother. Nothing seemed to fit. After a few days he decided to visit Arthur again. This time, accompanied by Lloyd Machon, another neighbour, he again inquired about Helen. Arthur was evasive, but gave the impression that she might be with her mother in Brantford. Later that day Broughton called Brantford and asked Helen's brother, Ross Cameron, if she was there. Her brother told him that she was not in Brantford, and the story of her disappearance so upset him that he decided to visit Arthur.

That same night Ross Cameron went to the Kendall farm in Elma Township. Arthur came out of the house and met him in the yard. He avoided Ross's direct questions about Helen and didn't seem to want to talk about her. The children, who were usually underfoot making a fuss when their uncle visited, were nowhere to be seen. Finally, Ross Cameron left the Kendall farm and went to the Sebringville Ontario Provincial Police Office, where he had previously arranged to meet Jim Broughton. The two men reported Helen Kendall as a missing person.

Arthur was questioned by the police but didn't give any new information. Helen's picture was distributed to police stations across Canada and the United States. She had blue eyes, blond hair, stood five feet seven inches tall, weighed 132 pounds and was considered to be an attractive mature woman. The Kendall children were also questioned, but were reluctant to volunteer any information of a concrete nature. Mary was too young to interrogate, but Ann and Jean were questioned extensively, and each time they were gently pressed for an answer about their mother's disappearance, they burst into tears. Margaret, the eldest daughter corroborated her father's story in every way, as did 12-year-old Jimmie. The police felt the children were not telling the complete truth and came to the conclusion that the Kendall children feared their father.

The little shack and the family car were examined, with no results. Everyone questioned knew of Kendall's relationship with Beatrice Hogue, but could offer no explanation as to what had happened to Helen.

On September 3, approximately a month after Helen's disappearance, John Krugel was cutting bush on his property not far from the Kendall farm when he came upon a cardboard box containing women's undergarments. He notified the police, who later identified the contents of the box as belonging to Helen Kendall. Arthur Kendall appeared to be as mystified as anyone else at the weird discovery. During the month of September, the police were actively looking for Helen Kendall's body. The bush surrounding the shack at Johnston Harbour was thoroughly searched, and likely areas were also combed, but all to no avail.

Months passed, and the authorities began to receive complaints about the care of the 11 children living on the Kendall farm. On January 7, 1953, police received a report from Dr. C.E. Connors of Listowel that Margaret had been attacked by her father with a whip. Evidently she had been warned not to stop off at the farm of Clarence Ronenburg on her way home from school, and when she did drop in on the farm, her father went over and gave her a horse-whipping. Kendall was arrested, but was later released when Margaret said that she had only received a slight punishment for disobeying her father.

The Children's Aid Society was successful in gaining custody of the Kendall children, who were taken away from the Kendall farm for a full year. Arthur appealed this decision, and the children were eventually returned to him.

Kendall and his family moved several times to get away from the rumours that dogged them wherever they went. In 1954, Thomas E. Hogue was granted a divorce from his wife, Beatrice, naming Arthur Kendall as co-respondent. The years sped by, and in 1959, Kendall's lawyer was successful in having Helen declared legally dead. Three months later, Arthur married Beatrice Hogue.

It was now nine years since the happy Kendall family left their farm for what was to be a pleasant vacation in the bush. Margaret, the oldest girl, was married to a private in the Canadian army, stationed in Winnipeg. Ann was living away from home, and Jimmie was a strapping 21-year-old working for Canadian Canners in Exeter. The two children still living with their father, Jean, 14, and Mary, 10, were of deep concern to Ann, who felt that they were being discriminated against, particularly now that they were the only Kendall children still at home.

The police received a telephone call from a friend of Ann's, advising them that Ann would now talk to them. They rushed to interview her. She stated emphatically that she and her older brother and sister had seen her father kill her mother. In front of the officers she called her sister in Winnipeg and told her what she had done. The answer came back sharp and clear, "Ann, I've wanted to do it for years, but I never had the guts!"

Ann then told her story in detail:

"After George Hislop and Gordon Neabel left, our sleeping arrangements were my mother and father in a lower bunk at the back of the cabin on the right as you walked in; my sister, Margaret, and I in the upper bunk above them. On the far left of the cabin at the back, Mary and Jeannie slept in the lower bunk, with Jimmie in the bunk above. A curtain hung between the bunks.

"I don't remember details of going to bed the night before we left Johnston Harbour, but my mother always insisted that we go to bed as soon as it was dark. About dawn—daylight was coming through the one and only window in the cabin—I was awakened by a commotion under our bunk and I heard Mother cry, 'No, Art, please don't.'

"I didn't hear my father say anything. I looked down over the bunk and I saw my father go from the lower bunk and lay a butcher knife on the table which was only one or two steps from the bunk. I saw blood on the knife. My dad was wearing only his work shirt, my mother her night-gown. When I awoke, Margaret was already awake and she put her hand over my mouth.

"I saw my father grab my mother around her shoulders; she was limp. He dragged her out the door. There was only a screen door on the cabin; I remember it slammed shut. I remember my mother's feet were dragging on the floor. I saw my father go past the window toward the bridge—east. I could see him dragging my mother on the road—walking in the direction of the mill.

"Dad was away about 20 minutes or half an hour. As soon as he came back he dressed, then he cleaned up the blood on the floor at the bunk. He took off the bedsheets and the pillowslips and he gathered my mother's clothes. He wiped the floor with my mother's clothes, then wrapped them up with the bedclothes and the butcher knife. He bundled them all up, put them in a shopping bag and went away. I saw him walk past the window. He was away a few minutes longer than the first time.

"As soon as he came back the second time he scrubbed the floor with a brush and rainwater from the tub filled from the cabin drainpipe. I had never seen him clean a floor before, either at the cabin or at home. While washing the floor he told us to get up and get dressed. It had always been a very strict rule in the house that we kids should never make a noise or get up until we were called. He then took Margaret away in the car to get drinking water from the spring. I remember he put the milk can we used for drinking water in the car."

Officers flew to Winnipeg to question Margaret. Her statement was in substance the same as Ann's. It concludes:

"Dad drove me to the fork in the road. As you go from the cabin toward the highway, you come to the mill gate, a culvert over the road where there is quicksand, a hill and a turn, then you reach the fork, where my dad stopped.

"He told me to tell anyone who asked about Mother that she left Thursday night when he was in Wiarton—the night he told us he took Mr. Pedwell for a shot in the arm. Dad told me to say that my mother and he had a quarrel, she threw a cup of hot tea at him, and after he left she walked out, taking her clothes in a shopping bag. I was to say that she told us she would never return.

"Dad told me not to make porridge; the old stove was in poor condition. I was to go to Charlton's store for corn-flakes. Dad didn't actually threaten to kill me but when he told me to do or say anything, I knew better than to disobey him.

"Dad drove me back to the cabin. Before he went to work he told us kids to pick wild strawberries for dinner. I walked to the store for cornflakes and I had to knock to wake up the Charltons. We kids had breakfast. We didn't talk about mother, but I recall a general feeling that she had gone to hospital. It was only when we reached Mrs. Hogue's place that night that I realized mother wasn't sick in Wiarton.

"Dad came home for dinner at noon. Ann and I had picked strawberries and we had killed a rattlesnake. We laid it out on the ground for Dad to see. I had made a stack of sandwiches and we had berries. There was no conversation about Mother. Dad went to work and quit earlier than usual. He came to the cabin and told us to put on our good clothes, we would have supper where we were going.

"He drove us fast to Wiarton. On the way, he loaded some wood in the car and unloaded it in Mrs. Hogue's woodshed. I remember my father saying, 'Beatrice, this is my family.' Then he shaved. We had supper—spaghetti and margarine—I had never tasted either before. Dad and Mrs. Hogue appeared to have known each other before and she also knew my brother, Jimmie."

Arthur Kendall was arrested on January 27, 1961, nine years after his wife disappeared. A preliminary hearing was held on March 3, and Kendall was committed for trial. His trial began in Walkerton on Tuesday, October 24, 1961.

Jimmie Kendall took the stand and told of the night his mother was murdered:

"The last night we were at Johnston Harbour, Dad left the cabin in the car, saying he was taking Mr. Pedwell to the doctor. At dawn I woke up when I heard my mother cry, 'Don't, Art!' She said it three or four times. I was sleeping in the top bunk. I remember looking over the bunk. My mother looked kind of stunned. She was wearing a light-colored nightgown. I saw my dad take my mother out of the cabin. He had his arms under her armpits and she was kind of limp. I believe my mother was still saying, 'Don't, Art,' as my dad took her down the road in the direction of the highway. I think she was still living when she passed the window. I haven't seen my mother since.

"I was frightened and I wondered if my dad was coming back to do the rest of us kids in. Dad came back alone within an hour. He was wearing hip rubber boots. He didn't speak. I noticed a butcher knife on the kitchen table with blood on it. Dad wiped the blood up off the floor with a rag. It took him about 10 minutes. I was scared."

Arthur Kendall sat unmoved as this three children testified against him. The jury took only two hours to find him guilty of capital murder. He was sentenced to hang on January 23, 1962. Seven days before he was to be executed, his sentence was commuted to life imprisonment.

Whatever happened to Helen Kendall's body? No one knows for sure, and it has never been found. The most popular theory is that Kendall disposed of his wife's body by placing it in Lake Scugog, which is located directly behind the Pedwell sawmill. The middle of the lake is blanketed with acres of green marsh grass, which lies about a foot underwater. The rooting of the grass is so tangled it can almost support the weight of a grown man. If Kendall parted this mass and lowered his wife's body under the tangled root system into five more feet of water, the body would never rise to the surface. Mr. Pedwell claimed that he lost many logs in this manner when he ran his sawmill.

Arthur Kendall has never once admitted killing his wife. While confined to the Agassiz Correctional Camp at Agassiz, British Columbia, he claimed his children lied at the trial in order to lay their hands on their mother's small estate. He asked some thought-provoking questions: Why did his children wait nine years to change their stories? They were questioned by mature members of the OPP. Surely they would have told the truth to these professionals, if indeed it was the truth? Why, Kendall asked, would he kill his wife in front of his children when there were so many other places to commit murder, surrounded as they were by wild bush country?

After serving 16 years in prison, Arthur Kendall was paroled. For many years he lived with his second wife, Beatrice Hogue, in Terrance, British Columbia. He has since died of complications resulting from a heart operation.

— DR. WILLIAM KING —

TODAY, THE TOWN OF Brighton, Ontario, is off the beaten path. Located about 100 miles east of Toronto, only a green sign on a superhighway indicates the exit to the peaceful little town.

Years ago, before the Macdonald-Cartier Freeway was built between Toronto and Montreal, Canada's two largest cities, it was necessary to travel through Brighton. In horse-and-buggy days, the town was a main stopover. It was here, back in 1858, that murder so very foul took place, a murder which would capture the attention of the entire country.

William Henry King was born in 1833 on a farm just outside Brighton in the township of Sophiasburg. His parents moved to Brighton, where young William spent his formative years. At the age of five, he was sent off to school, where he displayed a remarkable aptitude for learning. We must remember that we are delving into a time when schooling was not always available, even to those who were recognized as gifted children. As he grew up, William's main activity was helping out on the farm which, in a few short years, became relatively prosperous.

The young man with the driving ambition was pleasant and charming. He stood five feet eleven inches tall and sported a lush growth of sandy whiskers, in keeping with the style of the times.

At the age of 18, William attended teacher-training college in Toronto. Each summer he returned home to work on the family farm. During one of these summers, he started to date Sarah Ann Lawson. Ann, as she was known, left quite a bit to be desired in the looks department. She wore a perpetual frown, which gave her a rather stern appearance. Her personality was diametrically opposite to what one would describe as warm.

The powers that be have a way of evening things out. Ann's father was loaded. John M. Lawson owned a large, prosperous farm and was widely respected throughout the area. Can't you just hear the ladies of Brighton gossiping in the general store over a bolt of gingham: "That handsome King boy is after the Lawson money."

On January 31, 1855, William and Ann were married. While he continued his studies, his dutiful wife took in boarders to help defray the cost of his education. In Toronto, William obtained a first-class teacher's certificate. He returned to Brighton, where he taught for a few months before obtaining a position as a third-grade teacher at Hamilton Central School.

About a year after their marriage, Ann gave birth to a daughter, who was sickly from the day she was born. The child lived for only a little more than a month. It was around this time that a rather ugly rumour circulated about the King marriage. The good folks of Brighton whispered that William mistreated his wife. The rumours were given some credence when Ann did what so many other women have done before and since. She went home to mother.

William's driving ambition would not be stifled. He threw himself into a new career—medicine. With his father-in-law's financial assistance, he enrolled in

Philadelphia's Homeopathy Medical College. Meanwhile, Ann remained under her parents' roof in Brighton. William stayed in Philadelphia for three years, returning home each summer to teach in local schools between college semesters. During one semester, he wrote his wife several letters accusing her of infidelity, a totally bogus accusation. Ann showed the letters to her father, who was so upset he took them to his lawyer. When William apologized, his father-in-law agreed to return the letters. The wily Mr. Lawson took the precaution of copying the strange missives.

In 1858, William King returned to his home town. He was now a bona fide doctor, having graduated from the Homeopathy Medical College, Pennsylvania Medical University and the Eclectic Medical College.

Dr. King hung out his shingle. Right from the beginning, his practice prospered. And why not? Here was a local boy who had displayed the fortitude and determination to better himself. Besides, William dressed well, was always nicely groomed and had a delightful bedside manner. He and Ann reconciled. Everything was coming up roses, until that fall of 1858. Actually, it was exactly September 23 when the bloom came off the rose and love flew out the window, for on that day William King first laid eyes on Melinda Freeland Vandervoort.

It wasn't that the good doctor had eyes only for Melinda. Nothing could be further from the truth. He simultaneously made romantic overtures to a patient, Dorcas Garrett, of nearby Murray. That was a mistake. Dorcas, a Quaker, was just not that type of woman. William sent her a letter expressing undying love and insinuating that his dear wife was not long for this world.

He added that Dorcas should acquaint herself with the niceties of life befitting a doctor's wife.

As I said, Dorcas wasn't having any. She replied in no uncertain terms that she was dismissing him as her physician and at the same time demanded an apology. She threatened to expose him if he made any further advances. William apologized.

Melinda was another kettle of fish. William had sent her a letter, too. She responded to the doctor's letter by sending him a photograph with an accompanying letter containing such titillating lines as "You have unlinked the tender chord of affection until you have an alarming influence over my girlish nature," and, "One smile from your countenance can inspire a depth of veneration in my bosom never felt by me for any individual."

William had struck pay dirt. The pair corresponded. It didn't matter one iota that Ann King was two months pregnant. Her husband wrote Melinda that Ann was very ill and could die at any moment. If Melinda would just wait for another year, she would become the second Mrs. King. When these letters were written, Ann was in perfect health.

Four days after William wrote Melinda concerning his wife's condition, Ann took ill. She vomited continuously, suffered excruciating pains in her stomach and complained of a burning sensation in her throat. During the initial stages of his wife's illness, William provided her sole medical care. He told Ann's family that she was suffering from ulcerations of the womb and that everything possible was being done. So concerned was William that he rarely left his wife's bedside. For three weeks, William laboured over his patient. Some days she seemed to rally, but always slipped back into bouts of vomiting and retching. During the few times Ann was lucid, she implored her husband to stop giving her that hideous white powder five times a day. She complained that it "burned like fire" in her mouth.

Finally, as Ann grew weaker, William succumbed to Ann's father's urging and sought a second medical opinion. Dr. A.E. Fife was told by William that the patient was pregnant and had ulcerations of the womb. The doctor was not asked, nor did he request, to examine Ann. He prescribed ipecacuanha and camphor to alleviate the vomiting.

Nothing seemed to help Ann King. Once again, Mr. Lawson begged his son-in-law to bring in additional medical assistance. Dr. P. Gross was given the same information as Dr. Fife. He too prescribed something to help stem the persistent vomiting.

Who knows what thoughts raced through Ann's mind as she lay there in agony? Certainly she was aware that her husband was carrying on with the rather notorious 20-year-old Melinda Vandervoort. No doubt word drifted back to her of her husband's house calls to rural areas with the ever-present Melinda at his side. Sometimes, Melinda actually cared for Ann in the doctor's absence.

On November 4, 1858, Ann died. Dr. King was beside himself with grief. In fact, he carried on so much that witnesses were in fear for his life. The man convulsed, grew crimson in the face and required medical assistance.

Ann's parents never did like their son-in-law. Now that the worst had happened, they decided to find out once and for all if their suspicions were based on fact. While William was out of the house, Mrs. Lawson searched the premises. She came up with a photo of Melinda Vandervoort, along with suggestive letters from Melinda written to William insinuating how convenient it would be to have Ann out of the way.

On Sunday, November 7, Ann was buried. Dr. King was disconsolate. The following day, Ann's brother Clinton went to the county coroner with an array of incriminating evidence. He lugged along the accusatory letters his father had copied, as well as letters from Melinda to William and the letter written by William to Dorcas Garrett. As soon as she heard about Ann's death, Dorcas had turned it over to Ann's brother.

The Lawsons demanded an inquest into their daughter's death and informed William that an autopsy was to be performed. He was furious, but not so distraught that he didn't proceed directly to Sidney and the ever-loving arms of Melinda Vandervoort.

Once the ball started to roll, there was no stopping it. A coroner's jury was hastily convened and Ann's body exhumed. An autopsy revealed that there was no ulceration of the womb. The stomach and its contents were removed for analysis.

Meanwhile, William, no doubt realizing what the autopsy would reveal, had a meeting with Melinda at her home in Sidney. While at the Vandervoorts', William met Melinda's father for the first time. William told both father and daughter that he and Melinda were in trouble due to his wife's death. He would be arrested and so would Melinda. He implored Mr. Vandervoort for permission to flee with Melinda to Cape Vincent in New York State, where Melinda's aunt lived. William was lying, as he wasn't being sought by the law just yet, but the ploy worked. Mr. Vandervoort allowed his daughter to flee with Dr. King.

A warrant was soon issued for William's arrest. He was

apprehended, brought back to Canada, charged with murder and lodged in jail. Melinda, who had made her way to Cleveland, Ohio, returned to Brighton three weeks later.

On April 4, 1859, Dr. William King stood trial for the murder of his wife. Farmers travelled to the trial by horse and buggy. Those who couldn't get a lift walked to the tiny Cobourg courthouse where the trial was held. It was estimated that 1,500 people attempted to attend the proceedings, but only a fraction of that number gained admittance. King gave the appearance of tolerating the entire distasteful affair.

The Crown went about building its formidable case. The accused man had opportunity and motive. He had predicted his wife's death while she was still in good health and had invented a nonexistent illness to ward off other doctors and to account for her death. Professor Henry Croft of Toronto's University College testified that he had examined the deceased's stomach. It was found to contain 11 grains of arsenic. The liver contained small quantities of arsenic as well. This was vital evidence, as explained by Professor Croft from the witness stand: "Arsenic cannot be put into the liver after death." The main thrust of defence counsel's argument was that arsenic could have been placed in the stomach after death.

Ann's mother took the witness stand and tearfully related that she had watched William mix a white powder with water and administer it to her daughter. Most of the time Ann vomited and retched after each dose. She did admit under cross-examination that, on occasion, Ann's condition had appeared to improve slightly.

Melinda Vandervoort was called to testify. She accounted for her involvement with Dr. King using a few well-chosen answers. In response to what everyone was thinking, she replied, "I never had any improper intercourse with Dr. King." Melinda gave the following explanation for replying to suggestive letters she had received from the doctor, as well as sending him her photograph: "Mrs. King asked me to send the likeness to her. I directed the likeness to Dr. King. I thought that when I got the letter, it was written for amusement. I sent him this letter in answer for amusement."

No one really believed Melinda. After receiving Melinda's photograph, William dashed off a reply to his "Sweet little lump of good nature." In part, he wrote: "Could I indulge in the hope that those winning and genial smiles would ever be found in my possession, all troubles would then cease. It is a perfect infatuation to me. Can you keep from sacrificing yourself upon the hymeneal altar for the next year? I wish so."

Melinda responded with such tasty tidbits as: "Since I first had the pleasure of an introduction, my heart is constantly with you, and I'm not contented a moment. O could I forever be with you; I think I should be happy, for indeed I enjoyed myself to excess during my stay in your presence though suppose now I must eradicate such thoughts from my mind; for you are married, and my destiny must be to love and not share your interesting society."

The defence paraded before the jury an impressive array of doctors who testified to Dr. King's high moral standards, as well as his medical knowledge and skill. The defence made much of the fact that there was opportunity for arsenic to have been placed in the stomach contents after death. This claim was vehemently refuted by the Crown.

The jury retired to deliberate their verdict. When they had difficulty reaching a decision in a few hours, they were sequestered overnight. Promptly at 10 a.m., before a crowded but dead-silent courtroom, the clerk of the court asked the question on everyone's mind: "How say you, gentlemen, is the prisoner guilty or not guilty?" The foreman of the jury replied, "Guilty, with a strong recommendation to mercy."

On Saturday, April 9, Dr. King was once again led into the Cobourg courtroom for sentencing. When asked if he had anything to say before being sentenced, he replied, "I have this much to say, that upon my solemn oath I am not guilty of the charge laid against me. I have no doubt of this; my conscience is perfectly clear upon this point." The presiding judge then sentenced King to be hanged on June 9, 1859. Dr. King wept as he was led away to await his date with the hangman.

While in prison, William confessed to his spiritual adviser, Reverend Vanderburg, that he was guilty of having murdered his wife. Then, quite unlike most killers, he wrote out his confession in detail. Following are excerpts from his written statement:

"Having sinned against society as well as God I feel it my duty to confess my guilt to society with deep humiliation and sincere repentance and ask forgiveness for all my offences against my fellow men."

"My present unfortunate position is the result of an unhappy marriage."

In explanation of his motive, Dr. King wrote: "Miss Vandervoort and myself were greatly enamored of each other. Actions speak louder than words, and I knew that she loved me, and that I could not help loving her in return. She was both lovely and loving. I looked upon her with all her personal charms, and attracting graces and virtues, her attainments and literary acquirements, her mild and affectionate disposition, her genial smiles and affable manners, her good character and winning ways, and while she perfectly reciprocated all my affections, it was as impossible for me not to love her as it would be to fly to the moon.

"Here, then, I had found the object of my affections and the next thing was to get possession of that precious gem I had found, but there presented one obstacle in the way— my wife. It was only now that I allowed the thoughts to enter my mind of doing anything to shorten her life."

William further rationalized his actions by writing: "The law may compel man and wife to live together, but I defy it to compel them to love each other. Oh! how lamentable beyond description that so much misery and unhappiness should arise from unhappy marriages."

William refuted the experts' theories that his wife had died from the cumulative results of arsenic poisoning. He claimed he had given her chloroform. In describing his wife's last moments after she had fallen into a deep coma, he wrote: "Now I would have given worlds to have brought her to. I tried everything but could not succeed. O! what an awful feeling I then felt. How I repented, but, alas, it was too late. I just began to realize what had been done. Oh! the bitter pangs that I experienced cannot be imagined. The Devil had led me headlong into difficulty, but now came the remorse of conscience. Oh! how sharp, how pungent! I felt like death, and thought I would die."

Dr. King wasn't above passing out some free advice: "The way to avoid trouble is not to get in. Better far, not to marry at all than to do so to your sorrow. To those who are married my parting advice is to pray to God for grace to guard you against all manner of temptation. Love your wives if you can possibly do so and use them kindly and affectionately if you can; but both men and women have their proper spheres in this life and sometimes they get united and there is no harmony in the family circle; if you cannot love your wives my advice to you is to separate, for you will either do one of two things; viz: be tempted to commit a crime perhaps that was the most foreign to your mind before, and that may force you first into jail, then in the criminal box to be put on trial for your life and have the sentence of death passed on you and thence face the halter and die a violent ignominious death amid a congregated multitude and go to a premature grave, or, you will be compelled to live a life of torture and drag out a miserable existence."

June 9, 1859, rolled around all too soon for Dr. King. He arose at 4 a.m. and ate a hearty breakfast. He then spent some time in prayer with Reverend Vanderburg. Several doctors who were close friends of the condemned man visited the jail to pay their respects. The solemn procession of jailers and spiritual advisers made its way to the scaffold. A crowd, estimated to contain as many as 10,000 people, had trudged by foot and buggy to take in the spectacle.

The public hanging took place without incident and the crowd dispersed.

Melinda Vandervoort took up with a new beau in Cleveland, but soon tired of him in favour of a gentleman from Montreal. Evidently, he left her high and dry in Montreal, after which she returned to Brighton, where she lived for many years, an object of scorn to many of the residents who knew her story. She drank heavily and is reported to have died in the late 1890s, penniless and alone, in an asylum in Toronto.

— ALLAN LEGERE —

CHATHAM, NEW BRUNSWICK, is in the beautiful Miramichi country, tucked away off the beaten path. Max Aitkins, who achieved fame and fortune as Lord Beaverbrook, was brought up in the north-shore town of Newcastle. Ted Williams, the celebrated outfielder with the Boston Red Sox, was one of hundreds of sportsmen who sought out this small portion of paradise to fish the Miramichi River for the finest salmon in the world.

Well over 100 years ago, my grandmother and grandfather settled across the bridge from Newcastle in the adjoining town of Chatham. The young immigrants from Austria made Chatham their home for the rest of their lives. They had seven daughters and one son. One daughter, my aunt Addie, lived there through the seven months in 1989 when the reign of terror that was Allan Legere swept through the Miramichi.

As I sit in the kitchen of the homestead where my mother and my aunts played as children, it is difficult to imagine that an entire section of the province was caught in a grip of fear a decade ago. Back in 1989, as summer faded into fall and the leaves of the trees along the Miramichi burst forth in breathtaking hues of reds and golds, the entire nation would learn about a cruel killer, a man with an uncontrollable urge to mete out terrible retribution upon innocent and vulnerable victims.

It all really began three years earlier, on June 21, 1986. John and Mary Glendenning finished the day's work in their general store in Black River Bridge, about 20 miles outside Chatham. They walked across the yard to their home, as they did most days. Although Black River Bridge is little more than a sprinkling of homes on a back road, the Glendennings—John, 66, and Mary, 61—had prospered over the 30 years they had been in business. Everyone in the region knew their store then, as they do today.

The Glendennings were reported to keep large sums of cash in their home. You wouldn't call it gossip. It was the sort of rumour that is harmless unless it is heard by the wrong types. Allan Legere, 38, Scott Curtis, 20, and Todd Matchett, 18, planned on stealing that money. Several different versions of what took place in the Glendenning home on that pleasant summer night 12 years ago have been told by the participants. There is no doubt about the outcome.

The three masked men crashed into the Glendenning home. By the time they left, John had been viciously beaten to death. Mary had been badly beaten, but survived the attack. The men made off with the Glendennings' safe containing some $45,000. The empty safe was later recovered.

The two younger men were well known in the area as petty thieves. Legere, by far the most experienced criminal, was a professional break-and-enter man with a long police record dating back to his teens. The three men were soon traced, apprehended and speedily tried. Matchett and Curtis both pleaded guilty and received life sentences. Allan Legere went to trial, was found guilty of second-degree murder and was sentenced to life imprisonment with no possibility of parole for 18 years.

The brutal murder and the ensuing trial caused a sensation along the Miramichi. Still, it was a local crime, a botched robbery. The perpetrators were behind bars. Life goes on. In time, Mary Glendenning recovered from her injuries, although acquaintances tell me that even after this length of time she still suffers from the effects of the blows she received to her head.

On May 3, 1989, Allan Legere was escorted from the Atlantic Institution, a maximum security facility in Renous, New Brunswick, to a Moncton hospital to have his ears checked. Although handcuffed and chained, Legere managed to shed the restraints, dash out of a bathroom past his guards and escape. Citizens along the Miramichi didn't know it at the time, but seven months of living in fear were about to begin. Twenty-five days later, they would learn of the rage within the soul of Allan Legere.

Annie Flam was a 75-year-old merchant in Chatham. She had been a fixture in her grocery store on Water Street longer than most people could remember. Annie lived with her sister-in-law, Nina, in a section of the premises attached to the store. Surely the two women deserved to be left alone to live out their lives in peace. But such was not to be the case.

On the night of May 28, Annie Flam was raped and beaten to death. Nina was likewise sexually assaulted and beaten. She survived the attack. The old Flam residence was set on fire. Nina, badly burned, managed to crawl downstairs, where she was rescued by a passer-by. She would later relate in vivid detail how the cruel man had entered their home and attacked them. Because the intruder had worn a balaclava, Nina was unable to describe his face.

Could Allan Legere have been responsible? It had been 25 days since his escape. Could he have made his way from Moncton back to his hometown? People remembered the Glendenning killing. There were similarities, yet it seemed too incredible. Why would a man facing years in prison if captured return to the area where he was born and was known by sight? There were sightings of a shadowy figure stealing food and slipping into the woods. Allan Legere was certainly a suspect. Police poured into the area, but Legere, as if by magic, remained at large.

On October 13, the madman struck again, this time in Newcastle at the home of Linda and Donna Daughney on Mitchell Street. The town fire station is on the corner of Mitchell and Jane Streets. It was a firefighter who first spotted smoke emanating from an upstairs window of the Daughney residence. The fire was quickly extinguished before it could engulf the bodies of the two sisters. Linda, 41, and Donna, 45, had been sexually attacked and beaten to death. Police dogs and helicopters were used in the hunt for their murderer. There was little doubt they were looking for one man—Allan Legere, now a suspected serial killer.

Journalists travel the globe to cover major fast-breaking stories. Rick Maclean, the 32-year-old editor of the *Miramichi Leader*, could walk the distance from his office to the Daughney home in under two minutes. It was a unique opportunity to cover the story, capture the fear of the community and get into the mind of Allan Legere.

Now as we walked the short distance to the Daughney residence. Maclean explained that, in the towns and villages along the Miramichi, the average citizen had lived in a state of fear unlike anything they had ever experienced.

Little else was discussed. Day after day, his paper featured the three recent murders with the built-in anticipation that more would follow unless Legere was captured. At the time, Maclean had no way of knowing that across the river from his office window, the killer would strike again.

Father James Smith was uncharacteristically late to conduct the mass at the Nativity of the Blessed Virgin Mary Church. Parishioners gathered around the church, waiting for the 69-year-old priest to make his way across the yard from the rectory. Finally, someone peeked into the window of the rectory. Father Smith had been beaten to death. But death had not come with any degree of speed. An examination of the murder scene and the postmortem revealed that the priest had been tortured. His face had been carved with a knife which hadn't penetrated more than a quarter of an inch. He had been repeatedly kicked so viciously that his entire rib cage had caved in.

Was no one safe from the madman who seemed fully capable of outwitting more than 100 police officers? Jeeps sped up and down the Miramichi. Helicopters flew overhead, scanning the woods, while dogs led search parties through heavy brush. Many citizens installed floodlights in their backyards.

Father Smith's 1984 Olds Delta 88 was found abandoned near the train station 50 miles away in Bathurst. Authorities had correctly deduced that the fugitive had caught a train to Montreal. Perhaps he would never be apprehended. He might have been successful in crossing the border into the United States, they speculated.

Allan Legere, now the most wanted man in the country, had checked into the Queen Elizabeth Hotel in Montreal. He was relaxing.

Seven days after Father Smith's murder, the urge to return to the Miramichi compelled Legere to take a train to Saint John. It was a cold, blustery night. Legere commandeered a taxi driven by Ron Gomke. As he stuck a sawed-off .308 into Gomke's ribs, he announced, "I'm the one they're looking for. I'm Allan Legere."

The taxi driver did as he was told and headed for Moncton. Near that city's famed Magnetic Hill, Gomke, fighting the deteriorating road conditions, went off the highway into a ditch. Legere flagged down a passing motorist. By sheer coincidence, the driver happened to be Michelle Mercer, an RCMP officer on her way to her native province of Prince Edward Island.

Michelle stopped and offered Legere and Gomke a lift. Once they were headed for Moncton, the wanted man introduced himself and made Michelle aware of his .308. Although she was told to take the Chatham exit, weather conditions were so bad that Michelle missed the exit and ended up south of Moncton.

Michelle Mercer's mind was racing. She pointed out to Legere that fuel would soon be a problem. He agreed and allowed her to pull into the Four Corners Irving gas station. Legere took the keys of the car and pumped gas into the vehicle. He then stepped the few feet inside to pay for his purchase.

Unknown to Legere, Michelle Mercer had a second set of keys. In a flash, she was speeding down the highway. Within minutes she located a phone and reported her experience to police. Roadblocks were immediately set up.

Legere cursed as the car vanished down the road, but he still had one more card to play. At the side of the gas station, he spotted Brian Golding working on his Mack flatbed tractor trailer. Never one to miss an opportunity to introduce himself, the wanted man said simply, "I'm Allan Legere. Let's get going." His rifle spoke volumes.

Near Newcastle, the big vehicle was spotted on a road never travelled by flatbeds. The police were notified and were soon directly behind Legere, lights flashing. Golding hit the brakes and jumped out. A few seconds elapsed before Legere stepped down from the cab of the truck. "I'm Allan Legere," he said.

The hunt was over.

Legere was charged with four counts of murder. He was positively linked to three of his victims through genetic fingerprinting, better known as DNA. This relatively new investigative tool was utilized by matching the genetic structure of Legere's hair and blood to that of semen samples found on his victims at the crime scenes. He was also identified as the man who had attempted to sell the Daughney sisters' jewellery in Montreal. In addition, he had left his bloody footprints in Father Smith's rectory.

Legere was found guilty of all four murders and sentenced to life imprisonment with no possibility of parole for 25 years. Since his conviction, he has been moved out of New Brunswick to the super-maximum wing of the Ste. Anne des Plaines prison outside Montreal.

Notorious Allan Legere will long be remembered along the Miramichi. Rick Maclean's book, *Terror's End*, is the definitive study of the drama that paralyzed an entire province with fear. Mary Glendenning often suffers from bad headaches as a result of the injuries she sustained from her beating. Nina Flam, who refuses to discuss her horrifying experience, moved to Halifax, but still comes back to visit the area she called home for so many years. The

Chatham business community has placed a globe of the world in the new local library in memory of Annie Flam. Across from Father Smith's church, a home for the elderly has been renamed Father Smith's Manor.

As I left my aunt Addie, she remarked, "I'm not afraid anymore." She could have been expressing the feelings of the entire Miramichi.

– KEN LEISHMAN –

K EN LEISHMAN SEEMED TO have everything. He had an adoring wife, Elva, a modest but pleasant home in Winnipeg and five lovely children. Ken, a successful sales-man, tooled around in his Cadillac when he wasn't flying his own three-seater Stinson. A tall, good-looking man, with a lot of charm. There was only one problem. You see, Ken also robbed banks.

Born during the height of the Depression in rural Manitoba, Ken's early life was not easy. Mostly he worked on his grandparents' farm until he quit school in Grade 7 and struck out on his own.

He was 18 in 1949 and working in Winnipeg when he met Elva. Within a year they were married. Elva was a healthy girl who, for the next several years, was continually pregnant.

In 1952, Ken purchased a dilapidated little plane for $1,000 down and learned to fly. The following year he upgraded to a shiny new Stinson and obtained a job selling cookware. Ken Leishman hit the jackpot. He would load his plane up with pots and pans and take off for the boon-docks. Ken loved the farmers and the farmers loved the cookware. Within a year Ken was the company's top sales-man in western Canada. He bought another plane just for fun, and drove a big Caddy. Not bad for a 23-year-old. Elva was proud.

The good times lasted more than five years. Then, with-out warning, the cookware company Ken worked for went out of business. There he was—still good-looking, well-dressed, big car, plane, house, kids, everything intact, except for one thing. He owed money on everything. Ken was heavily in debt and Christmas was just around the corner.

That's when Ken got the bright idea which was to set him apart from all other criminals in the annals of Canadian crime.

On December 16, 1957, he kissed Elva goodbye and hopped a plane for Toronto. Debonair Ken was the picture of a prosperous salesman on a business trip. Except that his briefcase held a .22-automatic Luger.

Ken arrived in Toronto, rented a car and checked into the Park Plaza. He spent the day leisurely casing the Toronto Dominion Bank at the corner of Yonge and Albert Streets.

Next day, in mid afternoon, Ken walked into the bank and asked for the manager, Mr. A.J. Lunn. Posing as a Buffalo businessman, he was ushered into the manager's private office. As he took off his coat and placed his brief-case on a chair, he complained that the noise emanating from the bank was distracting. Mr. Lunn suggested that he close the door.

Both men settled into their chairs. When Lunn looked up, he was staring directly into the barrel of an automatic Luger. "Mr. Lunn, as you obviously realize, this is a hold-up." Lunn gulped, "Obviously."

Ken assured the bank manager that the gun was loaded

and he knew there was an alarm button, as well as a loaded revolver, somewhere within arm's reach. He warned the terrified manager not to move.

After some discussion it was decided that Lunn would make out a counter cheque in the amount of $10,000 and have Leishman sign it. The manager would initial the cheque and accompany Ken to the teller's cage.

Ken and the manager continued to talk for five minutes, during which time Ken elicited personal information concerning Lunn's family. When the two men emerged from the manager's office, it appeared to everyone within earshot that they were dear friends. The teller turned over $10,000 in large bills to Ken without question. Tucking the money into his briefcase, Ken remarked, "Come on, Al. I'll buy you a coffee."

The two men left the bank together. As they approached Richmond Street, where Ken had parked his car, he instructed Lunn to turn around and walk away. When the bank manager got up enough nerve to glance over his shoulder, Ken Leishman and the $10,000 were long gone. Before heading for Malton Airport, Ken dropped a Christmas card in the mail addressed to Mr. A.J. Lunn of the Toronto Dominion Bank. He signed it, "Merry Christmas from a satisfied customer."

Ken caught the next plane back to Winnipeg. "Successful trip?" Elva inquired. "Very," replied Ken. The next day he bought Elva a mink stole.

When the festive season drew to a close, Ken was still faced with the problem of making a living. He believed that a luxurious sports lodge north of Winnipeg would be a big winner with American millionaires. Such a project would take money to get off the ground. What better way to raise cash fast than another business trip to Toronto?

Posing as Mr. McGill, a Welland contractor, Ken strolled into the Canadian Bank of Commerce at the corner of Bloor and Yonge Streets. Manager H.F. Mason ushered him into his office, but things didn't go well for the businessman from Welland.

When confronted with the menacing Luger, Mason's response was a complete surprise. "This is ridiculous. You'll never get away with this," the bank manager said as he made for the door. Ken lost his nerve. He ran from the bank as Mason shouted, "Turn in the alarm."

Accountant K.C. O'Brien took off after Ken. He was joined by assistant accountant C.I. Walcott. Ken either stumbled or was tripped, but down he sprawled, with O'Brien and Walcott on top of him.

The jig was up. Ken Leishman, now dubbed The Flying Bandit, pleaded guilty and received nine years for armed robbery and three years for attempted armed robbery to be served in Manitoba's Stony Mountain Penitentiary.

Three years and eight months later Ken was paroled. He tried to go straight. He really did. But now he was a notorious man with a criminal record. Employers weren't falling over each other to take a chance on The Flying Bandit.

Four years passed before Ken got another one of his bright ideas. He found out that gold bullion was flown from Red Lake to Winnipeg about twice a month. In Winnipeg it was transferred to Air Canada for delivery to the Royal Canadian Mint in Ottawa the following day. Ken cased the operation carefully, and was amazed to discover that the entire transaction was conducted in a rather loose manner.

Ken contacted a lawyer friend, Harry Backlin, and three confederates, one of whom worked in Red Lake and could tell him when a shipment of gold was leaving for Winnipeg. Ken hung around the Winnipeg airport. He found out that all it took to receive the gold on Air Canada's behalf was a signed waybill. No one seemed to be particularly concerned about the gold. Ken actually jumped into an Air Canada van and made dry runs on the tarmac without being noticed.

Ken rehearsed his gang. They would wear Air Canada uniforms, have a forged waybill, pick up the gold in an Air Canada van and transfer it to their own car. Ken wouldn't go near the airport. The gold would be delivered to him. Normally the gold bars were taken from the plane to the Air Canada freight office, but Ken correctly figured that it would be released to his confederates directly into an Air Canada truck if they mentioned that it had to be sent rush to Ottawa that night.

The operation went off without a hitch. On March 1, 1966, Ken Leishman had engineered the biggest gold robbery in Canadian history. He stashed 12 crates of solid gold bars in Harry Backlin's mother-in-law's freezer. He told her it was moose meat. At $35 an ounce, the moose meat was worth $383,497.

Had Ken been patient and lain low for a year or so, he might have pulled off the perfect crime. But it wasn't in his nature to just let things happen. He had to act. With Harry's financial help Ken arranged to take a trip to Hong Kong with a small sample of gold to show prospective customers. He required a smallpox vaccination. Dr. W.G. French remembered the name Leishman, grew suspicious, and passed on his suspicions to the police. Ken was picked up in Vancouver. All but the small sample of gold was recovered.

Ken was lodged in Headingley Jail without bail. He languished there for six months, hating every day. The future looked bleak. This time they would throw the book at him. Ken had other ideas.

In September, 1966, he and a group of prisoners overpowered guards and escaped. With three companions he made his way to Steinbach, Manitoba, where he took off in a new Mooney Mark 21. The Flying Bandit was back in the air, heading south. Ken brought the aircraft down on a tiny airstrip near Tyler, Minnesota, where the tired men ate and rested.

Once again they took off. This time the desperate men landed on a farm near Gary, Indiana. The farmer welcomed them and was so thrilled with his unusual guests that he contacted a local newspaper and had their pictures taken. The men took a bus into Gary. The owner of the M and S Tavern became suspicious when they paid for a few beers with a Canadian bill. At the same time the farmer noticed a gun on the back seat of the aircraft. The Flying Bandit and his companions were surrounded and taken into custody.

Back in Winnipeg Ken could hardly figure out all the charges against him. The various sentences would add up to a lifetime behind bars. He had only one thought in mind—freedom.

A known escape artist, Ken was heavily guarded, but again he escaped from custody. Pleading ill health, he was allowed out of his cell to exercise. Using a bit of wire, he managed to open an outside door and overpower a guard. Using torn strips of bedsheets he shimmied over a 12-foot fence, badly cutting his hand on barbed wire in the process. The Flying Bandit had escaped once again, but not for long.

That same bitter cold night, Ken was apprehended in a phone booth by Constable Ed Finney of the West Kildonan Police Force. He had just finished calling his lawyer, who had tried to persuade him to give himself up.

On November 1, 1966, Ken received the relatively light sentence of seven years imprisonment for all his escapades incurred after the gold robbery. His luck held. The gold heist netted an eight-year sentence to run concurrently with the seven years.

While in prison Ken passed his Grade 12 matriculation. Four years later, in 1970, he was given day parole to attend Red River Community College. On May 3, 1974, Ken was released from Stony Mountain Penitentiary. Elva, who had stuck by him through thick and thin, was once more reunited with her wayward husband.

Ironically, Ken and Elva made their way to Red Lake, the very town from which his stolen gold had been shipped. They opened a gift shop called The Trading Post. Ken became one of the most popular men in town. All his children had grown up. He and Elva were grandparents many times over. Ken obtained his commercial pilot's license. In 1978 the former convict became president of the Red Lake Chamber of Commerce.

On Friday, December 14, 1979, Ken, a part-time pilot with Sabourin Airways of Red Lake, took off in a Piper Aztec for Sandy Lake. A woman had been injured tending her traps. Ken was to fly her to Thunder Bay.

The first leg of the flight went off without incident. At

Sandy Lake he picked up Nurse Jackie Meekis and patient Eva Harper. Ken and his passengers never landed in Thunder Bay. On May 3, 1980, a Canadian Armed Forces search team found the wreckage of the Piper Aztec. It had crashed 45 kilometres from Thunder Bay, disintegrating upon contact. All the occupants had been killed instantly. Their bodies had been ravished by wolves.

The Flying Bandit would fly no more.

— ARTHUR LUCAS AND RONALD TURPIN —

BEFORE THEY MET IN jail, Arthur Lucas and Ronald Turpin never knew each other. In death, they would be united forever.

Art Lucas was born in Cordle, Georgia, on December 18, 1907. Both his parents died of natural causes before he reached the age of seven.

Art was raised by an aunt and uncle in Byronville, Florida. He quit school in the sixth grade and went to work. By the time he was a teenager, he was running errands for small-time gangsters and making his living on the streets. Art had an IQ of 63, which is classified as borderline intelligence.

As the years passed, Art graduated to more serious crimes, specializing in narcotics and prostitution. While still a young man, he served a prison sentence in Leavenworth Penitentiary.

In 1953, Art married Dolores Chipps, a prostitute who hailed from London, Ontario. Dolores presented Art with a son. Apparently Art was so overwhelmed by the event, he kicked mother and child out of the apartment and ushered in Lillian Boykin, who practised the same occupation as Dolores.

In 1961, Art was making his living by procuring young girls to work in brothels in and around Detroit. He also wasn't above being paid to administer a beating to anyone who had crossed a fellow hoodlum. That's what he was doing in Toronto in November 1961.

A Detroit crook, Gus Saunders, had been fingered by an FBI informer, one Therland Crater. Crater, better known as Checkerboard, was to be a material witness against Saunders in an upcoming narcotics trial. Saunders loaned Art his pink Buick to drive to Toronto to teach Crater a lesson. Art taught well.

At 7 a.m. on Friday, November 17, 1961, a postman, Francis MacGuire, discovered Crater's body in the hallway of a Kendal Avenue boarding house. He called the landlord, Sygmant Turlinski, who entered Crater's apartment and found the nude body of 20-year-old prostitute Carol Anne Newman in a bedroom. Carol Anne, who sometimes plied her trade under the name Jean Rochelle, had been slashed across the throat. Crater had been shot in the back with a .38-calibre revolver. As an afterthought, his throat had been cut as well.

Toronto detectives were soon told by informants that the double murder had connections in Detroit. The word went out to the Detroit underworld for information. It wasn't long in coming. Red Thomas, a punk who had it in for Saunders, told police of Art Lucas's trip to Toronto in Saunders's pink Buick.

Detectives called on Art's wife, Dolores, whom he still saw on a regular basis. She told police that Art had killed Crater and Newman. Dolores stated that Art had travelled back to Detroit on the day of the murders. He had come to her house in an agitated state and told her, "I just killed two people."

Art had also told Dolores that a man named Crater was one of the victims and that the murders had taken place in Toronto. He had not intended to hurt the girl until she had screamed. Carol Anne was simply in the wrong bed at the wrong time.

Dolores said that Saunders had been informed on by Crater and deserved a beating, but she never thought her husband capable of killing anyone. Art had washed blood from his hands and had even rinsed blood out of a pair of shorts in a pail of water, which Dolores was able to turn over to police. The pink liquid in the pail proved to be diluted blood. Art was also very concerned because he was sure he had lost his ring in the bedclothes on Carol Anne Newman's bed.

Less than 24 hours after the double murder, police picked up Art Lucas at Lillian Boykin's Burns Avenue house in Detroit. Art denied having murdered anyone. He claimed that he had called on Crater to find a position for one of his prostitutes. He had had some drinks with Crater and had borrowed money from him, leaving his ring as collateral for the loan.

On April 30, 1962, Art stood trial for the murder of Checkerboard Crater. He was found guilty and sentenced to death with no recommendation for mercy.

RONALD TURPIN WAS BORN on April 29, 1933. His father was often away from home, working as a conductor with the Canadian Pacific Railway.

At age 13, Ronald was placed in a foster home. He

dropped out of school in Grade 8 and for a while worked as a clerk in Ottawa. In 1951, when he was 18, he stole a car. That little escapade earned him 18 months in Kingston Penitentiary. From that time on, Ronald earned his living as a small-time thief and counterfeiter, spending short periods of time in prison.

On October 25, 1961, Ronald, together with his girl-friend, Lillian White, arrived at 222 Wellesley Street, Toronto, home of prostitute Della Burns. Della was throwing a party.

The good times rolled for a while, but were abruptly interrupted around midnight when Della answered a knock at the door. Someone she had never seen before fired two shots at her, but missed. Della later told police that Ronald Turpin wrestled the gun out of the stranger's hands. He and Lillian left the party with the stranger's gun.

Unknown to Ronald, Della was under police surveillance in the murder investigation of one Lorne Gibson, an underworld character believed to have been killed by gambling competitors. Ronald and Lillian had run out the back door of Della's residence just as a police cruiser pulled up at the front. Della and the other guests told the officers what had transpired. Only one witness, Frank Benson, gave a different version. He claimed Ronald Turpin was the gunman.

Police felt that the weapon used in the attempt on Della's life might very well have been the one used to kill Lorne Gibson. In fact, they theorized that Turpin might have committed both crimes. The hunt was on for Ronald Turpin. Officially, he was wanted only for discharging a firearm with intent to wound.

Ronald and Lillian hid out in Sudbury. They continued to Buffalo, before succumbing to the urge to spend the

Christmas season in Toronto. They decided to stay on in the city they knew so well. The month of January was uneventful. Ronald operated in the open using various aliases. In February, he decided that he and Lillian should move along to northern Ontario. With this in mind, they purchased a beat-up old van.

On Sunday, February 11, 1962, Ronald and Lillian had a farewell drink with Della Burns. Ronald slipped away to raise a little money for the impending trip. He robbed the Red Rooster Restaurant of $632.84. The robbery had gone well, but now a police car was trailing him along the Danforth. Maybe, thought Turpin, it was because one of his headlights was damaged. Maybe the officer recognized him. We will never know the reason why Constable Frederick Nash had Ronald Turpin pull over.

Ronald identified himself as Orval Penrose and was asked to get out of his vehicle. An eyewitness, Leonard Boreham, saw the two men wrestle between the van and the police car. He watched as shots rang out and Constable Nash crumpled to the street. The other man jumped into the police car and attempted to drive away.

When a second officer arrived at the scene, Turpin was still behind the wheel of the police car. When the policeman approached, Turpin threw his gun at him and shouted, "Look after the police officer!"

Ronald was taken to hospital by ambulance. He was wounded in both arms and had a flesh wound in the cheek. Constable Nash died of his wounds. He left a wife and four children.

On May 28, 1962, Ronald Turpin stood trial for the murder of Constable Frederick Nash. He was found guilty and sentenced to death.

It was on death row in Toronto's Don Jail that Ronald Turpin and Arthur Lucas met for the first time. The two men who had been brought up in unstable environments and had led lives of crime awaited death together. They got to know each other well. Both leaned heavily on the spiritual comfort given them by Brigadier Cyril Everitt of the Salvation Army.

On Monday, December 10, 1962, the condemned men were led to the gallows. Brigadier Everitt was with them to the end. He read the twenty-third Psalm. The two doomed men stood back to back. The trapdoor swung open and they plunged to eternity.

Arthur Lucas and Ronald Turpin were the last men to be executed in Canada.

– AUBREY LUTZ –

AUBREY LUTZ RAN UP the steps of the RCMP office in Kentville, Nova Scotia, carrying his two-month-old baby daughter, Kimberley. He told Constable Edwin Malloy, "I've done a terrible thing. I shot four people. I want to make a full confession. I'll show you where the murder weapon is."

So began an odyssey which has affected the lives of so many in the peaceful Annapolis Valley community of Auburn. The impact of Aubrey Lutz's insane act so many years ago still resonates with the survivors of his shooting spree, as well as with their relatives and the citizens of Auburn.

Only a few short kilometres away in Grand Pré, busloads of tourists trek to view the statue of Evangeline, commemorating the expulsion of the Acadians from this area by the British in 1755. Thanks to Henry Wadsworth Longfellow's famous poem, Evangeline will forever symbolize the plight of the French and their search for a new home.

As Evangeline's story is told and retold, so too is the saga of Aubrey Lutz. On that fateful February 12, 1964, the 23-year-old Lutz left his parents' home with hatred in his heart and destruction in his eyes.

Life had been a living hell for Aubrey since his 18-year-old wife, Rosalie, had taken their baby daughter and returned to the home of her parents, Helen and Arthur Pudsey. She shouldn't have done that. It wasn't right. No matter what, a wife's place was beside her husband. The voices pounding at his temples told him that and much more. The voices told him that all his problems would be solved when every one of them was dead. Yes, even himself. First he would kill them and then turn the gun on himself. That would show Rosalie and everyone else that he truly loved her.

Aubrey carefully wrapped his .303 Enfield rifle in a white bag so no one could see what he was carrying. A neighbour of his parents', Arnold O'Neil, gave him a lift to his in-laws' house in Auburn. On the way he told Arnold, "I don't want too many people to see what I got." Once alone in the Pudseys' driveway, he unwrapped the rifle.

Aubrey's mother-in-law was in the kitchen. His sister-in-law, 15-year-old Audrey Jean Pudsey, was upstairs. Rosalie was downstairs, holding baby Kim in her arms.

Helen Pudsey took one look at the crazed Aubrey and his rifle, turned white and ordered Aubrey to leave her home. Audrey Jean heard the commotion and came downstairs. According to official documents, Audrey Jean wasn't in school that day because she was suffering from the flu. Others say she was at home to babysit Kim because the family was going to a lawyer's office to have Aubrey post a peace bond. Another sister, nine-year-old Ardythe, was in school, a circumstance which may very well have saved her life.

Aubrey told Audrey Jean he wanted to speak to her, but the frightened girl ran into the bathroom. Enraged at being ordered out of the house, Aubrey turned to Helen and slapped her in the face. Desperately, Helen made a futile grab for the rifle. Aubrey fired and Helen Pudsey fell to the kitchen floor. Aubrey then shot through the bathroom door, killing Audrey Jean instantly.

At that precise moment, Arthur Pudsey entered the house, took one look and ran outside to his car. Aubrey, in hot pursuit, shot him to death. Arthur Pudsey tumbled out of his car to the driveway. He was dead before he hit the ground.

Rosalie Lutz was so horror-stricken, she could hardly function. She placed her baby on a chesterfield as Aubrey came back inside. Once more, the Enfield roared. Rosalie slumped to the floor, seriously wounded in the shoulder. Her husband picked up the baby, jumped into Arthur's car and drove directly to the RCMP office in Kentville, where he encountered Constable Malloy and blurted out what he had done.

Meanwhile, back at the house of carnage, Rosalie crawled to the telephone and called a family friend, Geraldine Lutz. She in turn phoned her husband, Clinton, who worked at a nearby garage. He and another man, Laurie Ritchie, sped to the Pudsey home. They arrived in a matter of minutes and found Arthur dead in the yard.

Inside, Helen Pudsey attempted to raise herself on her elbows. She told Clinton that she was going to die. She whispered, "Get Sonny if it's the last thing you ever do." Sonny was Aubrey Lutz's nickname.

Clinton observed Rosalie, bleeding profusely, sitting against a wall near the telephone. An operator had called a doctor, who soon arrived at the scene.

Dr. Roy Moreash briefly examined Arthur in the yard and ascertained that he was dead. Upon entering the kitchen, he examined Helen, who was so near death that Dr. Moreash would later recall from the witness stand that he "focused all his attention on saving the life of the younger woman." An ambulance arrived and Rosalie Lutz was rushed to hospital. She would spend the next 16 months recovering from her ordeal.

Someone tried the bathroom door. It was stuck. When the door was pushed open, Audrey Jean's body was discovered.

Within minutes, three members of the tiny community of Auburn were dead. Another was in serious condition and 23-year-old Aubrey Lutz was giving a statement to RCMP in nearby Kentville.

What had gone wrong? What had triggered the kiling spree? To answer these questions, I travelled to the tiny community to speak to the individuals involved.

Aubrey Lutz was the product of an abusive father who drank heavily. He was generally argumentative and often beat his wife. At age 14, Aubrey, who was a slow learner, left school. The early signs were there, if anyone cared to notice. Aubrey was often moody. He displayed a bad temper. When he met Rosalie in 1962, he wanted to marry her immediately. She was only 16.

There was one major stumbling block. Rosalie's parents opposed the marriage. Aubrey discussed the matter with his spiritual adviser, Reverend Gordon McClare. He told the minister that Rosalie's parents were persecuting him. At times, his conversations with the minister were more ravings than discussions. On one occasion, he threatened to strike Rosalie in front of Reverend McClare.

The minister, convinced that Aubrey was mentally ill, refused to marry the young couple and suggested that Aubrey seek help at a mental health centre in nearby Wolfville. Aubrey didn't heed the advice.

In May 1963, with Rosalie two months pregnant, her parents relented and the young couple were married by Reverend McClare. Rosalie soon discovered that it was no picnic to be Mrs. Aubrey Lutz. During wild rages, Aubrey often smashed their furniture. On occasion he punched her and berated her for no reason. Kimberley's birth in December did nothing to improve matters. Rosalie couldn't take the abuse any longer. Fearful of her husband, she moved back home with her parents. That was the turbulent situation of the young Lutz family in February 1964, when Aubrey killed three of his imagined antagonists.

On April 16, 1964, Aubrey Lutz was charged with three counts of capital murder and, after a preliminary hearing, was committed to stand trial. A month later, on May 19, Aubrey refused to enter a plea. A not-guilty plea was ordered on his behalf.

At the outset of the trial, the presiding judge, Mr. Justice Frank H. Patterson, ordered that a hearing be held to ascertain whether Aubrey was unfit to stand trial due to insanity. A jury was impanelled to determine this issue. After hearing conflicting psychiatric testimony, they failed to agree and were discharged. A second jury found Aubrey Lutz unfit to stand trial. As a result of this decision, he was confined to the Nova Scotia Hospital to be kept in custody "at the pleasure of the Lieutenant Governor of the Province of Nova Scotia."

Aubrey Lutz, the insane man from Auburn, was out of sight in the mental institution in Dartmouth. Life went on for the survivors of his killing spree. Indeed, life went on for Aubrey Lutz. His mental condition deteriorated in the institution. Psychiatric reports reveal: "His behavior was characterized by violent episodes of throwing chairs at staff and patients and threatening people around him. He also frequently made suicidal threats and was a serious management problem."

Because of his behaviour, Aubrey remained on the Maximum Security Unit of the institution for nearly 15 years. During that time he was heavily medicated and received 494 shock treatments. At times he threatened to kill his doctor.

By 1978, Aubrey's behavior and mental condition showed some improvement. He was transferred to another section of the hospital. A year later, his doctor went before a medical review board and had the lieutenant-governor's warrant lifted. Aubrey became a formal patient.

During the 1980s, he displayed marked improvement and was transferred to a rehabilitation ward. Aubrey was no longer the aggressive, unmanageable individual he had been years earlier, although he still suffered from occasional hallucinations. His formal-patient status was changed to that of voluntary patient. He agreed with his doctors that, although his status had changed, it was not time for his release back into society. However, he now had a degree of freedom. He could leave the hospital grounds during the day and return at night.

In December 1990, Aubrey obtained a pass to spend the Christmas season with his parents. He returned to the Annapolis Valley for the first time in 27 years. The taste of a normal life was sweet to a man who had been confined for almost three decades. On December 27, he returned to the hospital and, against the advice of doctors, signed himself out. Aubrey Lutz, confessed killer of three innocent people, had never been tried, never been convicted and now was as free as a valley breeze.

Back in the Auburn area, the survivors of his killing spree had attempted to put their lives together. Little Kimberley, the two-month-old baby, was now 27 years old and a mother. Aubrey's wife, Rosalie, who'd spent so many months in hospital had long since divorced Aubrey.

Her sister, Ardythe, the nine-year-old child who, by the luck of the draw, was at school on the day of the murders, was happily married to Roger Huntley and was the mother of an adult daughter.

One can only imagine the feelings of the two sisters when they learned that the man who had killed their mother, father and sister was back in town. Ardythe and her husband, Roger, immediately contacted the RCMP. Aubrey was picked up and charged with three counts of murder.

On March 21, 1991, Aubrey Lutz stood trial for murders committed 27 years earlier. At issue was his mental state at the time of the killings. His lawyer, Joel Pink, spoke to me in his office overlooking Halifax Harbour. Pink agreed the procedure was unusual. "Had Lutz been convicted at the time of the crime and sent to prison, he would have been released long ago. There is no doubt in my mind that at the time of the crime he was legally insane." Pink also informed me that after receiving 494 shock treatments in the hospital, his client didn't remember anything prior to 1977.

Judge J. Gruchy heard the case without jury. After listening to all the psychiatric and other evidence, the judge ruled that the accused had a disease of the mind to such an extent that it rendered him incapable of appreciating the nature and quality of his acts on February 12, 1964. He found the accused not guilty by reason of insanity. The judge ordered that Aubrey be kept in strict custody at the Nova Scotia Hospital until the pleasure of the lieutenant-governor is known.

Back in Annapolis Valley live two sisters, forever separated by the actions of the madman with the Enfield rifle. Rosalie sat and sipped coffee with me as she described the day of horror so vividly etched in her mind. Philosophically, she says, "I believe everyone should leave him alone. I have forgiven my husband for what he has done." Rosalie had difficulty passing me a mug of coffee. She has limited use of her left shoulder and arm, even after 27 years.

Ardythe Huntley, who at nine years of age was left without parents and a sister she loved dearly, feels differently. After the shooting, she went to live with an aunt, but was soon shunted from foster home to foster home. To this day she is unwilling to talk about her upbringing after the death of her parents. She vividly remembers Clinton Lutz fetching her from school to tell her that her life had just changed forever. Ardythe firmly believes that Aubrey is capable of killing again and should be confined forever. She and her sister Rosalie are not on speaking terms.

Aubrey Lutz, who ended three lives and affected so many more, is back in the hospital where he has resided for the past 34 years. Every six months, a medical review board will study his case to ascertain whether he is capable of reentering society.

– DAVID MILGAARD –

DAVID MILGAARD LANGUISHED in a Canadian prison for over 20 years for a crime he did not commit.

On January 31, 1969, Gail Miller, a Saskatoon nursing assistant, left her home at 6:45 a.m. to catch a bus to work. It was bitterly cold out. Gail shivered in her overcoat and wrapped a scarf over her head. It was only a couple of blocks to the bus stop. She usually covered the distance in about 10 minutes.

At 8:20 a.m., Gail's body was discovered in a nearby alley. She was still wearing her overcoat, but her dress and underclothing were in disarray. She had been raped and stabbed to death.

During the course of a six-month investigation, police learned that David Milgaard, then a long-haired 16-year-old transient, had been in Saskatoon on the morning of the murder with two friends, Ron Wilson and Nicol John. They had been driving around looking for the home of another friend, Albert Cadrain.

David Milgaard has always claimed that after finding Cadrain, he and his friends left Saskatoon and drove west, stopping in Edmonton, Calgary and Banff, before returning to Regina. Milgaard has stated, "I have tried to challenge anyone to put me at the scene, to find some way, considering the times, that I could have committed the crime. I don't think you could."

But that's not the way the investigation evolved. Eventually, Wilson and Cadrain, the two young men with David that morning, and the young woman, Nicol John, were questioned extensively. All three gave damaging statements against David.

According to his friends, they arrived in Saskatoon between 5:30 a.m. and 6:30 a.m. looking for Cadrain's house. They lost their way and the car got stuck in the snow. Wilson and Milgaard left the car for 15 minutes to look for help. It was during this period of time that David supposedly raped and stabbed Gail Miller as she left her home around 6:45 a.m. It left him precious little time to commit the crime.

At 7 a.m., David was seen by a hotel manager asking for a map. A half-hour later, another witness observed David and his friends in a back lane. Their car was stuck again. They called a tow truck and left around 8:30. By 9 a.m. the trio had located Cadrain's house.

David was arrested and charged with Gail Miller's murder. Nicol John told police she had witnessed David killing Miller. She recanted her story on the witness stand and was declared a hostile witness.

David's two male friends didn't waver. For example, Ron Wilson stated that he had seen David with a maroon-handled paring knife in the car before they arrived in Saskatoon. It was this knife that police claimed was the murder weapon. Wilson further testified that once they reached Cadrain's house, he had seen blood on David's clothing.

In addition, prosecution attorneys pointed out that

semen found near Miller's body could have been David Milgaard's.

A year to the day after the murder, David was found guilty and sentenced to life imprisonment. Out of sight, out of mind. Very few people cared. The victim's family grieved. David Milgaard's mother, Joyce, believed her son was telling the truth. For years, she worked to prove his innocence against seemingly insurmountable circumstantial evidence.

In Stony Mountain Penitentiary, David insisted on his innocence. His lack of remorse may very well have quashed any chance he may have had for an early release via the National Parole Board route. They like to hear a man say he is sorry for committing his crime.

In 1988, noted forensic pathologist Dr. James Ferris issued a report that concluded there was no physical evidence linking David to the crime. The federal Justice Department agreed to review the old murder, but did not consider the report in itself sufficient to reopen the case.

Still believing her son's innocence, Joyce Milgaard retained lawyer David Asper to act as her counsel.

Eventually, events took an unusual and dramatic turn. It was learned that another man, Larry Fisher and his wife, Linda, were living in a basement apartment in Albert Cadrain's house on the night of the murder.

Larry Fisher normally caught the same bus as Gail Miller. On the morning of the murder, his wife woke up well after 9 a.m. to find her husband still at home, dressed not in his working clothes, but in clothing he normally wore on weekends.

Two years after the murder, Fisher was convicted of a series of rapes in Saskatoon and Winnipeg. He was sentenced to 12 years in prison, but was released in 1981. Once free, he was convicted of raping a 52-year-old North Battleford woman. During the course of one of his rapes, Fisher had used a paring knife.

Linda and Larry argued incessantly and eventually divorced. In 1980, Linda Fisher told her story to police. She even mentioned that later on the day of the murder, she noticed that one of her paring knives was missing. That same day, a neighbourhood youngster knocked on her door. The little girl had found Larry's wallet on the street. Police took Linda's report, but apparently nothing was done.

Ten years later, a friend of Linda Fisher's contacted lawyer David Asper and told him Linda's story. Now there was another suspect in the murder of Gail Miller. Asper maintains, "The evidence the police presented at David Milgaard's trial cannot be true. The Crown's theory is preposterous."

The Crown's chief witness, Ron Wilson, has admitted that he lied at the 1969 trial. He now claims that he never even heard of the murder until March 1969, two months after the crime, when Saskatoon police questioned him. Initially, he denied knowing anything about the killing.

In May, he was questioned again, and one more time professed ignorance of the killing. After hours of questioning, he broke and, out of sheer fright, said what his interrogators wanted to hear. He was shown five knives and was told to identify the maroon-handled paring knife. Under extensive questioning, he lied and said that he had seen David with the knife in the car before arriving in Saskatoon.

At first he told police that he had not seen any blood on

David's clothing. But later he lied, stating that he had seen blood on David's clothing after the murder. In reality, Wilson now said, his mother had washed David's clothes when they returned to Regina and she had not seen any blood on them.

Since Wilson's statement, Albert Cadrain has stated that he too was coerced into giving damaging false evidence against David at the time of the trial.

As a result of the witnesses stating that they lied from the witness stand, a second review of forensic evidence was completed by Manitoba's chief medical examiner, Dr. Peter Markesteyn. He, too, has concluded that the physical evidence presented at the long-ago trial fails to link David Milgaard to the crime.

After spending 23 years in prison for a crime he didn't commit, David Milgaard received an apology from the province of Saskatchewan. He has received $250,000 from the province as interim compensation until a final settlement is negotiated.

– TERRENCE MILLIGAN –

JANE WHELPLEY AND Terrence Milligan both attended high school in Saint John, New Brunswick. The teenagers never met in the Maritimes and had no way of knowing they would travel more than a thousand miles to meet, marry and encounter tragedy in Toronto.

Detective Donald Wright arrived at Terrence and Jane Milligan's apartment only half an hour after the police received a phone call from Terrence telling them that his wife was dead. It was 8 a.m. Sunday, June 11, 1967. Upon entering the apartment located at Eglinton Avenue East and Birchmount Road in Toronto's east end, Wright found Jane Milligan dead in the bathtub.

Wright felt that all was not as it should be. The bathtub had a barren look that was not typical. Wright's trained detective's eye noticed that there was no soap or facecloth near the tub. Jane Milligan's body was sitting in the tub with her back to the taps. While there is no rule that dictates how a person sits in a bathtub, Wright correctly deduced that the vast majority of people sit facing the taps. A mantel radio was lying in the tub in a foot of water beside the body.

The obvious conclusion was that death was due to electrocution. Wright scanned the scene and noticed that an extension cord had been used to plug the radio into an outlet in the living room. This allowed Jane to place the radio on the edge of the tub. Without using the extension cord she could have plugged the radio into an outlet in the bathroom, enabling her to place it in a safer location.

Would it be natural for Jane to go through the inconvenience of using an extension cord in order to place the radio on such an obviously dangerous perch?

Milligan told Wright that his blond, 19-year-old wife had awakened him about 6 a.m. She asked him if he wanted breakfast. He declined and went back to sleep. When he awoke at 7:30 a.m., he called out to her but received no answer. He got up to look for her. He told Detective Wright that he found his wife dead in the bathtub. He said he pulled out the plug of the radio before touching her body.

Within 10 minutes, under the inquisitive but still gentle questioning of the detective, Milligan changed his story.

He now said that he didn't even notice the radio, but touched his wife's body for any signs of life. When Wright suggested that he must have received a shock, Milligan volunteered that he was mistaken—no doubt he had unplugged the radio first.

Over and above Milligan's elaborate stories, Wright was amazed that the 22-year-old could be so composed after finding his wife dead only minutes before. The couple had been married less than a year. Milligan, who seemed to be a lucid, clean-cut young man, casually mentioned to Wright that he had a $15,000 double indemnity policy on his wife's life. He stood to collect $30,000 from the unfortunate accident.

After two and a half hours in Milligan's company, Wright came to the private conclusion that he had walked into a murder case. Within days, Detective Wright had his vacation postponed. He was assigned to the Milligan investigation.

Wright canvassed the neighbourhood for a profile on Terry Milligan. The Milligans' immediate neighbour, Mrs. Marion Bakes, said she had often heard fighting from the young couple's apartment. She said that early on the morning of Jane's death, she heard a rubbing noise, like the sound of flesh against porcelain, but had heard no loud music from the adjacent apartment. Wright recalled that when the radio was recovered from the water, the volume indicator was at the high position.

While Wright was becoming more convinced than ever that he had stumbled across murder, the pathologist's office released the cause of death—asphyxiation, probably due to electrocution. Wright couldn't believe it. He was sure the scene had been set up to give the impression of death by accidental electrocution. The detective was convinced that the cause of death was drowning.

Jane Milligan was buried, and that very same day Detective Wright received a call from the emergency ward of Toronto General Hospital. Terry had collapsed on a busy downtown-Toronto street. Wright was called to the hospital, hoping that his suspect may have broken and was ready to confess. He did not find a repentant Milligan. Instead, the baby-faced suspect accused the police of trying to concoct evidence to convict him of murder. Later it was discovered that Milligan had an IQ of 135, which placed him in the near-genius class. This day the bereaved husband not very cleverly took Wright into his confidence and inquired where he could find a prostitute.

Wright checked into Jane Milligan's background and found nothing unusual. She had finished Grade 12 and had been employed as a teller in a Scarborough bank.

While all the incriminating circumstantial evidence uncovered by Wright indicated foul play, the pathologist's report could not be denied. It stated emphatically that death was due to asphyxiation, probably caused by electrocution. There is something about an official report that seems to defy questioning. Despite this, Detective Wright decided to delve further into the pathologist's report. This may have been the single most important decision of the entire investigation. Wright found out that the pathologist had made only a cursory examination of the remains. He had been in a hurry to go to a medical convention in Montreal. A few scribbled notes were, in the main, what went into making up the report. Fortunately, Jane's vital organs had been retained after her body was buried.

A second examination of the organs was conducted, and

a quite different cause of death was discovered—death due to drowning, no evidence of electrocution. In addition, the new report included other information not previously mentioned. There were bruises to the body below the left eye, on the left elbow, and hip.

An inquest was called for July 27, 1967, and the police feverishly tracked down witnesses. Wright questioned employees at two electrical plants where Milligan worked. Both Sangamo Co. Ltd. in Leaside and Crouse-Hindes Co. of Canada Ltd. in Scarborough had large staffs. Wright located some workers who knew Milligan well and were willing to testify that he referred to his wife as "the old bitch." In fact, some specifically stated that Terry used to go out of his way to let them know that his wife was terribly careless about placing her radio on the edge of the bathtub.

On June 21, Milligan was served with a subpoena to appear at the inquest into his wife's death on July 27. When given the subpoena, he informed the authorities that he was leaving Toronto to live with his uncle on a farm in Prince Edward Island.

On July 27, Milligan returned to Toronto for the inquest. The jury determined that Mrs. Milligan's death was due to "homicide at the hands of her husband." Terrence Milligan was arrested and charged with non-capital murder. Detective Wright's job was now over. He turned over his thick file on the Milligan case to Detective Sergeant Jim Crawford and Detective Sergeant Jack Evans, whose job it was to prove murder in a court of law.

The two detectives went over all the ground that Wright had already covered. They received the co-operation of Sangamo and Crouse-Hinds officials, and had offices made available to them in each plant. They stayed almost a week at each location, questioning employees. They found out that Milligan had planted the idea of a radio in the bathtub in the minds of several of his co-workers. He had insinuated that his wife was careless with the radio. Yet none of his neighbours in the east end of the city had ever heard him even mention this fact. Was he cunning enough to avoid bringing up the subject to his neighbours, perhaps fearful that they would mention it to his wife?

Crawford flew to Prince Edward Island with a search warrant to go through Milligan's belongings on his uncle's farm. One of his discoveries was a paperback book entitled *The Doomsters*, by Ross MacDonald. The two victims in the story meet their deaths by having a radio thrown into the bathtub. Crawford, mindful that Milligan had spent the month before his arrest in Prince Edward Island, plodded across the countryside looking for friends of the accused. The islanders quickly identified the six-foot, four-inch Crawford as the big cop from the city. Soon he located friends of Milligan's who told him that Terry was not your typical bereaved husband. He had taken out girls and attended dances only days after his wife's funeral.

Evans and Crawford tried balancing Milligan's radio on the edge of the bathtub and found it very difficult. I know. I tried the same thing with the same radio on the same bathtub. Anyone with average intelligence would know that the slightest touch would either knock the radio to the floor or into the tub. Using any degree of common sense, you just wouldn't put a radio in such a precarious position.

Crawford and Evans had a plumber take the entire bathtub out of the apartment. The experiment was completed in eight hours so as not to inconvenience the new tenants. They transported the tub to the basement at police headquarters. Police officer Janet Ebert, clad in a bathing suit, entered the bathtub. The water level was the same as the day Detective Wright walked into the Milligan apartment. Ebert sat in the tub with her head under the water. Later she verified that her head kept coming to the surface. She even tried to concentrate on keeping her head underwater, but try as she might, there was a natural pressure for her head to bob to the surface.

Milligan's trial for non-capital murder began on Monday, May 13, 1968. The prosecution succeeded in establishing that Jane met her death by drowning, not electrocution. The Crown paraded witness after witness to the stand, each one adding to the intertwined series of incidents that completely incriminated the accused.

David Keeler, who lived close by the Milligan apartment, testified how Terry had knocked on his door that fateful morning with the words, "My wife's drowning, let me call the police."

William Green, an electrical engineer, testified that anyone receiving an electrical shock while sitting in the bathtub would certainly scream. Mrs. Bakes, the Milligans' immediate neighbour, who could hear the squeak of flesh on porcelain through the walls, testified that she heard no scream.

Eric Armstrong, a fellow employee of Milligan's at Sangamo, told of a strange conversation he'd had with Terry when he drove him home three weeks before his wife died. Armstrong said of the conversation, "He mentioned the fact that his wife was worth a lot of money, and he wouldn't mind doing away with her."

Even the manager of the cemetery where Milligan

had picked out a plot for his wife, took the stand. He quoted Milligan as saying, "It is probably better than she deserves."

Crawford and Evans had done their job well. The jury took ten and a half hours to find Milligan guilty of non-capital murder. The judge congratulated them on their verdict, and Terrence Milligan received life imprisonment. He has since been released.

Staff Sergeant Jim Crawford, now retired, vividly remembers the case that took place over 30 years ago. The huge man whose dogged police work was most responsible for placing Terrence Milligan behind bars, says with a distinct note of satisfaction in his voice, "It was certainly one of my most interesting cases."

– WILLIAM MILLMAN –

THE QUAINT PROVINCE OF Prince Edward Island conjures up images of tranquil sandy beaches, rolling fields of potatoes and Anne of Green Gables. Murder and its evil ramifications do not often visit the peaceful island. It was 110 years ago that P.E.I.'s most infamous homicide took place.

Will Millman met 16-year-old Mary Tuplin at a New Year's Eve dance. The farm boys had scrubbed the rich red dirt from their bodies, slicked down their hair and, equipped with a bottle of black rum, set off for the event of the year. Their counterparts, the fresh-faced daughters of the hard-working farmers, donned their very best frocks and, sometimes accompanied by their parents, took off to welcome in the year 1887.

As the dance progressed and the rum bottles emptied, the piano playing sounded more melodious, the fiddling smoother; the farm girls looked more desirable than ever. At midnight, Will kissed Mary. It was a lingering, sensual kiss. The young people danced on.

Around 3 a.m., Will walked Mary home and was asked into the house. In those long-ago days, a peck on the cheek and goodbye at the door meant it was great fun but it was over. An invitation into the house meant there was more. How much more only added to the intrigue. Will stayed only 20 minutes before tearing himself away. He made a date with Mary for the following week.

When Will arrived at the Tuplin farm the next week, the entire family was there to greet him. The Tuplin children giggled and made faces. Their sister Mary had a sweetheart. Will was ill at ease the entire evening. The night wore on, and finally the young children were put to bed. Eventually, Mr. and Mrs. Tuplin retired for the night, leaving Will and Mary alone.

In the wee hours of the morning, John Tuplin, like many a father before him, shouted down to his daughter to get upstairs. A few moments later, he heard Will leave and his daughter scurry to bed.

Having partaken of Mary's charms, Will lost interest. It had been a conquest, nothing more. Promises made in the heat of passion were soon forgotten. Will bragged about having had intercourse with Mary to his friend, Francis Power. He never pursued Mary after that one night in the house in early January. In fact, Will took up with other young ladies around Margate and, quite possibly, never gave another thought to Mary Tuplin.

Months passed. The harsh winds of winter gave way to

the rebirth of spring and summer on the picturesque island. It must have been a shock to Will when he heard that Mary Tuplin was pregnant. What's more, it trickled down to Will that many thought he was responsible for her condition.

Will attempted to find out if the rumour was true. On Sunday, June 26, while attending church, he mustered up enough courage to ask the sexton, Tom Bryenton, if he had heard anything about Mary being pregnant. Will knew Bryenton could be discreet and he also knew Bryenton was a good friend of the Tuplin family.

Tom Bryenton confirmed the worst. Mary was pregnant and rumour had it that Will was responsible. By coincidence, Tom and his wife would be visiting with the Tuplins that very evening. Mary's younger brother was seriously ill, which was the reason for the visit. Tom promised Will that he would ask his wife to have a chat with Mary to find out the truth.

That evening, Mary's father scowled as his daughter left the house for a private chat with the sexton's wife. Mary confirmed that she was pregnant and that her only lover had been Will Millman.

The sick Tuplin child died within hours of the Bryentons' visit and was buried two days later. The family, grief-stricken at their loss, returned home from the cemetery. Later on that evening of June 28, Mary walked out of her home, and was never seen alive again.

When Mary failed to return home, John Tuplin searched for his daughter. It was only 9:30 p.m., but Mary had left the house shortly after 6 p.m. It may not seem like a long time now, but in rural P.E.I. of a century ago, it was considered serious for a young girl to be missing for more than three hours. Near exhaustion, John went to bed. Early the next morning, he continued his search.

Two related incidents took place which convinced everyone that Mary had met with foul play near South West River. Her white handkerchief with the initial M embroidered in one corner was found on the riverbank. A 45-kilogram rock was missing from John Cousins's oyster boat, which had been locked up on the bank of the river adjacent to the Millman property.

For six days the river was dragged before Mary's body was recovered. An autopsy indicated that she had been shot twice in the head before being weighed down with the rock taken from Cousins's boat. The autopsy also indicated that Mary was pregnant. The day after the discovery of the body, Will Millman was taken into custody and lodged in the Charlottetown jail.

On January 12, 1888, Will stood trial for Mary's murder. He had little chance to dispute the strong evidence against him. His friend, Francis Power, stated that he had loaned Will his loaded pistol before Mary disappeared. When Will returned it, two of the five bullets had been fired.

Francis's brother Patrick testified that two days after Mary went missing, Will had asked him to say that he was with Will on the night of Mary's disappearance. Dorothy Adams, Donald Tuplin and James Somers all swore they had seen Will near the Tuplin farm on the night in question.

Defence council attempted to prove that there wasn't enough time for Will to have committed the crime. The testimony presented by Will's parents was suspect. They had attended a meeting at the Irishtown Church on the night of Mary's disappearance, leaving Will at home at 7 p.m. When they returned from the meeting at 10:20 p.m., Will was preparing for bed. As two witnesses swore they heard the fatal shots between 9:30 and 10:00 p.m., it left precious little time for Will to have shot Mary, placed her body in the boat, poled a half kilometre, secured the body to the rock and thrown both over the side. He would then have had to pole three-quarters of a kilometre to get home before his parents returned from their meeting.

However, Justice William Hensley indicated in his summation that he felt Will had had plenty of time to commit the crime. That cooked Will's goose. It took only three hours for the P.E.I. jury to find him guilty. Will was sentenced to death.

On April 10, 1888, a large crowd gathered in front of the Charlottetown jail to witness the hanging of William Millman. It went off without a hitch. And so ended the saga of the two children of the soil who met on New Year's Eve over a hundred long years ago.

– JOHN MYCHALUK –

THE HARD-WORKING FARMERS of Wakaw, Saskatchewan, had no reason to believe that the spring of 1916 would be any different than those of previous years. It was true that hail in the Wakaw area had destroyed 35 per cent of the crops that year, but the Ukrainian immigrants, most of whom couldn't speak a word of English, had overcome such hardships in the past.

Life would go on. Soon the heat of summer would bring tourists from Prince Albert and beyond to partake of the excellent fishing and boating on the crystal-clear lakes sur-rounding the village.

Then it happened. The Royal North West Mounted Police division headquarters at Prince Albert received a telegram from Constable Dey of the Wakaw detachment: "Six people reported dead near here. Murder suspected. If possible send help."

And so began the investigation into one of Saskatchewan's most diabolical and cold-blooded murder cases.

Inspector Duffus and Detective-Sergeant Prime, together with two other Mounties, journeyed to Wakaw to assist Dey. They discovered that the home of Prokop Manchur had been burned to the ground. His barn, which had sheltered horses and oxen, had also been destroyed by fire, cremating many of the animals trapped inside. Inexplicably some oxen were lying dead just outside the barn doors.

As the ruins cooled, the Mounties searched for bodies. They found Prokop Manchur, 46, in the kitchen, burned almost beyond recognition. They recovered the charred remains of his two daughters, Antone, 15, and Paulina, 20, in the same area.

The primitive farmhouse had not yet given up all its dead. Entrance to the cellar was gained by lowering a ladder through the floor of the living room. Here the Mounties found Prokop's wife, Mary, and the youngest member of the family, two-year-old Olga.

Mary's legs were grotesquely caught in the bottom rungs of the ladder, while her head, what was left of it, rested on a large stone on the floor. A portion of the unfortunate woman's brains lay on the floor. Her baby lay beside her.

This was no accidental fire. Constable Dey realized that murder had taken place that April day in the farmhouse of Prokop Manchur. While pondering the magnitude of the tragedy, Dey was informed that yet another body had been found. The soot-covered body of John Mychaluk, Prokop's brother-in-law, was discovered a short distance from the farmhouse. The body had not been burned. There was no doubt as to the cause of death. A bullet had entered Mychaluk's forehead and travelled directly through his head. Another had pierced his chest. It was the opinion of the coroner that either wound would result in instant death.

The bodies of the Manchur family were examined, and revealed the horror of their last moments before someone had set fire to their home. Mary had two bullet wounds in her arms. Baby Olga had also taken two bullets to the body. The three victims who had met their deaths in the kitchen, Prokop and his daughters, had all been shot.

Who had wiped out an entire family? The Mounties went to work.

Initially it was ascertained that John Mychaluk's body had been dragged out of the farmhouse through a window by neighbours who were the first at the scene of the fire. This accounted for the soot and grime on the unburned body. Mychaluk had a room in his brother-in-law's farmhouse and had lived there for some time.

The investigators deduced that Mary Manchur had fled to the cellar with her baby in a futile attempt to escape the carnage taking place in the kitchen. The murderer caught up with her while she was still on the ladder. No doubt the force of the two bullets in her arms sent her plunging onto the stones below, splitting open her head. The killer must have then taken aim and shot the baby in cold blood.

After killing all the occupants of the farmhouse, the killer set the house and barn on fire. Several oxen made their way out of the blazing inferno only to be shot down by the mad, but obviously cool, assassin.

Paulina's husband, Mike Syroshka, was the first individual to come under suspicion. Paulina's marriage to the farmer had failed, and she had come to live in her father's house. It was alleged that he had treated Paulina cruelly. After three years of marriage, at the instructions of her father, she had left him and returned to the family farm. Syroshka didn't take the separation well. He had been heard to threaten the entire family if Paulina didn't return to him.

When questioned, Syroshka admitted that bad blood had existed between him and the entire Manchur clan, but he vehemently denied any connection with the crime. He claimed that he had not set foot on the Manchur farm for over a year.

On the night of the fire, at exactly midnight, he, his mother and other members of his family, had watched the reflection of the fire from his parents' farm. Syroshka willingly showed the Mounties the clothing he had worn on the night of the tragedy. They found no stains nor any other evidence to connect him to the multiple murder. Besides, when Syroshka confided to the Mounties that he had loved Paulina they were inclined to believe him.

The Mounties now turned their attention to the burned-out ruins and a .32 Winchester rifle found amidst the debris. When the rifle was recovered, there were eight live cartridges in the magazine and one exploded cartridge in the chamber.

A meticulous examination of the burned-out house recovered bullets which had been embedded in a wall. These bullets matched those recovered from the bodies of the victims. Empty cartridge cases were found in the ruins. They were all .32 Winchester centre-fire cartridges. It was apparent that one person, using the Winchester, was responsible for all the murders.

No one could identify the rifle. Friends and acquaintances swore that they had never seen any member of the Manchur family or John Mychaluk in possession of such a weapon.

The first break in the case occurred when Prokop Manchur's father informed the police that he had found a sheepskin coat near his son's farmhouse on the night of the fire. He had thought nothing of it at the time, but now, realizing that it might be connected to the murders in some way, he turned the coat over to police.

The garment was quickly identified as belonging to John Mychaluk. He was seen wearing it on the night of the tragedy. Inside a pocket of the coat the Mounties found a box containing three .32 Winchester centre-fire cartridges. Also tucked away in the box was the name of the store in Wakaw where the cartridges had been purchased.

While shown this evidence, the Wakaw shopkeeper's memory was jogged. It was he who had sold the cartridges and rifle to Mychaluk.

The investigating officers now turned their attention to the possibility that Mychaluk may have been in some way involved in the murders. There were powder burns around his wounds, indicating that he had been shot at close range.

It was alleged that Mychaluk had made improper advances to Paulina Manchur. Was it possible that she was about to expose him, thereby providing him with a motive for murder? Some claimed that Mychaluk had argued heatedly with Prokop Manchur over money. Did these arguments precipitate the annihilation of the entire family?

These theories all pointed to Mychaluk as the killer, except for one indisputable fact. According to the coroner, either the bullet to Mychaluk's head or the one to his chest would have caused instant death. Dead men simply can't get off a well-aimed second shot.

To Inspector Duffus goes the credit for solving the mystery. So sure was he that Mychaluk had wiped out the entire Manchur family before turning his own rifle upon himself that he was convinced that the coroner had erred. Inspector Duffus knew that if by chance the chest wound had not caused death there would be internal haemorrhaging. Only an autopsy would prove his point.

Duffus was correct. An autopsy revealed that Mychaluk's chest cavity was swimming with blood. There was now no doubt in the coroner's mind that Mychaluk had lived for some time after receiving the chest wound.

John Mychaluk had killed all the Manchurs and then turned his rifle upon himself. Instead of ending his life instantly with a bullet to the heart as he had planned, the bullet missed its mark and he remained alive. Now, certainly dying, but conscious enough to feel the heat of the flames advancing toward him, he managed to lean the Winchester to his forehead and pull the trigger.

On April 14, 1916, a coroner's jury found the Manchurs' deaths to be the sole responsibility of John Mychaluk who, immediately following the murders, had committed suicide.

MANSON, BUNDY, GACY, DAHMER—the names are synonymous with horrific acts perpetrated by evil men. Their exploits have been recounted in books, on television and in movies. Yet one of Canada's most terrifying tales of wanton murder has gone relatively unnoticed by the country's media. The unspeakable deeds of Dale Nelson took place during the course of one night in Creston Valley, a rather isolated area in southeastern British Columbia.

Dale was in his early thirties back in 1970 when the crimes took place. A logger by profession, he lived with his wife, Annette, and their three children in a modest house along Corn Creek Road. Dale was a good husband and a kind, caring father, except when he drank with his logging buddies in Creston. On those occasions, he would become aggressive, rowdy and unpredictable. Earlier that same year, Dale had gone into a deep depression and had made an unsuccessful attempt to take his own life. He underwent a psychiatric examination, after which he was returned to his family.

Dale's main hobby was hunting. He was an expert marksman in an area where hunting is the chief diversion from the back-breaking labour of the logging and farming industries. Everyone in the area knew Dale. Many were related to him. Sure, he had his moods and drank a bit, but there was nothing really wrong with Dale Nelson. When he wasn't intoxicated, there was no finer fellow in the valley.

On September 4, 1970, Dale drove his blue Chevy into town. He picked up a six-pack of beer and a bottle of vodka at the liquor store and proceeded to the Kootenay Hotel, where he was well known. No one noticed anything unusual about Dale's behaviour. He downed eight beers and chatted with friends, mostly about the upcoming hunting season.

After leaving the bar, Dale drove over to Maureen McKay's home to pick up his 7-mm bolt-action rifle, which he had previously loaned to her. He then made his way to Creston and purchased ammo for his rifle, as well as a further supply of booze from the liquor store. Even though he had been drinking on and off all day, Dale was in surprising control of his faculties. He strolled into Creston's King George Hotel and consumed another half-dozen beers. Around 10:30 p.m., he was invited to one of the hotel rooms, where he and two friends drank more liquor.

The various people who crossed Dale's path that day had no way of knowing they would later be witnesses at a sensational murder trial. Clerks, drinking buddies and casual friends all thought Dale was in a good mood. He displayed no hint of what was to follow.

It was now past midnight. Ironically, the hunting season had opened moments earlier. Dale drove to the home of Shirley and Alex Wasyk. He knew that Alex was not at home, but had no way of knowing that one of the Wasyk children, Laurie, had accompanied her father. That left Shirley at home with daughters Debbie, 12, Charlene, 8, and Tracey, 7.

Debbie was alone in her bedroom when Dale Nelson came calling. She recognized his voice. After all, Dale was her cousin and often took her hunting. Suddenly, Debbie heard her mother scream, "No, Dale, don't!" The cry was followed by silence. Debbie sneaked out of her room to get a better view. She saw Dale lead Charlene into Tracey's bedroom, where her sister lay asleep. Debbie kept quiet and sneaked into her mother's room. She gasped when she saw her mother lying on the bed with her hands tied behind her back. A fire extinguisher lay close by. Trembling with fear, Debbie untied her mother's hands. When she heard Tracey scream, she picked up the fire extinguisher and dragged it to her room. She threw the extinguisher through the window and jumped out, just as she heard Dale at the bedroom door. Debbie ran to Maureen McKay's and hysterically blurted out her tale of terror. Maureen called the RCMP detachment in Creston.

The Mounties arrived at the Wasyk home to find that Shirley and Tracey had both been murdered. Shirley had been savagely beaten to death with the fire extinguisher. Tracey had been stabbed repeatedly. Charlene had been taken from the house, but had been set free. Dale's Chevy was still parked beside the house.

Fearing for the lives of Mrs. Nelson and other potential victims, the Mounties drove to the Nelson home and evacuated Annette and her children. In all, they were away from the Wasyk home for a total of 15 minutes. When they returned, they were stunned to find that Tracey's body was missing, along with Dale's Chevy. Obviously, he had been hiding outside in the deep brush watching as the RCMP officers drove away.

Officers realized they were dealing with a man who had just taken two lives for no apparent reason. He was armed with a rifle, was a crack shot and was driving in pitch darkness through the countryside with Tracey's body.

Ray Phipps, 42, and his common-law wife, Isabelle St. Amand, 27, lived a few kilometres down the road in little more than a shack. Three of the children, Paul, 10, Cathy, 8, and Brian, 7, were Isabelle's by a previous marriage. Eighteen-month-old Roy was the child of Ray and Isabelle. It was Isabelle who called the RCMP detachment in West Creston. Among other disjointed phrases, she whispered, "There's a man here with a gun." The RCMP rushed to the Phipps' home. They were too late.

Ray and Isabelle Phipps had both been shot in the head. The baby, Roy, had been shot as he lay in his crib. Paul and Brian had also been shot in the head. Eight-year-old Cathy was nowhere to be found, which led the Mounties to surmise that Dale, who had taken seven lives in a few hours, had driven away with the little girl in his Chevy.

As dawn broke, Mounties from several neighbouring detachments poured into Creston Valley. Systematic spot checks of houses in the area were conducted by the Mounties, who had no idea where Dale would strike next.

The following afternoon, Dale's vehicle was spotted from the air by the pilot of a Piper Cub engaged in the search. The unoccupied car was stuck in a ditch. Investigators found a bloodstained hammer on the front seat. The woods surrounding the Chevy bore grisly results. Parts of Tracey's body were discovered scattered throughout the immediate area.

Darkness fell on the valley with the monster still at large. Next day, the search intensified. Men stayed home from work. Rifles were taken down from racks. The hunting season was officially open, but the quarry on everyone's mind was Dale Nelson.

Late in the afternoon, Dale was located in the woods close to his own home. He offered no resistance. The question on everyone's mind was the fate of Cathy St. Amand.

Without hesitation, Dale informed his captors that the girl was dead and pointed out the location of her body on a map. The RCMP found the child's body in the exact spot indicated by Dale.

From the time of his arrest, Dale underwent a series of psychiatric examinations. When he stood trial for the murders of Tracey Wasyk and Cathy St. Amand, there was only one question to be decided: Was Dale Nelson sane or insane? He had admitted committing all eight murders, but could give no reason other than his intoxication.

The British Columbia jury found Dale sane and guilty. He was sentenced to life imprisonment. Twenty-eight years have elapsed since the madman ran amok through the peaceful countryside. Dale Merle Nelson has spent every one of those years in a B.C. prison. As you read this, he is still incarcerated. Should he ever be paroled, he will immediately be charged with the remaining six murders.

— EARLE NELSON —

THE BOSTON STRANGLER managed to kill and mutilate 13 innocent women, terrorizing the city of Boston for several years. Albert DeSalvo confessed to being the strangler, and was committed to an institution. He had terrorized an entire city to such an extent that women feared to walk the streets alone.

Way back in 1927, Earle Nelson operated in much the same manner as DeSalvo, except that he killed more frequently and moved from city to city, cutting a swath of rape and murder across the United States and into Canada.

Everyone who has researched the Nelson case agree on

one thing—Earle Nelson was not normal. The best documented portion of his life began when he crossed the border from the United States into Canada.

William Patterson worked in a Winnipeg department store. He and his wife lived at 100 Riverton Street. The couple planned to sell their home, so while Bill Patterson was at work his wife showed prospective buyers through the house. To attract potential purchasers, they had placed a For Sale sign prominently in a front window.

On a bright June day in 1927, Bill came home from work and was startled to find that his wife was not at home. His two children had spent the afternoon playing in a neighbour's backyard. Patterson couldn't believe that his wife would leave the children unattended. He phoned the police and reported his wife missing.

In the meantime, despite his concern, Patterson had the practical problem of caring for his two children. He prepared the youngsters for bed. Later, in his own bedroom, he noticed that someone had forced open a suitcase in which he and his wife kept their savings. When Patterson kneeled down to take a closer look, he caught sight of his wife's coat under the bed. When he extended his arm, reaching for the coat, his hand came to rest on the neck of his dead wife.

The distraught man raced to a neighbour's house, blurted out the story of his tragic find and collapsed. The police were at the scene in a matter of minutes. Near Mrs. Patterson's body they found an old blue jacket and a pair of cheap cotton pants which did not belong to Mr. Patterson.

One of Patterson's brown suits was missing, along with $70 from the suitcase. It was obvious that the killer had left his old clothing at the scene of the murder, having first changed into Mr. Patterson's suit.

226 · MAX HAINES

In the pockets of the cotton pants the police found newspaper clippings of rooms to let in Winnipeg. An examination of Mrs. Patterson's body revealed that she had been raped and strangled. The police recognized the similarity between this crime and those being committed by a monster who was roaming through the United States, raping and murdering as he went. The For Sale sign, the woman alone, the rape, strangulation and theft, all pointed to the same man.

Was it possible that the man known as "The Strangler," or "The Gorilla Man" was in Winnipeg? The answer soon became apparent. So sure were the police that they had among them one of the most notorious killers in history that they commenced to canvas every home in Winnipeg advertising a room for rent on the chance that they might come up with the killer.

On the day following the murder, the police found Mr. Patterson's brown suit in a pawnshop. In its pocket they found his cigarette lighter. The pawnshop proprietor distinctly remembered the man who had left the suit. He was an excellent customer. He had purchased an entire new outfit consisting of a light gray suit and overcoat. The customer had then asked the pawnshop owner for the location of a good barber. The merchant had accompanied the man to his own barber. The stranger had laughed and joked with the barber while in the shop. It is estimated that he had killed Mrs. Patterson only hours before.

A full description of the wanted man was sent to every law enforcement agency in the United States and Canada. By June 11, the stranger had managed to hitch-hike to Regina, where he rented a room under the name Henry Harcourt. He was shocked to find his description all over the front pages of the Regina newspapers. In order to change his appearance, once more he bought old work clothes at a local pawnshop, and by June 13 left Regina on foot.

Back in Winnipeg, a second body was discovered. Lola Cowan, a 14-year-old schoolgirl, had been enticed to her killer's room on the promise that he would purchase some flowers the girl was selling. Lola was contributing to her family's income by selling flowers after school. When her body was found under a bed, it was obvious that she had been sexually attacked and strangled. The stranger had slipped out of his room on June 9 without paying his rent.

With the news of the discovery of the second victim, the entire West was gripped by fear. Citizens bolted their doors and peered suspiciously at strangers from behind closed drapes. A living fiend was in their midst.

Although a complete description of the killer was widely distributed, and he had left a hot trail, it wasn't until Wednesday, June 15, that he was spotted. Leslie Morgan owned and operated a general store in Wakopa, Manitoba, a tiny community of six houses about 250 miles southeast of Regina and 16 miles southwest of Killarney. Morgan served a soft drink and some cookies to a stranger. He was sure he had just served the strangler, and informed the Manitoba Provincial Police in Killarney. The police caught up with the fugitive a few miles south of Wakopa. He was arrested without incident and taken to Killarney. At 10:40 p.m. he was placed in jail. It took him exactly 20 minutes to pick the locks on his cell door and escape.

Nelson made his way to the Killarney railway station, figuring that he might be able to hop a train. He remained hidden until 8:10 a.m., when he came out of hiding to board an incoming train. He had no way of knowing it was a special train loaded down with police arriving expressly to take part in the manhunt. Nelson was quickly apprehended, handcuffed and escorted to Winnipeg under heavy guard.

Earle Nelson was born in San Francisco on May 12, 1897. He attended school for a short time, but dropped out to become a transient labourer. By 1912 he had twice been confined to an insane asylum in California. After his second release, Nelson married. His wife soon began to notice his childlike behavior. In fact, Nelson liked to play with children, and got along well with them. He would wander away from his wife and home for weeks at a time. When he returned, he would behave as if he had been absent for only a few minutes. Finally, because of his erratic behaviour, his wife had him confined for a third time. He escaped from the institution and was never recaptured.

When Nelson was safely behind bars in Winnipeg, police officials from a score of American cities requested his fingerprints so that they could be matched with prints left at the scene of similar crimes in their cities. From these fingerprints and eyewitness reports, Nelson's path of terror was traced.

It is believed that he started killing on February 20, 1926, in San Francisco. In succession, he went to San Jose, returned to San Francisco, then on to Santa Barbara and Oakland. In all, he murdered five women between February 20 and August 16, a period of just under six months. Next, Nelson struck in Portland, Oregon, where he strangled three women in three days. He travelled back to San Francisco, on to Seattle, Washington, then returned to Portland. Nelson travelled continually throughout the winter of 1926-27. He strangled a woman in Council Bluffs, Iowa, and killed two women and a baby in Kansas City, Missouri.

In 1927, killing as he went, Nelson struck in Philadelphia, Buffalo, twice in Detroit, and in Chicago. From Chicago he travelled to Winnipeg where Mrs. Patterson and Lola Cowan became victims number 21 and 22. It is difficult to pinpoint the exact number of the strangler's victims, as it is believed that he may have killed more women whose murders, for one reason or another, were not attributed to him.

Earle Nelson did not look or act like a gorilla. All through his trial, which was held in Winnipeg on November 1, 1927, he was mild-mannered and polite to everyone who came in contact with him. He had used his rather pleasant disposition many times before to put unsuspecting women at ease. While posing as a prospective roomer, he would always impress his potential victims with his polite chatter about church affairs. Many women who managed not to become victims came forward at the trial to testify how Earle Nelson had impressed them.

His trial was probably the most sensational ever held in Winnipeg. The courtroom was jammed, and thousands could not gain entrance to the courthouse. In an attempt to save his life, Nelson's wife and aunt were on hand to testify to Nelson's insanity. Throughout it all Nelson remained composed and swore he never killed anyone. The evidence against him was overwhelming and he was found guilty.

On a chilly January morning at daybreak, Father J.A. Webb of St. Mary's Cathedral administered the last rites of the Catholic Church to Nelson. At precisely 7:41 a.m. his body plunged through the trapdoor of the gallows. Earle Nelson was 30 years old. The date was Friday, January 13, 1928.

– BILL NEWELL –

BILL NEWELL WAS A ladies' man. Good-looking, muscular, oozing confidence. Born in Toronto on May 20, 1914, Bill led an ordinary early life. His most outstanding accomplishment appears to have been in athletics. He was pole-vault champion of Scarborough Collegiate Institute.

Bill married Winnifred Moores in 1934. He and Winnifred had a daughter, Doreen, but the marriage didn't last. A year before his divorce he was living with attractive Aune Paavola, the daughter of strict Finnish immigrants. Three weeks after his divorce from Winnifred became final, Bill married Aune, who had given birth to his son, Bill, Jr., some six months previously.

Aune Paavola accepted Bill at face value. It was true his charming manner was often interspersed with impulsive temper tantrums, but she tried to overlook such minor faults. However, Aune eventually became disenchanted with Bill's uncontrollable temper and his wandering ways. The couple separated. Bill rebounded without missing a bounce. Within a year he was living with another Finnish-Canadian woman, Elna Lehto.

It was 1940. Russia had invaded Finland. In a grand gesture, Bill joined a Canadian force in Finland's defence. Two months later, on April 5, he was back in Toronto. It was an embarrassingly short tour of duty, but Bill came up with a plausible explanation. He claimed that he had received serious wounds around one eye, which had forced him to return to Canada.

As usual, Bill was lying. It was later learned that he had refused to sign an agreement to serve with the Finnish forces. As a result, he was deported to Canada. So much for Bill Newell's distinguished two-month war record in helping to defend Finland.

On August 26, Bill joined the Royal Canadian Air Force and was sent to Brandon, Manitoba, for training. For the first time in years Bill had a steady income. It was the distribution of his Air Force dependents' allowance cheques that gave rise to his problems.

Aune was still Bill's legal wife. She and her son, Billy, were certainly entitled to some kind of living allowance. Then there was Bill's first wife, Winnifred, who had the full responsibility of raising Doreen. Also squarely in the picture was Bill's current companion, Elna, who, according to the Canadian Armed Forces, could not claim common-law status as she and Bill had not been living together for a full year. The only way Elna could share Bill's income would be if Aune signed an agreement to that effect or consented to a divorce.

Using his muddled affairs as an excuse, Bill obtained a transfer from Brandon to St. Thomas, Ontario. On September 20, 1940, he returned to Toronto on leave and spent almost every evening with Aune.

Bill made arrangements. On Saturday, September 28, he spent the night with Aune. He planned to take her and her roommate, Orvokki Hakamies, to a concert at the Active Service Canteen. At 8 a.m. he left Aune and returned to Elna, but stayed only a few hours. At noon he took Aune to lunch, telling Orvokki that they would return in an hour or so.

When they left Aune's home at 15 Grange Street at 1:30 that Sunday afternoon, there is little doubt that Bill Newell was leading his wife to her death.

Mrs. Toini Ranpors, the girls' landlady, thought Bill looked gallant in his crisp new air force uniform. She watched the good-looking couple as they walked east on Grange and turned south on Beverley. They had a bite to eat at the Active Service Canteen about 2 p.m., walked down to the docks and caught the 2:50 ferry, the *Sam McBride*, to Centre Island.

They strolled hand in hand down Manitou and Iroquois Avenues onto a footpath to the northeast section of a filtration plant located there. They were within a stone's throw of St. Andrew's Cut, one of several lagoons intersecting the island's coast. It was an isolated, lonely place.

Aune had believed that there was still hope for a reconciliation with her husband, but now she knew it was no use. Bill was pressing for a divorce or, failing that, was attempting to have her sign off her rights to his family allowance cheques. Aune would have none of it.

Suddenly Bill pounced on his wife. Aune struggled as he twisted a rope around her neck. Bill pulled until she lay dead. All was quiet in that isolated, overgrown section of Centre Island. Bill's mind raced with the details of what still had to be done.

Without warning, unexpected intruders came upon the scene. Charles and Marion Maynes, who lived on the island, were canoeing through St. Andrew's Cut. Bill saw them first. He propped Aune's body up to a sitting position, tied a string to a stick and pretended to be fishing.

Mrs. Maynes later testified she thought it strange that the woman sitting so erect seemed to be staring straight ahead. She noticed the airman fishing and looked away.

Slowly the Maynes disappeared from view. Bill carried his wife's body off the path and stripped it of everything that might identify her. He covered Aune's body with her black coat. Then he gathered as much brush as he could find and dumped it over her inert form. With luck, Bill thought, the body might not be found until spring.

Bill caught the 4:30 ferry back to the mainland. At 8:45 he met Orvokki Hakamies and inquired if Aune was at home. When Orvokki replied that she didn't know where Aune was, Bill continued on to his living quarters with Elna at 172 Howland Avenue.

Aune Newell was immediately reported missing. Next day Bill returned to St. Thomas. On Tuesday, in an attempt to allay suspicion, he wrote a pleasant letter to Aune.

Bill managed a 48-hour leave. This time Elna met him with the disconcerting news that there were radio reports of his wife's disappearance. She suggested that he contact police. Bill took the advice and told Detective Sergeant Fred Skinner that, in his opinion, his wife was not missing, but hiding somewhere to avoid being served with divorce papers. He also told Skinner that he had last seen his wife the previous Sunday at 7 p.m., when he had bumped into her at the corner of Yonge and Adelaide Streets.

On Sunday, October 6, Harry Lemon, a parks department employee, whose job it was to make a circuit of Centre Island every Sunday, spotted a woman's shoe. It captured his attention because it appeared to be new. Harry looked further and found a garter, a purse, a stocking and finally the body of Aune Newell. Exactly one week had elapsed since she had been strangled to death.

Bill was immediately picked up and held as a material witness while detectives gathered evidence. Bill's letters to Aune indicated that his main concern was to obtain a divorce and custody of his son, Billy, so that his service cheques could be diverted to Elna. A piece of rope was found at the scene. It matched rope found at 172 Howland Avenue, where Bill lived with Elna.

Bill stood trial three times for the murder of his wife. The first two trials resulted in hung juries. He was an obstreperous prisoner, continually fighting with guards. During court proceedings he shouted at the presiding judge and witnesses.

New evidence was presented at the handsome airman's third trial. A torn YMCA envelope with an RCAF crest had been found near Aune's body. The reassembled envelope revealed a sketch of the remote death site. Elna identified the handwriting on the map and notes as being Bill Newell's. He had written to her many times using similar envelopes. One was found among his belongings. Elna also testified that Bill had written to her suggesting that the murder of his wife was the solution to his problems.

Bill Newell was found guilty and sentenced to hang. All appeals failed. On February 12, 1942, Bill had a breakfast of bacon, eggs, toast and coffee. He refused a sedative and, proclaiming his innocence to the end, walked erectly to the Don Jail scaffold, where he was executed.

To all outward appearances, the Rallos were a loving, close-knit family. Their home at 16 Lantana Court in Hamilton, Ontario, was typical of a young family seeking the good life.

Jon Rallo, 33, the head of the family, had done pretty well for himself, working his way up in the municipal government to a responsible position as office manager in the engineering department. Attractive Sandra Rallo was four years younger than her husband. The Rallos had two children—Jason, 7, and Stephanie, 5.

Neighbours on Lantana Court liked the Rallos. They often socialized. So did Sandra's parents. Like grandparents everywhere, Doug and Margaret Pollington doted on their grandchildren and looked forward to the children's periodic visits to their home in nearby Cambridge.

Nothing is perfect. There were rumours that all was not smooth in the Rallo marriage. Jon had accused Sandra of having an affair with another man. She, in turn, had her suspicions about her husband's fidelity. They had gone through a rough period, but it was over. By 1976, their marriage appeared to be stable. Appearances can be deceiving.

On the night of Monday, August 16, a friend called at the Rallo home, saw the entire family and left at 11 p.m. From that moment, no one other than their killer was to lay eyes on Sandra, Jason and Stephanie Rallo.

Jon didn't show up for work the next morning or the next. In fact, the first anyone was to hear of the fate of his family occurred when he called on his father-in-law, Doug Pollington, at 11:30 a.m. on Wednesday. Mr. Pollington was shocked at Jon's appearance. He was wearing old clothes, needed a shave and behaved in a nervous manner.

Jon explained that Sandra had left him for another man. She had taken the children with her. He went on to say that it all happened while he was asleep in the basement. When he woke up Tuesday morning, his entire family was gone. In their place was an unsigned typewritten note.

Doug Pollington was astounded as he read:

> I'm writing this letter to say goodbye and ask you to try and understand what I am doing, Jon. I've met someone who I love very much. He's a rich lawyer from out West who I met while working last year. He can give us everything we would ever want.

Jon later told his mother-in-law that Sandra had left everything behind except her wallet. The Pollingtons were skeptical. The note, the abruptness of Sandra's decision to walk out of their lives, was not typical of their daughter. They consented to Jon's request to contact a lawyer rather than the police.

While they were telling their story to Hamilton lawyer Dennis Roy, another drama was being enacted on the shores of Jordan Harbour, not far from St. Catharines. Shawn Labonde, 14, and his brother were fishing when they came upon a duffel bag in the water. The boys opened the bag and then opened a green garbage bag they found inside. There, before their terrified eyes, was the nude body of a little girl. Unaware of the gruesome find, Doug Pollington informed Hamilton police that his daughter and her children were missing. Next day, the little girl in the garbage bag was identified as Stephanie Rallo.

Sergeant Gary King of the Hamilton police, together with William Towstiak of the Centre of Forensic Sciences in Toronto, searched the Rallos' west end Hamilton home. Towstiak, a veteran of 21 years of scientific sleuthing, found an abundance of incriminating evidence in the Rallo home. Blocking a doorway to a bedroom was a mattress stained with minute drops of blood. The broadloom which had covered the master-bedroom floor had been torn up and was nowhere to be found.

Towstiak also found seven small drops of blood on the deep maroon drapes in the bedroom. Later, he would testify they were "consistent with blood splashed, with being thrown with some force." The blood proved to be the same type as that of Sandra Rallo.

More blood was found on the walls leading to the basement. Traces of blood were found in water trapped in a floor drain. In a bedroom closet, the forensic detective discovered Jon Rallo's bloodstained slippers.

Rallo was taken into custody and charged with first-degree murder. Meanwhile, police actively searched for the bodies of the two missing members of his family. On August 26, an OPP officer scanning the Welland Canal from a helicopter spotted a parcel floating in the water. It proved to be Sandra's body, wrapped in garbage bags. Medical examination indicated that Sandra had been beaten and strangled. Little Stephanie had been smothered to death.

Jon Rallo stood trial for the murder of his wife and two children. Prosecution attorneys presented a formidable case. They were able to trace the garbage bags used to dispose of the bodies back to the manufacturer and prove that they came from an open package of bags found in the Rallo home. A guard at a local garbage dump identified Rallo as the man who had disposed of several bags of garbage on

August 18. Broadloom removed from the Rallo home had been recovered from the dump.

Rallo took the witness box in his own defence. He admitted that he'd had an affair with a colleague at City Hall, but steadfastly claimed that his wife had taken the children and left him for another man. He stated that he had no idea how his wife and daughter ended up in garbage bags. He dismissed the condition of his home with a shrug, saying he had become so despondent when he read his wife's letter that he had dismantled the bed. He'd ripped up the carpet because the dog had recently soiled it. The bloodstains? Sandra had had a nosebleed.

No one believed Jon Rallo. He was found guilty of three counts of first-degree murder and sentenced to three terms of life imprisonment with no possibility of parole for 25 years.

Before being sentenced, Rallo addressed the court: "What has kept my head above water these past 16 months is the fact that I know I did not do it, Stephanie knows I didn't do it and Jason, wherever he is, knows I didn't."

The search for Jason's body appeared to be over when skeletal remains of a young boy found near Barrie were erroneously identified as Jason. Some time after the body was buried, it was discovered that the dead boy was Jamie Shearer, a youngster from Alberta who had disappeared a year earlier. The boy's mother was questioned by OPP officials. She insisted that her son was staying with friends in Toronto. Before she could be questioned a second time, she committed suicide. Jason Rallo's body has never been found.

I T WOULD BE A DAY to remember—the impressive cere-mony at O'Keefe Centre, calling her to the Bar—dinner with her mother—drinks with friend Krystyn Rutkowski at the Hotel California in Toronto. It would be a day to remember—the last day of new lawyer Barbra Schlifer's life.

In the wee hours of April 11, 1980, Barbra bade good-bye to her friend Krystyn and left the Hotel California. She took the subway and then a streetcar to her apartment at 98 Leuty Avenue in Toronto's east end. Barbra was weighed down with a purse, an umbrella and a shopping bag containing *New Yorker* magazines.

It was approximately 1:40 a.m. The doors to the apart-ment building on Leuty Avenue were open. There on the stairwell, Barbra met a sleeping teenage boy. She ordered him out of the building. She may have recognized him as a lad she had helped out with a few dollars some days earlier. The boy made no effort to leave. Instead, he pulled out a knife and proceeded to sexually assault the terrified young woman, all the while threatening her with the knife and warning her that if she screamed, he would kill her.

As the assault continued, 12 stab wounds were inflicted on Barbra Schlifer. Finally, she slumped to the floor. The frenzied attacker raced from the building, tossing some of Barbra's belongings into a deserted water-filled bathtub in an adjoining lane. He tossed other material under a car. From deep down in his gut, the killer screamed into the still spring air. Then he was gone.

Sandra Wherry lived in an apartment beside Barbra's. She went to bed between 1 a.m. and 1:30 a.m. that morning.

Sandra fell asleep immediately and slept soundly. Next morning, she left her apartment at 8:40 a.m. and was startled to see blood smeared on the walls. Her eyes followed the bloodstains to the stair alcove. She spotted Barbra Schlifer's body and called police.

Ten minutes later, homicide detectives were at the scene. Barbra Schlifer, who only the day before had culminated years of study by graduating as a lawyer, now became the centre of an intense murder investigation.

In the days that followed, Mariana Theresa MacGuire, who lived in a house beside the lane adjoining Barbra's apartment building, came forward. She had arrived home at midnight the morning Barbra was murdered and had gone to bed, which was located near an open window. A few minutes after she retired, Ms. MacGuire heard a noise outside in the lane.

"It was a yell from a man, it was a low scream, sort of like a vent of frustration. It was very loud and it startled me." Ms. MacGuire drew her curtains and peered out her window. A man ran down the lane from Leuty Avenue and hunched behind a chain-link fence. The man appeared to be carrying a white plastic grocery bag. He rose and ran to Leuty Avenue and was soon out of sight.

At 8 a.m. on the morning of the murder, Mushtaq Meer walked out of his home at 2108 Queen Street East to take his dog for a walk. Meer strolled into his backyard and was startled to see several magazines and the contents of a wallet strewn on his lawn. In a deserted water-filled bathtub on his property, he discovered pornographic magazines. All the material was soaking wet. Meer gathered it up and took it inside to dry.

By 11 a.m. he had seen the police in the area and had

heard of the murder. He walked over to a police officer and told him about his find. Mushtaq Meer had found Barbra Schlifer's ID and the pornographic magazines which the teenager had been reading on the stairs as he waited for Barbra to come home.

A block away, Eugene Deline opened his business, Queen Compact Cars. He, too, was well aware of the murder, which was the talk of the neighbourhood. When he found a bloody T-shirt, an umbrella and a plastic bag among his used cars, he immediately informed police. Eugene Deline had recovered Barbra Schlifer's umbrella and the killer's shirt.

Fernand Robinson was nine days short of his sixteenth birthday when Barbra Schlifer was murdered. He had been in trouble most of his young life. From 1977 on, he lived in a group home in east end Toronto. After a short stay with his parents in Rexdale, he was sent to the Ontario Correctional Institute in Brampton. Fernand was a troubled boy. He embellished, lied and fantasized.

One Sunday, when his father visited him in Brampton, Fernand told him that he had been at an apartment building in Toronto. He said that he'd been cold and hungry, but the woman had told him to leave. Fernand told his father that he had killed her. Mr. Robinson, who was hard of hearing, thought his son said that the victim's name was Barbra. He had not read about the murder and thought his son was making up another one of his wild stories. Although he didn't believe Fernand, he advised him to tell someone at the institute. Fernand Robinson was a boy with an urge to confide his guilt to someone, yet he didn't want to face the consequences.

Five months passed, but Fernand wouldn't let the issue

die. While being interviewed by Dr. Gerald Heasman, of the Ontario Correctional Institute in Brampton, Fernand mentioned that he often dreamed of murder. He said he felt terrible because of what he had done. The doctor would later state that Fernand told him, "I am guilty. I did not mean to do it." At this point, Dr. Heasman warned Fernand that he would have to report their conversation. The boy wasn't dissuaded. He went on to tell Dr. Heasman that his victim had been a lawyer and that he had been sleeping on the stairs of an apartment building. The doctor passed this information on to his superiors.

Staff Sergeant Bill Wolfe and Staff Sergeant Gordon Fenton interviewed Fernand. He told them he knew nothing about the case and was reluctant to discuss the matter with them.

But the urge persisted.

Fernand was transferred to the Guelph Correctional Centre. On Christmas Eve of 1980, correctional officer Bonnie Zimmerman was in charge of 12 segregated inmates, all housed in individual cells.

Around midnight, Fernand woke up and shouted for Mrs. Zimmerman. Each time she went to his cell block, he was stark naked. She told him to put on his security gown and refused to talk to him. After each episode, she returned to her office area. On the third visit to his cell, he screamed and shouted, but finally confided to Mrs. Zimmerman, "Do you remember the female lawyer that was murdered in Toronto recently?"

Mrs. Zimmerman was aware of the case. She replied, "Yes."

Fernand said, "I killed her."

Mrs. Zimmerman looked at the nude man, who had

shouted at her for the better part of an hour. She didn't believe him. Finally, she told him to go to bed. Fernand responded by going into a rage, shouting obscenities at the correctional officer. Mrs. Zimmerman had heard too many fantastic stories to pick out Fernand's latest rantings as the truth. Over a year later, when she heard that he was a suspect in the case, she remembered the incident and came forward.

During July 1982, Fernand wrote out a rambling confession, full of fictional characters and easily proven untruths. However, this statement, in which he confessed to the murder of Barbra Schlifer, contained several facts that only the killer could know. The 48-page handwritten statement is one of the most heartless accounts of senseless murder ever put to paper.

Staff Sergeant Wayne Oldham and David Boothby of Metro Toronto's homicide squad received the notebook on August 9, 1982. They travelled to Kingston Penitentiary, where Fernand Robinson was then confined.

Fernand's confession to the two officers followed the same fictional account as his written longhand statement. However, under astute questioning by the two officers, he finally stated that he had made up all the fictional characters in his earlier narrative. Now he confessed to being the only one involved in the murder of Barbra Schlifer.

On May 2, 1984, Fernand Robinson was found guilty of murder in the first degree. He was sentenced to life imprisonment with no possibility of parole for 25 years. He is presently serving that sentence.

If anything positive can be said to have resulted from a senseless murder, the founding of the Barbra Schlifer Commemorative Clinic is such a phenomenon.

In 1985 the clinic was founded to assist female victims of violence. Located at 188 Dupont Street, Toronto, the clinic bustles with activity as dedicated intake counsellors cope with the scores of women who either telephone or show up at their door.

The need to assist these women is urgent. "Most have nowhere else to turn," points out counsellor Laurie Bryson. The vast majority seeking help are abused women, but there are others. Adult survivors of childhood sexual abuse and child assault also reach out for assistance.

Clinic advocate Joan Burrell is quick to assert that the public's idea of an abused woman may be someone who has received a slap on the face. Nothing could be further from the truth. The clinic has assisted women who have been blinded, crippled and made deaf by attacks on them.

The men who wreak such havoc may not appear to be monsters. But they lead double lives. Outwardly they are upstanding members of the community. In the privacy of their homes, they batter their wives and/or their children.

Male children whose fathers were abusive toward their mothers often become batterers themselves. In many cases, a man behaves normally until marriage or until he enters a structured relationship. He may then proceed to beat his mate. Usually, as time passes, the abuse increases in intensity.

Pregnancy often precipitates abuse. Certain men resent their wives' focus on their unborn children. They feel cheated and jealous. Their feelings often explode into violence.

The Barbra Schlifer Commemorative Clinic offers a variety of services to women, from legal and counselling services to individual and group counselling for abused women. They even provide a cultural interpreter service for women who are unable to express their problems in English. Presently they provide cultural/language assistance in five languages—Hindi/Punjabi, Italian, Portuguese, Spanish and Vietnamese.

A young woman was murdered in an apartment stairwell. Her death has given hope to hundreds of women who never had the privilege of knowing Barbra Schlifer.

– JANE STAFFORD –

JANE STAFFORD LOOKED at the 280-pound hulk of a man snoring in the cab of the family's Jeep, the man who had been the source of her hell on earth for five long years. Then she said to Allan, her 16-year-old son, "Get me a gun." Allan brought out a 12-gauge shotgun, passed it to his mother and returned to the house.

Jane, relating the sequence of events to me, stated, "I put the gun in the window of the cab and just fired."

It was the night of March 11, 1982, when Jane Stafford, 33, blew the head off Billy Stafford, her common-law husband. Jane didn't know that in the months to follow, her case would be discussed across the nation. She didn't know that many would claim that Jane's terror crystallized the plight of abused women everywhere. Jane knew only one thing that March evening. The beatings to herself, her family and her neighbours had to stop before Billy killed her or someone else.

Jane Stafford has not had an easy life. Born in Brooklyn, Nova Scotia, not more than 30 miles from Bangs Falls, she has rarely left the beautiful South Shore area where she was raised. She vividly recalls her career-army father abusing her mother, so that later, when she became the victim of her second husband's abuse, she felt this was the natural order of things.

Jane left school in Grade 9. She had married and given birth to son Allan by the time she was 15. For 10 years she lived with an alcoholic husband. Her second son, James, was born before she obtained a divorce in 1976.

While still married, she met Big Billy Stafford, a friend of her husband's. Soon after her divorce she moved in with Billy.

For a short while, her common-law husband, a part-time fisherman and lumberman, treated her with some semblance of decency. Jane didn't know that Billy Stafford had already had two disastrous relationships with women. His first wife, Pauline, almost drowned when Billy submerged her head in a bucket of water. He terrorized their five children with lighted cigarettes and knives, until one day, while Billy was fishing, Pauline and the children took off for Ontario. She only returned after Billy's death.

Billy's next relationship with a woman fared no better. His first common-law wife left for Calgary after sampling Billy's lifestyle.

Now it was Jane's turn. Jane gave birth to Billy's son, Darren. When I met Darren, who is now six years old, he played hide-and-seek with me in the Nova Scotia Legal Aid offices. He appears to be a normal youngster, but Darren's short life has been full of the trauma of having a monster for a father. When Darren was only two, to amuse himself, his father would pick up his son by the hair and hold him aloft before dropping the terrified child to the floor. Sometimes Billy would hold a gun to the boy's head and tell him, "I'm going to blow your head off." On other occasions he would hold a knife to the boy's throat.

Allan Ferrier, the Nova Scotia legal aid lawyer who defended Jane, told me, "Darren has received psychiatric treatment and counselling for almost two years and there is every reason to believe he will be fine. However, he shocked psychiatrists when he told them he wished he was as big as his father and that his father was as small as he, so that he could be mean to Billy like Billy was mean to him."

Billy directed his abuse toward Jane after Darren's birth. He had apparently wanted a girl and knew he wouldn't have one after Jane had a hysterectomy. Jane's life became a series of degrading acts and beatings.

When I met Jane Stafford I thought one of her outstanding features were her flawless, even, white teeth. I mentioned this and was shocked at her reply: "Oh, they're all false. That happened when Billy kept striking me with the butt of his rifle until I was unconscious. My oldest son, Allan, found me on the floor and thought I was dead. The few teeth which weren't knocked out later had to be extracted by a dentist. I told the dentist I was in a car accident and struck my head on the steering wheel. I was laid up in bed for two weeks after that beating."

Cover-ups, such as lying to the dentist, served to isolate Jane, but many knew what kind of man she was living with. Most of them were fearful for their lives if they messed around with Big Billy. Once he forced the captain of a scallop dragger he was working on to bring his vessel to shore. Billy was charged with mutiny on that occasion, but no one would testify against him. The charges were eventually dropped, but Billy found himself blacklisted by the fishing industry. Sometimes friends would become the object of

Billy's anger. For no apparent reason, he would beat them up and throw them out of his home. Once he beat up Jane's father. Soon friends stopped dropping in at the Staffords'.

Billy drank daily, used drugs and terrorized anyone who crossed his path. Police were told to approach the Stafford home armed and with caution. They rarely did.

Just for fun, Billy, who sometimes claimed he was placed on earth by the devil, would load the truck with his family and roar down the highway on the wrong side of the road. Eyes popping, mouth frothing, he laughed in the face of death while his passengers cringed in fear.

But it was against Jane that most of Billy's anger was directed.

On two occasions he fired his .22-calibre rifle at Jane, once while she was tending her garden and once while she was working in the house. Billy explained that he was just seeing how close he could come to her with bullets.

There were other, far worse, indignities and sexual abuses, some of which were too abhorrent to be told here.

James escaped most of his stepfather's abuse because he stayed with Jane's parents much of the time. Allan was beaten up once a week.

Why didn't Jane leave? Why didn't she simply run away? Jane explained to me, as she had explained to the court, that Billy had often bragged to her that he had once murdered a man by throwing him overboard. In fact, a man was lost at sea while Billy was aboard, but nothing ever came of Billy's involvement. Billy assured Jane that if she ever left him he would kill her parents. Jane didn't doubt him for one minute.

Life went on. Billy called the shots and Jane and her children danced to his tune. There were rules. When you drove in the Jeep, you were not allowed to get out before Billy. If you did, you were beaten. Some evenings Jane and Billy played cards. It was a strange game. If Jane played the wrong card, she was beaten to the floor and made to struggle back onto her chair and continue playing. No Bible or prayer books were allowed in the Stafford home.

Most people knew that Billy was in some state of drunkenness every day. They knew he got into minor scrapes with the law. Some, who asked to remain anonymous, thought that he might kill someone some day. But only Jane knew first-hand the violence that was Billy Stafford.

During the last few years of her life with Billy, Jane was helped and consoled by Margaret Joudrey, an older woman who lived in a trailer adjacent to the Stafford property. For years Billy had been arguing over the boundary line of the two properties. When Margaret's common-law husband passed away without a will, it became a legal possibility that Margaret did not hold title to the property. Billy taunted his neighbour with this fact at every opportunity.

The turbulent existence that was Jane Stafford's life came to a head on March 11, 1982. That morning, Billy rose early and worked in the woods with his eldest stepson, Allan, and Ronald Wamboldt, 44, an alcoholic who was rooming with the Staffords. Wamboldt had often unintentionally displeased Billy, and he too had been the recipient of periodic beatings.

The men returned from the woods around noon and started drinking. By 4:30 p.m. Billy and Ron were drunk. Billy was becoming progressively wilder. They decided to visit a friend, Leona Anthony, in Charleston, five miles away. Darren and Allan were left at home. Jane drove the truck to Charleston, where the drinking continued.

By 8:30 that evening, Ron Wamboldt was dead drunk. He remembers none of the events of that night. On the way home, Jane drove the Jeep. Ron sat next to the passenger door, while Billy was propped up in the middle. Billy bragged that once they got home he was going to burn out Margaret Joudrey. Then he would beat Allan to a pulp. No doubt it would be Jane's turn next.

Jane guided the truck onto the dirt road leading to her modest home. She pulled into the yard. Ron staggered out of the vehicle, entered the house and fell into bed. Billy was asleep in the cab. Jane hesitated before leaving the Jeep, knowing she would be breaking one of Billy's rules if she left the truck before he did.

Jane beeped the horn. When her son Allan appeared, she asked him to fetch a gun. She stepped down from the truck. Sixteen-year-old Allan gave his mother the shotgun and returned to the house. That's when Jane admits to thinking, "To hell with it. I'm not going to live like this anymore." She said, "I put the gun in the window and just fired."

Billy Stafford would inflict no more indignities on his common-law wife. The shotgun blast had blown off his head. Bloody pieces of bone and brain fragments splattered the interior of the cab. Some blood splattered on Jane's clothing. Bits and pieces of Billy's skull lay on the cab floor.

Dazed, Jane acted in an irrational manner. Jane Stafford, who had never harmed a living creature in her life, shouted to her son to go to Margaret Joudrey's to phone her parents and tell them to meet her at the small rural settlement of nearby Charleston. She also told Allan to get rid of the shotgun. Without hesitation he threw it in the Medway River.

Jane jumped into the cab beside the bloody body of what had once been Billy Stafford and drove five miles to Charleston, where she met her parents. Jane parked the truck with its grisly cargo beside the road. She accompanied her parents to their home, changed clothes, and had them drive her back to Bangs Falls. That night she stayed with her sons.

Next morning, a resident of the area, Carl Croft, walked past the truck and spotted the headless corpse. He called police. Later that day, when Jane was informed that Billy's body had been found, she fainted.

Three days after the shooting Jane Stafford was arrested and charged with first-degree murder. A friend put her in touch with Allan Ferrier, a legal aid lawyer.

Ferrier, 33, a graduate of Dalhousie Law School, had never been in private practice. His career had been spent with the province's legal aid department. The Stafford case was his second murder trial. His first defence in a murder case had resulted in an acquittal.

Ferrier, a laid-back Maritimer, wears blue jeans and a T-shirt to the office. As I sat in Ferrier's office, he explained that he realized the Crown would allege that his client's life was not in danger at the time of the killing. After all, the victim was snoozing in the cab of his truck. However, Ferrier quoted Section 37 of the Criminal Code, which reads: "Everyone is justified in using force to defend himself or anyone under his protection from assault, if he uses no more force than is necessary to prevent the assault or the repetition of it." Ferrier argued that Jane Stafford was defending her son, who was under her protection. She also had no other recourse, nowhere to turn, no one to help her.

The Nova Scotia jury of 10 men and 1 woman had 4 verdicts to consider: guilty of first-degree murder; guilty of second-degree murder; guilty of manslaughter; or not guilty. They took 18 hours to find Jane Stafford not guilty. When the verdict was read, the crowded courtroom burst into applause. Scores of friends and spectators tried to hug Jane, slap her on the back, wish her well. It was as if abused women everywhere had won a moral victory.

Later Jane's aquittal was appealed by the Crown and she stood trial once more. This time she pleaded guilty to manslaughter and was sentenced to 6 months' imprisonment. Two months later she was released.

Ten years after Billy's death, Jane parked her car in an empty lot on the Halifax waterfront. She fired a 38-calibre slug into her heart and died instantly.

— ABRAHAM STEINBERG —

ALMOST 70 YEARS AGO, at a little after 6 p.m., on the night of March 5, 1930, someone activated firebox 566 at the corner of Dundas and McCaul Streets in Toronto. The person who sent in the alarm was never identified, and probably had no way of knowing that he was opening the curtain on one of Canada's most baffling murder cases.

Within minutes, fire companies from Adelaide, Queen and College Streets were dispatched to Goldberg Bros. Monument Works at 153 St. Patrick Street. Firemen burst into the premises and quickly extinguished the flames. Fireman James Ridout was groping in the darkness, trying to find his way back to the door when his hand fell on something peculiar. He directed the beam of his flashlight to the object and quickly realized that he had come upon the body of a man slumped over a desk. The upper portion of the body had been terribly burned, with the face charred beyond recognition.

In this manner, James Ridout found the body of Samuel Goldberg, 35, who was part owner of the monument firm. An autopsy performed on Goldberg revealed that a bullet had gone through his head. No weapon of any kind was found at the scene, but a small tin containing coal oil and a larger can of motor oil were found on the floor near the desk. Goldberg's clothing had been soaked in the oil.

The police, acting swiftly and efficiently, questioned friends and relatives of the deceased. Goldberg's wife, Sala, now a widow with two children, Norma, 3, and Nathan, 21 months, could shed no light on the tragedy. Goldberg's partners in the monument business were his two brothers, Harry and Abe, and his uncle, Abraham Steinberg. Harry and Abe were both absent from the office that day and were never suspects in the case.

Abe Steinberg said that he left the office at 5 p.m. Because he was considered to be the last person to see Sam alive, the police questioned him for three hours, and finally arrested him on a holding charge of vagrancy.

Bits and pieces of information were uncovered during the police's preliminary investigation. Goldberg, who neither smoked nor drank (important details since fire was involved in the incident), was shot at close range. A quantity of charred paper was found on top of Goldberg's desk. The fire had been confined to the area surrounding the desk. No fingerprints were found anywhere near the body.

In the meantime, Abe Steinberg was released on bail of

$5,000. Then, on March 7, two days after the murder, Detective Sergeant Arthur Levitt found a revolver while sifting through rubbish at the rear of Goldberg's office. The .38-calibre Colt had not been tossed away. It had been carefully placed under an old cement bag and pushed into the snow between a garage and a fence. The gun contained three fired and two live shells. Within days the police were able to trace the Canadian distributor of the U.S.-manufactured weapon. The gun had been sold on April 16, 1910, to the firm of Wood, Vallance & Co. in Hamilton. They in turn had sold it shortly thereafter, but here the trail stopped. The police could not trace the gun further.

The city of Toronto, and indeed most of Canada, was now humming with news of the mysterious murder of the mild-mannered, respectable businessman. Then, on March 25, Abraham Steinberg was charged with the murder of his nephew, a charge, which, if proven, carried an automatic death sentence.

The police revealed that a lead slug had been found at the scene, and after the gun was located it was established that it had fired the fatal shot. An empty cartridge case from a .38 Colt revolver was found on a lot adjacent to the Goldberg property. Through the unglamorous task of sifting through garbage and searching through snow, the detectives had uncovered the murder weapon, the lead slug and even the cartridge case.

The police were successful in finding some young people who identified the murder weapon as belonging to Abe Steinberg. Two years previously, when Steinberg had owned a dry goods store in Chesley, Ontario, his son Phillip had shown his father's gun to several friends. They now came forward to identify the gun. One youngster remembered that the gun had a chip out of its handle and picked the murder weapon from a row of nine guns.

The police also discovered that some money had been short in Steinberg's accounts with the firm. When asked by the other partners about this matter, Steinberg had come up with the missing money. Since the incident took place, the Goldberg brothers said things were never the same, and tensions ran high at the monument firm. They emphasized the bad feelings between Steinberg and their murdered brother.

On October 6, 1930, Abraham Steinberg stood trial for the murder of his nephew. During the trial, it was revealed that when Steinberg's house was searched detectives had found overalls stained with human blood. Again the bad feelings between the accused and the murder victim was rehashed. In a sensational move, the Crown called one James Creighton who had spent time in the Don Jail with Steinberg. According to Creighton, Steinberg told him that he and Goldberg were always arguing. Steinberg had also told him that on the day of the murder he went to the monument works carrying a gun for protection. During a heated argument, Steinberg had accidentally killed Goldberg. Then he set the place on fire.

Rabbi Jacob Gordon told the court that a man had knocked on his door at about 6 o'clock on the evening of the fire. The stranger requested that the rabbi use his influence to prevent an autopsy from being performed on Goldberg's body. The rabbi explained that religious custom prohibited a body from being cut. The visitor told the rabbi that there had been a fire at Goldberg Bros. and that Sam Goldberg had been burned to death. The rabbi then explained to the visitor that he could not prevent an autopsy if it was required and was the law of the land. The prosecution hinted strongly that Steinberg might have been the rabbi's visitor.

In Steinberg's defence, his wife took the stand and swore that the overalls found in their home did not belong to her husband. She said he had never worn nor owned a pair of overalls. Defence attorneys admitted to the bad feelings between Steinberg and Goldberg, but put forth the rather plausible argument that disagreements between partners were a common occurrence and did not necessarily lead to murder. The defence also tried to discredit the Creighton story, and hinted of favours given in return for the co-operation of the witness. Lastly, Rabbi Gordon emphatically stated that he could not identify Steinberg as the man who had visited him the night of the fire.

On October 10, 1930, after four hours of deliberation, the jury failed to agree on a verdict and was dismissed. Steinberg stood trial for murder a second time on February 1, 1931. This time, the defence came up with several witnesses who testified that Steinberg was in his friend Max Rotenberg's store between 5:10 p.m. and 7 p.m. on the night of the killing and could not have been his nephew's murderer. Countering this evidence was that of Max Milgram, who swore he saw Steinberg in the vicinity of the fire between 6:30 and 7:45 p.m.

Steinberg was found guilty and was later sentenced to be hanged on April 21, 1931. His lawyer lodged an appeal and was turned down. A second appeal to the Supreme Court of Canada was lodged. As a result of this move, a stay of execution was granted so that the appeal could be heard. The Supreme Court dismissed the appeal, and a new execution date of July 14, 1931, was set. Despite a petition containing 40,000 signatures pleading for Steinberg's life, the federal cabinet denied clemency, stating that "there be no interference with the death penalty."

As the execution date approached, Steinberg maintained his innocence. His religious counsel, Rabbi Samuel Sachs, disclosed that Steinberg never veered from his claim of innocence.

On July 14, at exactly 8 a.m., Steinberg was hanged for the murder of his nephew. A clock in the Steinberg home which had not chimed for over a year rang out the hour at precisely 8 a.m. on that fateful day.

All that day, Rabbi Sachs desperately tried to find a synagogue or fraternal organization to accept Steinberg's body. None would, and in the end, Abraham Steinberg, draped in the prayer shawl which had been given to him as a boy in Poland, was laid to rest in a potter's field.

— DAVID TODD —

DAVID WILFRED TODD was something of a loner, a born watcher rather than a doer.

Todd was born on May 3, 1934, in Hamilton, Ontario. From the outset he wasn't interested in school and only continued until he completed Grade six. After his brief academic career, he started on a variety of labourers' jobs not designed to tax his mental abilities nor make him a fortune, and by the time he was 25 he had held more than 30 different menial jobs, each of which he quit for one reason or another. Sometimes his reasons were not all that good— he loved to skip work and wander the streets of Hamilton, just bumming around looking into shop windows.

Todd stood five feet eight inches, with receding curly hair, a rather weak voice and a limp handshake. When people spoke to him, he had the annoying habit of staring back blankly, and it was difficult to know what he was thinking.

Grace Filmore was taller than Dave, but the height difference didn't seem to bother her, and she dated him throughout the spring and summer of 1959. Though some of Grace's friends made no secret of the fact that they thought Dave wasn't good enough for her, she married him on August 17, 1959. At this time, Dave was 25 and Grace 20.

After their marriage the young couple lived in Hamilton, where Dave held a job as a desk clerk at the Windsor Hotel for three years, which was something of a record for him. When the manager of the hotel left to open his own restaurant, Dave took a job with him. It didn't work out, however, because Grace objected to the long night hours, and after three months he left to join Hamilton Cotton Company, where he stayed one full year.

Like many young couples, the Todds felt that Toronto held more opportunities for them, and in 1965 they moved to Ontario's capital. They had just moved into 1 Deauville Lane, when Dave got a steady job at Dunlop Rubber. He remained gainfully employed at Dunlop until the company closed its plant in 1970. Grace, who worked for the North American Life Insurance Company in Hamilton, managed to get a transfer to the company's Toronto office.

When Dunlop closed its plant, putting Dave out of work, the Todd marriage went steeply downhill. Instead of actively trying to find a job, Dave became paranoically suspicious of his wife's actions. Entirely without justification he began to suspect Grace of being unfaithful to him. He continually phoned her office to make sure she was there, made a point of picking her up at work so that she wouldn't have the opportunity to go with anyone else.

Occasionally, Grace's company had a party and she and Dave would attend. Grace was charming and mixed easily with her colleagues, but Dave would sulk in a corner, watching his wife. Grace loved to dance. Later his comment was, "I would be lucky to see her for about an hour without some other guy getting her on the floor." The conversation at the office parties often revolved around salaries, while the unemployed Dave, hands deep in his pockets, became red-faced at what he considered the bragging of his wife's co-workers.

At home they started to argue incessantly. Dave accused Grace of taking birth control pills to prevent her from becoming pregnant by another man, though she explained that the pills were to relieve her menstrual pains.

Dave later claimed that at this time Grace would have nothing more to do with him in bed. She had never refused him before, but now she turned her back on him. He retaliated, truthfully or not, by bragging to her that he had slept with another woman. Grace probably didn't believe him, but the bickering went on. All their small differences, which hadn't seemed to matter earlier, came to the surface and festered, causing irreparable chasms in what had been a relatively happy marriage.

And so it went. Sometimes Dave would console himself by consuming 24 beers in one evening. After so much beer he occasionally fell asleep on the sofa. Finally he ended up sleeping there alone while Grace had the bed to herself. This became more or less the permanent arrangement.

Throughout all the arguing, Grace worked, earning the money on which they both lived. She took care of all the bills and even accompanied her husband when he bought a new pair of pants. Grace saw to it that Dave always had a few dollars in his pocket, but she often quarrelled with him for spending his allowance on liquor. When they went out in the evening for a few drinks at the nearby Mississippi Belle, it was Grace who picked up the bar bills.

The few acquaintances they used to meet at the well-known club later remarked that even here Grace came off as being far more socially accomplished than her husband. He again took up the wallflower stance, and peered in from the perimeters of conversations. In fact, poor Dave Todd believed that now that he was steadily unemployed he was losing his wife's love and respect, yet he continued to do nothing about his joblessness. He hovered over her obsessively—keeping his eye on her, ever watchful to catch her in one of the unfaithful acts that were taking place only in his mind.

Everyone who ever knew Grace stated that she was a respectable woman in every way.

Sometimes Dave, in his shy, introverted fashion, would try to initiate some activity he knew they both enjoyed. On Thursday night, July 29, 1971, he had talked Grace into going on a camping trip the next morning. She agreed, and things were looking bright for the Todds when they rose on Friday.

Just before Christmas 1971, Charles Cassidy, a 21-year-old acquaintance of Todd's, told him that he could move in with his family at 4 Vendome Place. Cassidy's family included his sister Catherine, 15, and his mother. Todd had been having trouble getting together the rent at his previous residence at Deauville Lane, and was going around mumbling something about his wife leaving him. Cassidy knew that Todd had recently obtained a job as a truck driver, and felt that, if given a break, he would straighten out.

The Cassidy family thought it strange that Todd had brought along an electric freezer. Not only was it an unusual piece of furniture to have near the dining area, but it was locked, sealed and never used. It just sat there, humming away.

On the night of January 12, 1972, Charles Cassidy, his sister, their mother and two friends, John Moore and Layne Jackson, were spending an evening at home watching television. The program they were viewing was a thriller, "One Step Beyond." The young people joked about the story because of the weird plot, which at one point revealed a body in a trunk. Right in their dining area they had a mysterious freezer humming away, while its owner slept peacefully in an upstairs bedroom. Well, they thought, it is quite one thing for a piece of fiction to have bodies in trunks, but in real life those things just don't happen. Still, the thought of something sinister in the freezer was too fascinating to resist. A screwdriver was produced; the screws holding down the hinges of the freezer door came out easily. Laughing and joking, the young people peered into the freezer. There, among the turkey pies and vegetables, was the tanned, solidly frozen body of Grace Todd.

Placid, timid David Todd readily confessed to killing his wife, but steadfastly maintained that he'd never meant any harm to come to her. He was charged with non-capital murder. A jury heard the psychiatric evidence in a report given by Dr. Peter Watts Rousell. Here, in the doctor's own words, is what Todd told him took place that Friday morning, July 30, 1971:

"She had taken a shower the next morning and they were having another verbal fight. She had made the quip about his being an old man and he quoted her, in addition to these remarks, as saying further 'You couldn't satisfy any of the whores around town. We are not man and wife. I tolerate you; I don't love you.' He quotes her as going on—he, of course, accusing her of walking out on him, which he went on to say was exactly what she was going to do after she had had an hour's sleep following her shower. She lay down on the chesterfield; she went on, 'By the time I am back to work, I will be under a new roof and when I get out today I am going to walk into the first man's bed I can get into.' He says 'I took it that she had another man because she had been mixing all of a sudden this two years.' It was very evident as he described it, that this was in his mind because of his telephoning her so frequently, always asking her, as he described to me himself, who was in the office with her at any given time, and he says frankly, 'I was at the point of watching everybody, even my brother-in-law and my brothers.' Concerning his brothers also, he disliked their putting their hands on her when talking to her or holding her arm. He said he was becoming rather depressed, wanting to avoid large crowds; just wanting to be with Grace where they would be alone; where he could have her all to himself. This was one of the chief reasons for camping as a vacation, to be alone with her, then he didn't have to worry about anybody else putting their hands on her. He indicated to me that they had planned to go to Simcoe. As this morning argument, Friday July 30, occurring about 11 a.m. had built up and she had told him she was going to walk out, that she was going on no camping trip with him, he said 'I accused her of running out on me with another man and she laughed in my face. She again referred to his being a watch-dog and she was referring, of course, to his picking her up at work and the constant telephone calls. He had not been sleeping during that year prior to the tragedy, staying on the chesterfield to satisfy his wife but occasionally putting away a case of 24 beer, almost, while he was on that chesterfield in one night. This would bring a further rebuke from his wife that he was being a drunk and if he had not finished all the beer, to go back and finish what was left. His appetite was not so good. One year ago he says he weighed 200 pounds and, as one can observe Mr. Todd now, he gives his present weight as 150 pounds and is certainly no 200. Most of the weight has been lost since his wife's death. Apparently she criticized his weight too, calling him 'hippo,' 'pear-shaped,' and telling him he was a disgrace to be seen in the street with, being so fat. She told him to go on a diet. Apparently most of this weight had in fact gone on during the last two years prior to the tragedy.

"Meantime, returning to the fateful morning of July 30, with his wife's bitter statement, he said he was burning inside, wanting to scream, get something out of his system, a feeling going up into his chest and his head but somehow couldn't just let go. When she allegedly further taunted him that Friday July morning that he was pussyfooting and screaming about women and he couldn't satisfy any of them anyway, at

264 · MAX HAINES

this point he had been telling her, while she lay not looking at him on the chesterfield, he being behind her, 'Won't you look at me while I am talking?' He indicated to me that he asked her three times and Grace had turned her back to him as she lay on the chesterfield. Having just said she was going to leave him after an hour's sleep, at this point he reached over and got the gun which was loaded, as he knew, and cocked. He says, 'I walked across and picked it up and I pointed it at her. Then she turned; I guess she was scared. She twisted and put her arm up and somehow I flipped it and it went off.' As he described this to me, he made this gesture. She—imitating her lying on the chesterfield, raising the right arm, head turning and as I understand it from his description, he was standing I think behind her, but this is the gesture that he imitated for me as he quoted those words; the turning to the right and looking back, bringing up the right arm. His wife, of course, fell back on the chesterfield. He said, 'I tried to talk up to her to say I was sorry and then I felt her pulse, her stomach and I got some towels to try and stop the bleeding.' He also indicated to me that he was crying at this point. He thought of an ambulance but just sat, scared, for an hour, wondering what to do. For the time being, he says, 'I put her in the freezer. I was going to call Bob Rowe who I respect; he is a man's man, to get his advice, but I didn't. I was in the house for an hour. The car was full of things. I brought some of them up. I was talking to Larry Hough [Todd's friend] while I was unloading the car. I went to the bar but Bob was not at the bar and tomorrow never came when I would do something.' In June 1971 he indicated that he had told Larry Hough that when they returned from vacation, that is, he and

Grace, that Larry could move in with them. Then it seems that Larry and friends came up and then of course with the freezer present, he had to start telling stories to 'cover up.' I was particularly struck by the cover-up stories so frequently alluding to Grace running off with another man, of course it became his preoccupation all the way along. He himself slept on the chesterfield and regarding his state at that time, bearing in mind that the freezer with his wife's body was so close to him, he said, 'I felt my wife was with me. I dreamt good dreams, all the good times we had had together in the past. I was going to look at her twice, but somehow I couldn't. Someone was coming in.' At this point, when he was retreating into the happy and comfortable past, into what might be called his world of fantasy, of course the intrusion of the harsh reality of that freezer was always in front of him; the reality of keeping the secret of the body kept intruding on him. He invented more and more stories to cover her disappearance. The cash was running out. He was no manager of money. He admitted to feeling hopeless, as he has felt all the way along, drifting along, letting things happen. He has never thought of suicide during all this time. He felt very tired, he complains, after that. He lost a lot of weight, 50 pounds, he quoted in all and is uptight. It is notable at this point of my examination he is giving a fairly straight, apparently, description of his actions and that is over this long period of time."

J. Crossland, Q.C. acting for the Crown, wanted to know what caused mild-mannered David Todd to kill his wife. Dr. Rousell gave the opinion that after examining Todd, he felt that the accused didn't have the capacity at the time of the killing to form the intention. Crossland asked for the doctor's reasons for his opinion:

Dr. Rousell continued:

"This accused man, Mr. Todd," Dr. Rousell told the court, "in my opinion first of all can be labelled under a true psychiatric diagnosis as an inadequate personality. Now, although this is a true diagnosis, it does not imply that such a person is in any way insane within the legal meaning . . .

"The man himself, a wallflower, a quiet, always pleasant, easy-to-get-on-with individual, yet so inadequate in so many ways, could function and in fact, as his work record bears out, did function very well provided that he had that strong woman on whom he depended so much. She—it was in a sense very much like a mother-child relationship that really lay between them, so he is basically a clinging person, who when he has got somebody strong behind him, can function, and function very adequately in a job so long as he doesn't have to take too much of the responsibilities. That is his basic personality diagnosis: inadequate personality."

The doctor then traced Todd's escalating possessiveness up to the morning of Friday July 30th, 1971:

"When there was the same set of accusations and recriminations, as he described it, on both sides but with one difference and the difference was that this time she said, as he quoted, 'I am leaving you; I am not going camping with you. I will be under another roof when I come back from vacation,' so in the situation we have his description of his pointing the gun at her, trying to force her, in my opinion, as he expressed it to me, to make her stay and her subsequent actions as he described them which led to the gun going off and the subsequent tragedy that followed . . . after all, his basic motive was to keep his wife. Following her death the only way he could, in his mind, keep her was to go into what is called a psychosis and this is a different matter because this does fall within the legal definition of insanity and a psychosis, by definition, is a disorder of thinking, feeling and behaviour accompanied by what is called a break with reality . . . Following Grace's death, David Todd, in my opinion, became, so to speak, split into two different states of consciousness and behaviour. First, the harsh reality of everyday living and having a roof over one's head, the presence of his wife's body in a freezer a few yards from him, knowing that money had to be obtained, knowing that he felt he had to conceal what he had done, this is the level of reality which is impossible to get away from. It was there. On the other hand, there is the seemingly incomprehensible behaviour of this person who sleeps only a few yards—and makes a point of it—from the freezer containing the body of his loved one and his fantasy life, as he quotes from reality, dreams and indulges in all his happy memories, if you like, almost denying inside himself that she was dead, so in one way he keeps her alive through his happy memories and hangs onto the body and yet, in another way, he has to cover up and make up stories so he is forced into reality by the harsh things of life one moment and retreating from reality into his happy fantasies the next, and the mind in such chaos as a person—occurs in a person who is under extreme tension. He started to change his behaviour. He went around with the young people far more and of course had to cover up with his stories about the refrigerator to them, and he lost 50 pounds in weight which, of course, is a leading symptom of . . . a major nervous breakdown in the way I have defined it. An instance of his communication over the happiness aspect of it was his remark to, I think it was Mr. Moore, that she had come in one night and kissed him on the cheek. This is a fairly good example of the type of fantasy, wishful thinking, removed from the harsh reality of the situation which he appears to have been going through."

David Wilfred Todd changed his plea to guilty of manslaughter and was sentenced to 10 years in Kingston Penitentiary with the stipulation that he receive psychiatric treatment. Having served his sentence, he has long since been released from custody.

– STEVEN TRUSCOTT –

BACK IN 1959, the Truscott family was living a secure middle-class life in the PMQS, Private Married Quarters, at the Royal Canadian Air Force station near Clinton, Ontario. Warrant Officer Dan Truscott had been elected man of the year on the base. In addition, he was president of the Sergeant's Mess. Dan's wife, Dorothy, had her hands full raising four children. Ken and Steven were active teenagers. Life was good, but all the hopes and aspirations of the entire family were to be altered forever on the sweltering hot night of June 9, 1959. That was the evening 12-year-old Lynn Harper was murdered.

At ten minutes to six that Tuesday evening, Dorothy called to 14-year-old Steven who was playing ball on the lawn. She wanted him to dash down to the store for a pound of coffee before it closed at 6 p.m. Steven jumped on his bike and completed the errand in a matter of minutes.

Dan and Dorothy had plans to go out that evening. It was Steven's turn to babysit his younger brother and sister. After supper, Steven left the house at 6:30 p.m., promising his mother he would return by 8:30.

The youngsters' activities in that area around the air force base that night were probably typical of those in every small town in the country when the temperature approaches 90 degrees and there are few organized activities. Many of the young people just hung out. Some played catch, but most headed for the swimming hole in the Bayfield River. The bridge across the river was a great place to view the goings-on, as kids of every age splashed and swam in the cool river water. Because of the intense heat that evening, the river was getting a bigger play than usual.

Steven cycled over to the schoolyard, where he met Lynn Harper. The two chatted for a while. According to Steven, Lynn expressed a desire to see some ponies owned by a man who lived in a white house on Highway 8, approximately a mile and a half away.

A Mrs. Nickerson, who happened to be in the school-yard that evening, would later confirm that it was shortly before 7 p.m. when Steven and Lynn met. No later than 7:15 p.m. she observed them leaving together on foot, Steven pushing his bicycle. Three lads at a football field saw Steven and Lynn proceed from the school area to the county road. Lynn jumped on the crossbar of Steven's bike and the two continued down the road. The pair drove past a woodlot known as Lawson's Bush, over some railroad tracks to the Bayfield Bridge. Arnold George waved to them from the riverbank. Douglas Oats nodded as Steven and Lynn drove by. Gordon Logan, perched on a rock in the river, looked up and saw Lynn and Steven as they crossed the bridge. A few minutes later, Gordon saw Steven standing on the bridge alone.

Steven would later claim that he had given Lynn a ride to Highway 8 as he had promised. He rode his bike back to the Bayfield Bridge, where he glanced over his shoulder in time to see her hitch a ride and get into a grey 1959 Chevrolet. He believed the vehicle bore yellow licence plates.

Steven cycled down the county road toward his home. He talked to boys he knew at the football field and joined other friends in the schoolyard. His brother Ken was among them. Ken reminded Steven that he had to be home at 8:30 to babysit. It was now around 8 p.m. Steven told his brother he would be home in plenty of time. The teenagers chatted as teenagers will to pass the time. At 8:25 Steven was back home.

It had been a quiet, uneventful day at the Truscott household. Not so at the home of Flying Officer Leslie Harper and his wife, Shirley. The Harpers were eating dinner when their daughter Lynn arrived home at 5:30 p.m. Lynn sat down and ate as her parents finished their meal. There was some discussion about Lynn going for a swim in the RCAF tank, but her parents forbade her to go, as one required a permit to swim there without a parent present. Lynn left the house to procure the permit, but as she was unable to get one, she returned home. She did the dishes and left the house. The Harpers never saw their daughter alive again.

The next morning, Leslie and Shirley Harper were very concerned. Lynn had not come home all night. She was only 12 years old. What could have happened? She had never stayed out all night before. That morning, Flying Officer Harper made inquiries. One of the men he met at the station was Dan Truscott. Truscott didn't know for sure, but thought his two boys might have seen Lynn. He suggested that Harper drop over to his house and question Ken and Steven. Steven quickly volunteered that he had given Lynn a lift on his bicycle to Highway 8 and had seen her hitch a ride.

Leslie Harper experienced a sinking feeling of apprehension. Police were informed that Lynn Harper was missing.

Constables were dispatched from nearby Goderich. It was soon established that young Steven Truscott had been the last person to see the girl. On being questioned, he told officers the details of giving Lynn a lift on his bike. He was interrogated a second time and demonstrated where he was standing when he saw the vehicle with the yellow licence plates. Steven's story has never varied in the 39 years since the incident took place.

The man who lived in the white house on Highway 8 was questioned. Although Lynn had expressed an interest in his ponies, he convinced police that she had not visited him the previous evening. In addition, many of the children who had been swimming in the Bayfield River were interrogated. Some remembered seeing Steven, but others didn't recall seeing him at all.

A search was conducted for Lynn Harper. It was tragically successful. Her almost-nude body was found in Lawson's Bush. Lynn had obviously been raped. She still wore an undershirt. Her sleeveless blouse was wound in a roll and knotted around her neck. There was a scratch on her leg extending from above her knee to her foot. Strangely, her clothing, including her shoes and socks, was in a neat pile beside her body. Lynn's killer had even closed the zipper of her shorts. Her panties were found some 30 feet away along the tractor trail leading into the bush. Three branches had been twisted off and placed over Lynn's body. A fourth branch was partially twisted off, but left hanging there. There was no evidence of a struggle anywhere near the murder scene.

A day after the body was found, an autopsy was performed by Dr. John Penistan, the regional pathologist. He was assisted by the RCAF base physician, Dr. David Brooks.

The contents of Lynn's stomach were poured into a glass jar and examined by Dr. Penistan. Knowing exactly when Lynn had eaten her last meal, and estimating the rate of digestion, he established the time of death between 7:15 and 7:45 p.m. two days previously. Lynn had been strangled to death with her blouse.

Steven Truscott was questioned several times. He told the same story over and over. It was apparent he wasn't believed. The time of death placed Steven with Lynn. Steven was subjected to a medical examination by Dr. J.A. Addison of Clinton, who had been briefed on the situation before the examination. Also present was Dr. Penistan. It was a fateful examination for the 14-year-old Steven. He was found to have a skin irritation, or more specifically, a lesion on his penis. The doctors concluded it was the result of performing a rape. In the wee hours of the morning, Steven Truscott was formally charged with the murder of Lynn Harper.

From the very moment Steven was charged, there was a presumption of guilt. Locals in the surrounding towns figured it was a case of one air force brat killing another air force brat. No local man was involved. That Truscott kid did it. Everyone saw him drive away with the little girl on his bicycle. He must be guilty.

On September 16, 1959, Steven Truscott stood trial for the murder of Lynn Harper in adult court in Goderich. Dr. Penistan and Dr. Brooks described the autopsy they had performed on Lynn's body, particularly as it pertained to the contents of her stomach. The stomach contents, in a glass jar, contained ham, chicken, peas and onion, which were not totally digested and were identifiable to the doctors with the naked eye. From their observations they established Lynn's time of death as between 7:00 and 7:45 p.m. on June 9 (Note that doctors also set time of death as being betweem 7:15 and 7:45, an apparent inconsistency).

Testifying for the prosecution, the doctors placed the time of death exactly when Lynn was in Steven's company. Their conclusions would have to have been exact for Steven to have murdered Lynn. Years later Steven would claim that he had been chatting with boys in the schoolyard at approximately 7:25 p.m. and was back with them at 8 p.m. This would have left him only 35 minutes to drive Lynn to Lawson's Bush, lug his bike into the bush, rape and strangle Lynn, tear branches off bushes and be back on the county road without anyone seeing him leave the road or come back. It would have been quite a feat. It was a hot night. Children and adults were outdoors, yet no one saw this happen. If the doctors were mistaken by a matter of an hour, Steven would have been in the company of other people and could not have been the killer.

Defence attorney Frank Donnelly introduced highly qualified Dr. Berkeley Brown, an expert in internal medicine, particularly diseases of the digestive system. He testified that the stomach takes much longer to empty than the time estimated by the doctors for the prosecution. He also pointed out that other factors, such as fat content of the food, temperature, stress and fatigue slow up the digestive system. Examining the frozen contents of the jar in court, Dr. Brown said that they were ready to leave the stomach and had been digested for at least three or four hours. If Dr. Brown was correct, Steven would have been at home at the time Lynn was raped and murdered.

The jury did not accept Dr. Brown's testimony. His credibility might have been questioned because he had not been present at the autopsy. Some may have thought his theories probably came from book learning. After all, the local doctors had actually examined the body of Lynn Harper.

Dr. J.A. Addison of Clinton had physically examined Steven. He testified that he had detected a lesion on Steven's penis, which he felt had been the result of the commission of a rape. When he had questioned Steven regarding the lesion, Steven claimed he didn't know how he had come by it. No doctor for the defence had examined the accused. Later, Mr. Donnelly put forth several explanations as to how a 14-year-old boy might develop a sore in such a sensitive area.

The prosecution, in an attempt to discredit Steven's story that he had seen Lynn get into a grey Chevy with a yellow licence plate, questioned officers, who claimed they couldn't identify the make of the car from the bridge. Photos taken from the bridge were produced. In the photos, the car appeared so small that it was hardly possible to make out the licence plate, let alone its colour. However, no officer was asked if they could see a yellow licence plate with the naked eye from the bridge. The court was left with the impression that Steven had made up the story of Lynn hitching a ride at the intersection of Highway 8.

Thirteen-year-old Jocelyne Goddette related that Steven had made a date with her to see a newborn calf in Lawson's Bush. He told her to keep the date a secret. On the evening of the murder, at a few minutes before six, he called at her house, but Jocelyne had not had her supper and could not go with him. Later, she visited Mr. Lawson's barn, but couldn't find Steven. She proceeded to the tractor trail, walked into the bush calling his name, but couldn't locate him. She pedalled to Lawson's farm and remained there for some time before returning home.

Upon cross-examination, Mr. Donnelly brought out several discrepancies in Jocelyne's story, but the inference left with the jury was clear. She was the intended victim. When Steven didn't get her, he settled for Lynn.

A series of children testified. Some verified Steven's story, others refuted it. Arnold George told different versions of the various times he had seen Steven that night. At one point he claimed that Steven had asked him to lie about waving to him from the riverbank.

For the defence, 11-year-old Douglas Oats verified Steven's story. He remembered saying hi when Steven and Lynn crossed the bridge. Then he went under the bridge and did not see Steven return. Under cross-examination, the youngster would not budge. He had seen Steven cross that bridge and head toward Highway 8, as he had stated the very first time he had been questioned after Lynn went missing.

Gordon Logan, 13, testified that from his perch on a rock in the river, he had witnessed Steven and Lynn cross the bridge. About five minutes later, he moved to the river-bank. It was then that he had seen Steven back on the bridge alone, just hanging around.

Oats and Logan were refuting what seemed clearly to be an open-and-shut case. Would the jury believe local doctors who had performed an autopsy on the victim or would they believe a doctor who hadn't seen the body? Would they believe trained police officers or adolescent boys?

The answers to these questions were soon revealed. The Huron County jury foreman spoke loud and clear, "We find the defendant guilty as charged with a plea for mercy."

The presiding judge passed sentence, "Steven Murray Truscott, I have no alternative but to pass the following sentence upon you. The jury have found you guilty after a fair trial. The sentence of this court upon you is that you be taken from here to the place from whence you came and there be kept in close confinement until Tuesday, the eighth day of December 1959, and upon that day and date you be taken to the place of execution and that you there be hanged by the neck until you are dead, and may the Lord have mercy on your soul."

Fourteen-year-old Steven Truscott was hustled away to await his date with the hangman. The verdict was appealed, but the appeal was dismissed by the Supreme Court of Ontario. An application for leave to appeal was presented to the Supreme Court of Canada. The application was refused. On the same day that the application was refused, Steven's sentence was commuted to life imprisonment.

Because of his age, Steven was initially incarcerated at the Ontario School for Boys near Guelph. After spending three years at Guelph, he was transferred to Collins Bay Penitentiary in Kingston to serve the rest of his life sentence.

In 1966, author Isabel LeBourdais wrote a book entitled *The Trial of Steven Truscott*. In it she pointed out the many weaknesses in the prosecution's case. The book was widely read and was the driving force in having the federal government convene a precedent-setting hearing before the Supreme Court of Canada. The court was to consider the following question: "Had an appeal by Steven Murray Truscott been made to the Supreme Court of Canada as is now permitted by Section 597A of the Criminal Code of Canada, what disposition would the Court have made of such an appeal on a consideration of the existing record and such further evidence as the Court, in its discretion, may receive and consider."

In their joint opinion, eight of the nine justices of the Supreme Court put much stock in Jocelyne Goddette's story of her date to meet Steven on the evening Lynn was murdered. Steven denied that he had called at Jocelyne's house with the invitation to join him. In addition, the justices reviewed the evidence of 12-year-old Richard Gellatly, who had been at the river on the night in question and had returned home for a pair of swimming trunks. He claimed he had met Steven and Lynn riding toward the bridge at around 7:25 p.m. Richard pedalled home, but did not see Steven and Lynn on the road, nor at the bridge. The inference was clear. The boy would certainly have seen them if they had been on the road or at the bridge.

The justices went on to review other witnesses the Crown had produced who had not seen Steven and Lynn on the road during the crucial time frame. Because of this, the justices believed that after crossing Richard Gellatly's path, Steven and Lynn had gone into Lawson's Bush.

The children's evidence was in direct contrast to that of Douglas Oats and Gordon Logan, who expressly stated that they had seen Steven and Lynn cross the bridge. However, the justices questioned the credibility of the two boys. In the case of Gordon Logan they doubted the lad's ability to make the observations he claimed from a rock in the water some 642 feet from the bridge. In the case of Douglas Oats, the justices felt that he was mistaken as to time. They felt he had really seen Steven at 6:30 p.m., which detracted from the importance of his evidence.

The justices agreed that if a car was placed at the intersection of Highway 8 in the exact position that Steven maintained, he could indeed have identified the vehicle and the licence-plate color. They quickly pointed out that they didn't believe that a driver, when stopping to pick up a hitch-hiker on Highway 8, would back into a county road.

The majority agreed with Dr. Penistan's estimated time of death based on his observations:

1. The extent of decomposition, which is entirely compatible with death approximately 45 hours prior to identification, having regard to the environmental and climatic conditions.

2. The extent of rigor mortis. This had almost passed off, a finding again compatible with death at the suggested time.

3. The limited degree of digestion, and the large quantity of food in the stomach. I find it difficult to believe that this food could have been in the stomach for as long as two hours unless some

complicating factor was present, of which I have no
information. If the last meal was finished at 5:45
p.m., I would therefore conclude that death
occurred prior to 7:45 p.m. The finding would be
considered with time of death as early as 7:15 p.m.

The justices noted that defense witness Dr. Brown had
never before testified as to the time of death of a deceased
person.

In regard to the lesions on his penis, Steven testified to
the justices that the condition had existed for six weeks
prior to June 9, 1959. The justices believed the experts
who testified that the rape of Lynn Harper would have
aggravated such a condition, causing it to be in the state
found by Dr. Addison when he examined Steven on June
12, three days after Lynn's death.

After reviewing all the evidence placed before them, the
justices, by an eight to one majority, declared: "Our answer
to the question submitted is that had an appeal by Steven
Murray Truscott been made to the Supreme Court of Canada, as is now permitted by section 597A of the Criminal
Code of Canada, on the existing record and the further evidence, this Court would have dismissed such an appeal."

One member of the Supreme Court disagreed with the
majority decision. Justice M. Hall stated: "Having considered the case fully, I believe that the evidence should be
quashed and a new trial directed. I take the view that the
trial was not conducted according to law." Justice Hall
went on to say: "That does not mean that I consider
Truscott guilty or innocent."

In his review of the trial evidence, Justice Hall pointed
out many irregularities, such as a portion of the Crown's
summation in regard to Steven's not being able to connect

with Jocelyne Goddette. He said, "I suggest to you gentlemen that if they were late having supper it was a God's blessing to that girl." In addition, Crown counsel often referred to Lynn going into the bush with Truscott and to her doom.

In reference to Douglas Oats's and Gordon Logan's testimony, which most agreed would have acquitted Steven, the judge at trial, after presenting this evidence clearly to the jury, concluded with: "In other words, I will put it to you this way. In order to convict this boy, you have to completely reject that story as having no truth in it, as not being true. You have to completely reject that story."

Justice Hall would have quashed Steven's conviction and directed a new trial.

At the conclusion of the hearing, Steven Truscott was returned to Kingston Penitentiary, where he completed his sentence. After serving a total of 10 years in prison, he was paroled at the age of 24.

Today, Steven Truscott is happily married and lives under an assumed name in Ontario. He is an exemplary citizen and is a proud father and grandfather.

As this book goes to press, there is a movement afoot to re-examine the old physical evidence in the Truscott case in the hope that, by DNA testing, the doubts that remain concerning Steven Truscott's guilt or innocence can be resolved.

— JAMES WHELAN —

THOMAS D'ARCY MCGEE WAS born in 1825 in Carlingford, Ireland. At 17, heeding the adventurous call of the New World, he made his way to Boston, where he obtained employment with a Catholic Irish newspaper, the Boston *Pilot*. By the time he was 19, he was editor of the paper.

The following year, McGee returned to his homeland, and became an avid foe of Great Britain's union with Ireland. He was a leading figure in the Fenian Brotherhood, an organization devoted to achieving Irish independence from England.

In 1848 McGee had to flee the country; some say he left disguised as a priest. He made his way once more to the United States, and moved to Canada in 1857. A year later he was elected to the Legislative Assembly of Canada, representing Montreal West.

Once in Canada, it was assumed by Irish patriots that McGee would continue to expound his Fenian sympathies, but such was not the case. McGee split with the Fenians, believing their policy of violence too extreme. An adversary of the Fenian Brotherhood, he was considered a traitor by many Fenian sympathizers.

On the evening of April 6, 1868, exactly nine months and six days after Canada's Confederation, the Honourable Thomas D'Arcy McGee, one of the finest orators ever to address the House of Commons, was at his eloquent best. A little after 2 a.m., the House adjourned. McGee, accompanied by Robert MacFarlane, a fellow Member of Parliament representing Perth, Ontario, left Parliament Hill. MacFarlane and McGee parted company at the corner of Metcalfe and Sparks Street. McGee walked toward his boardinghouse on the south side of Sparks between Metcalfe and O'Connor.

McGee reached his destination, the Toronto House at 71 Sparks Street, owned and operated by Mary Ann

Trotter. Mrs. Trotter, as was her custom, lay asleep on the cot in the dining room. She thought she heard a noise at the door. Believing it to be her 13-year-old son, Willie, a parliamentary page boy, she rose to open the door. Just as she did so, she witnessed the flash of a discharging revolver and saw the form of a man fall at her doorstep.

The Honourable Thomas D'Arcy McGee, one of the 33 Fathers of Confederation, was the Dominion of Canada's first murder victim. As he bent over to insert his key into the lock of the boardinghouse door, his assailant silently pointed a revolver at the back of his neck. The Smith and Wesson revolver roared as the bullet entered McGee's neck and exited through his mouth. He died instantly.

In the days immediately following the assassination, several men were arrested as co-conspirators in the young country's most infamous single violent act. All would eventually be exonerated and released. All except one—James Whelan.

The bewhiskered Whelan had been employed in Ottawa as a tailor since November. He had previously followed his trade in Quebec City and Montreal.

When questioned within 24 hours of the assassination, he had a fully loaded revolver in his coat pocket. One chamber appeared to have been recently fired. Whelan was taken into custody. After a lengthy preliminary hearing, he was held over for trial.

On September 7, 1868, Whelan stood trial for the murder of the Honourable Thomas D'Arcy McGee. News of the trial dwarfed all other events in the young dominion. One of the founders of the country lay dead. His suspected killer came under microscopic examination.

The prosecution attorney, James O'Reilly, contended

that Whelan had attended the House of Commons on the night of the murder, leaving before McGee. He had lain in wait for his victim in a gateway and had shot McGee in front of the door of his boardinghouse. O'Reilly claimed that the plot to kill McGee had been hatched in Montreal. He asserted that Whelan had once visited McGee's home in Montreal. On that occasion he met John McGee, the victim's brother, and told him of a plot to set fire to the McGee residence. The threat was taken seriously and reported to police, although no attempt was ever made to torch McGee's home.

Most damaging of all, O'Reilly stated that one Jean Baptiste Lacroix had actually witnessed the shooting. To back up his contentions, O'Reilly presented strong witnesses. John McGee confirmed Whelan's early-morning visit to the McGee residence in Montreal.

Detective Edward O'Neill of Ottawa testified that he had found the .32-calibre revolver in the right-hand side pocket of Whelan's coat. In the opposite pocket he recovered a box of cartridges. Although the revolver was fully loaded when it was confiscated, O'Neill stated that upon examination it was clear to him that it had been recently fired.

"I looked in the cylinder and the six chambers, and I found six cartridges. Five of these cartridges looked like they'd been in there for some days. But one seemed to be put in recently." O'Neill went on to explain that one cartridge was bright, while the other five were dark and dull.

Jean Baptiste Lacroix told of walking home at the time of the murder. He saw a man at the door of the Toronto House and saw another man sneak up behind him. A shot rang out. The moon was full. Lacroix, from a distance of fifteen yards, saw the whole thing. When he heard the shot he stepped into the shadows. The assassin walked quickly past his place of concealment and Lacroix was able to identify him. It was James Whelan. Other witnesses took the stand, claiming that at various times they had overheard Whelan threaten to kill McGee.

Whelan was defended by the Honourable John Hillyard Cameron, believed by many to be the ablest lawyer in the country. The courtroom was silent. Shy, black-haired Euphemie Lafrance, a servant at Storr's Hotel on Clarence Street, took the stand. When in Ottawa Whelan lived at the hotel.

Miss Lafrance stated that she knew Whelan, and that one of her duties was making up his bed. One morning she found a revolver under his mattress. She picked it up and it accidentally discharged, wounding her in the area of the left elbow. She displayed her scar to the court. Miss Lafrance claimed the accident occurred shortly before the McGee murder. This evidence effectively explained the reason for the one shiny bullet in Whelan's revolver.

Prosecution witness Lacroix's reputation was vigorously attacked. An array of tough lumberjacks who had known Lacroix for years took the stand and swore that the Crown's chief witness was a notorious liar. Their testimony had a forceful effect on the court, particularly when it was learned that Lacroix did not reveal his eyewitness account of the crime until he knew that a $20,000 reward had been offered for the apprehension and conviction of the killer.

The trial, attended by Prime Minister John A. MacDonald and his wife, lasted seven days. Whelan was found guilty. When asked if he had anything to say before sentence was passed, Whelan gave a long dissertation covering his history and the events of the night of the murder, all the while professing his innocence. He even absolved the jury for their wrong verdict, stating that based on the erroneous circumstantial evidence placed before them he too would have reached a guilty verdict.

On Thursday, February 11, 1869, accompanied by Father John O'Connor, James Whelan walked directly to the scaffold built for his public execution. His last words were, "God save Ireland and God save my soul." Father O'Connor pressed a crucifix to the condemned man's lips. The trapdoor sprung open, the crowd gasped, and James Whelan was no more. His was the last public execution to take place in Canada.

A plaque commemorating the Honourable Thomas D'Arcy McGee's assassination can be seen opposite 143 Sparks Street in Ottawa.

– DOUGLAS ROBERT WORTH –

THIS IS THE STORY of two losers. One, abused in prison as a teenager, turned out to be a sexual sadist, pedophile and murderer. The other, a tragedy of our times, was his 12-year-old victim.

Douglas Robert Worth was born on January 7, 1952, in New Glasgow, Nova Scotia, just down the road from his parents' home in Stellarton. Times could be tough in that part of Nova Scotia when the coal mines were down or the Trenton Steel Works were operating part-time.

Doug, one of 10 Worth children, got into trouble at age 16 when he stole a car and received a two-year jail sentence. A month before his sentence was up, while out on a day pass, he stole a car and raped a girl in New Glasgow. He received two years for breach of prison regulations, two years for stealing a car and two years for rape. Doug Worth was well on his way to a lifetime of crime.

In 1974, Worth was released from prison on mandatory supervision. Now a bitter young man who claimed that he had been sexually abused while incarcerated, he left the Atlantic provinces to roam the rest of Canada. Worth made his way to Oakville, Ontario. In August 1975, he assaulted a police officer. For this offence he was jailed for 30 days.

Upon release, Worth travelled to Kenora, Ontario, where he tried his luck at breaking and entering. His luck was out to lunch, as it had been all his life. He was convicted of two counts of breaking and entering and found himself once more behind bars, this time for 90 days.

The displaced Maritimer then made his way to Edmonton. It didn't take long. In 1979, he was convicted of raping a 19-year-old girl and was sentenced to eight years in jail.

While serving time in a Fort Saskatchewan prison, Worth met Mary Kelly, who was visiting a relative in the pen. When Worth received a day pass, he spent it with Mary. He didn't return on schedule and was transferred to a maximum-security prison in Edmonton and later to Kingston Penitentiary in Ontario.

Doug Worth spent every day of his eight-year sentence in prison. He was released on June 11, 1987, exactly eight years to the day after he was sentenced. Kingston penal authorities put him on a plane to Edmonton and told Edmonton officials that one bad apple was headed their way.

In Edmonton, Worth moved in with his old flame, Mary Kelly, a divorced mother of three. Her daughter and son, both in their twenties, moved out when Worth moved in. The third Kelly offspring, a boy of 14, stayed with his mother.

Although he had taken a meat-cutting course while in prison, Worth obtained work as a roofer. Kelly worked in a restaurant. At home, she was physically abused by her common-law husband. Worth beat her at the least provocation. Sometimes he choked her. But she never left him, nor did she report the abuse to authorities.

In September 1987, Worth and Kelly quit their jobs, sold their belongings and, together with Mary's teenage son, moved to Orangeville, Ontario, where Kelly's adult daughter lived. The very next night, a Friday, Kelly and her daughter went to a bingo game. They won $600. Worth was elated. He confiscated the winnings, as well as $800 they had received for their belongings back in Edmonton, and took off to visit his family in Nova Scotia. A month later, her returned to Orangeville minus the $1,400.

Worth tried his hand as a labourer with a construction crew. A month after returning from Nova Scotia, he decided to leave Kelly and move into a rooming house at 244 Main Street North in Brampton. Mary Kelly, despite the beatings, was very upset at Worth moving out. She and her son moved back to Edmonton.

Trina Campbell stood four foot eleven and weighed 85 pounds at the time of her death. If ever a youngster was born to a life of hard knocks, it was Trina.

Born in Melford, Saskatchewan, to an alcoholic mother and father, she and her two brothers were taken by child welfare workers when her parents parted company. Trina was nine years old when her mother was killed jumping from a truck while intoxicated.

In 1984, the Campbell family of Streetsville, Ontario, adopted all three children. Trina was enrolled in school and did well enough, but she was a troubled youngster. She often stole things from her home. When confronted, she ran away. In short, she was a problem child.

Finally it was decided that Trina would function best in a group home located in Brampton. She often ran away from the group home as well. In the wee hours of the morning of December 11, 1987, she was found in a local doughnut shop and was taken back to the group home by Peel Regional Police.

That day, it was decided that Trina would attend school as usual. She was picked up by a bus and returned around five in the afternoon. There is some evidence that Trina spent the next few days in a dilapidated house frequented by vagrants and runaways. The 12-year-old was reported missing to police.

A few days later, a man who had spent time in prison with Doug Worth spotted him on the street in Brampton. Worth had a young girl in tow. He was leading her by the arm. It appeared that the girl was being coerced by his old prison buddy.

Later, he and Worth met in a tavern and had a few beers. The friend noted that Worth had blood on his hands and shirt. When he inquired, Worth said he'd been in a fist fight. The friend asked, "What about the girl I saw you with earlier?" Worth replied ominously, "She got everything she deserved."

What had happened to Trina Campbell? According to later testimony, Worth told Dr. Robert Woodhill, a psychiatrist, that he had met Trina in a store and figured from her actions that she was a runaway. He befriended her, and took her to his rooming house, where he sexually attacked and killed her.

On December 14, 1987, Doug Worth took the body of Trina Campbell out of his room to a field behind the house. He covered the body as best he could with bushes. That same day, he sought a new place to stay. A few days later, he found a room in a private home. Worth moved in, then took off for Stellarton, Nova Scotia, to spend Christmas with his family.

During the holidays, Worth drank more than usual and was notably depressed. He was a man with a problem and that problem lay in a field behind a rooming house in Brampton, Ontario. Worth had to tell someone.

Worth confided in his brother-in-law, Wayne Lewis, but he didn't tell the exact truth. He told his sister Sharon's husband that he'd been in a fight with a man he had met in a bar. He had been forced to kill the man, a drifter with no family. Something in Worth's psyche wouldn't let him admit that he had murdered a child. Worth told his brother-in-law that he had been seen with this man and if the body were discovered he would be apprehended. He planned to return to Brampton to bury the body.

On January 2, Worth returned to Brampton. Two weeks later, Mary Kelly returned from Alberta and moved into her own accommodations. She started seeing Worth again, but he hadn't changed. He still beat her.

The pair rented a car to visit relatives in St. Catharines. During the visit, Worth attacked Mary and tossed her out of the car. This time, Mary reported the beating. Worth was picked up, but soon released. He patched up his difficulties with Mary.

By mid-February, Worth had fed Mary a string of lies to cover his latest plan. He told her, "I've done something really bad. Don't get the wrong idea. It's not a body, it's not a woman, it's not a man. I just stole some guns." Worth explained that he had to move the guns from their hiding place because there was a witness who knew where he had stashed the weapons.

There were no guns, only the tiny nude body of Trina Campbell, which had been lying behind his old rooming house under some bushes for over two months.

On March 4, 1988, Doug instructed Mary Kelly to rent a Dodge Colt from Budget Rent-A-Car in Brampton. They would move those guns he was always talking about. Instead of acting immediately, the urge to return to his native Nova Scotia overcame him. He and Mary made a quick trip there and returned March 11.

Two days later, Mary drove Doug to the field behind his former rooming house. He left the car carrying an empty hockey bag. Mary waited in the parked vehicle. Approximately a half-hour later, Doug returned with a bulging hockey bag and placed it in the trunk. He was perspiring and appeared to be nervous and pale.

All the while, Peel Regional Police were trying to locate the missing Trina Campbell. Ten thousand flyers describing Trina were distributed throughout the country.

Doug and Mary made their way to the Orangeville area with their macabre cargo. It had been a hard night's work. Doug was tired. He and Mary parked and soon fell asleep. One can only imagine what went through Doug Worth's mind when he was awakened by an Orangeville police officer. The officer, who had no idea that he had stumbled upon one of the most bizarre killers in Ontario's history, advised the occupants to move on. Doug mumbled to Mary, "We're all right, long as he doesn't look in the trunk."

The Dodge Colt made its way to Terra Nova, where Doug told Mary to park until daylight. When dawn broke, they were noticed. A customer walked into the Terra Nova general store at 7:50 a.m. He told Mr. Bernier, the owner, that there was a suspicious-looking couple parked down the road. Mr. Bernier called the OPP detachment at Shelburne, but when he was placed on hold, he grew impatient and hung up.

Only months later did the folks of Terra Nova learn that they had had a murderer among them that morning.

It was time. Doug took the hockey bag out of the trunk and lugged it into a nearby field. Mary observed what she thought was blood oozing out of the bag. When she mentioned this to Doug, he told her it was transmission fluid.

Police believe Doug visited the body behind his rooming house many times. When he discovered it wouldn't fit into his hockey bag, he systematically dissected the body with his hacksaw. Doug had taken that meat-cutting course while in prison and so knew something about what he was doing.

Now divested of the body, the pair made their way back to Brampton. Realizing that blood had dripped out of the bag and stained the trunk of the rental car, Doug had Mary's young son and another lad wash it out. The boys noticed the bloodstains and they too were told the stains had been caused by transmission fluid. The boys couldn't remove the stains from the rug. The next day, Doug asked Mary to cut out the stained portion of the rug. She told him she had done as he had instructed, but in fact she hadn't bothered. The vehicle was returned to the car rental agency.

On March 30, 1988, Doug, Mary and her young son left their rooms in Brampton, stealing anything of value. They made off with jewellery, towels, cigarettes and loose change. Once again, Doug Worth was going back to Nova Scotia in a rented car.

Doug discussed his most pressing problem with his sister and brother-in-law. He admitted to Sharon and Wayne Lewis that he had dismembered a body and moved it from behind his old rooming house. Doug was curious about how long it would take a body to decompose. He also told his sister he thought teeth were the only way police could identify a decomposed body.

Without funds, it was impossible for him to get back to Ontario to dispose of the head. He thought it would be a good idea to bring his victim's head back to Nova Scotia and bury it deep in the woods.

Usually, Doug referred to his victim as a man, but a few times in relating his story he slipped up and called his victim a girl. Somewhere along the line, he saw a poster of Trina Campbell. Doug almost flipped out, not over what he had done, but from the urgency he felt about to disposing of his victim's head.

Doug and Mary moved from Stellarton to their own apartment in Pictou. On April 22, a teenage lad overheard Doug, Mary and the Lewises discussing a murder and the moving of a body. He told the story to his guidance counsellor, who took the tale seriously and contacted the RCMP in Pictou. They, in turn, contacted Peel Regional Police. Was there anyone who had been reported missing around December 14 of the previous

year? There was only one outstanding missing person—
12-year-old Trina Campbell.

Under the direction of Inspector Rod Piukkala of the
Peel Regional Police, an investigation into Doug Worth's
background was conducted. It was soon discovered that
Doug had a long police record which included rape. The
vehicle used to transport the body was located at Budget
Rent-A-Car in Brampton. Inside the trunk were the telltale
bloodstains. Laboratory analyses of the most sophisticated
nature were conducted at the Centre of Forensic Sciences,
which determined that the stains had been made by
decomposed human blood.

Everything fit: the missing Trina Campbell, the bloodstains and the youngster's story in Pictou. Still, police had
no body, no confession and no real proof murder had been
committed.

Piukkala dispatched detective sergeants Edward Toye
and Len Favreau to Nova Scotia. With the help of the
RCMP, they would learn more about Doug Worth without
revealing to friends and relatives that he was the prime suspect in what they felt certain was a murder case. The
undercover officers learned of Doug's hatred of women
and his reputation in the area, but as no new developments
took place, it was decided that the RCMP would keep tabs
on Doug while the Ontario officers returned home.

Toye and Favreau were scheduled to fly back to Toronto
on the night of May 6, 1988. Unexpectedly, at 10 a.m. that
same day, Wayne Lewis walked into the local police station
and told authorities the whole story. He said that Worth
wanted to return to Ontario to retrieve the head of the
person he had murdered and dismembered. Doug hadn't
left because he was broke. Toye and Favreau cancelled

their flights. When Wayne Lewis's wife, Sharon, was informed that her husband had told what he knew, she corroborated his statement.

The Lewises agreed to co-operate with investigating officers. Outfitted with recording equipment, they engaged in a conversation with Doug in which he gave what amounted to a confession. Police rented an old car and gave Wayne $300. Wayne, under instructions, gave the car and the money to Doug so he could return to Ontario to complete the task of disposing of the head. Doug thanked the Lewises profusely. He inquired if they had a spare shovel. They didn't.

Within 45 minutes, Doug and Mary were on their way to Ontario. With Piukkala acting as anchor man, the pair was tailed all the way to Quebec City, where fresh surveillance officers were put on the job of following them. In Port Hope, Doug unsuccessfully attempted to purchase a shovel. In Brampton, he scoured a few construction sites, obviously looking for a shovel.

The man with the gruesome mission made his way north and parked close to the spot where the body had been placed. He was waiting for daylight, unaware he was under surveillance by police. He left the car carrying a gym bag, while Mary waited. He wasn't long returning with the bag, which was placed on the back seat. Doug stopped at a Shell station to dispose of a pair of gloves, which were immediately picked up by the trailing officers. He and Mary proceeded down Highway 10. Ironically, they drove past the Peel Regional Police headquarters before being pulled over. Inside the gym bag was the decomposed head of Trina Campbell.

During his trial, it was revealed that Doug had often

bragged in prison that after his release he would "go to a public school in Kingston with an axe and chop as many children as he could." He once told prison psychologist Sharon Williams he would "wreak havoc on society" as revenge for his years in prison. On another occasion, he stated he would "make serial killer Clifford Olson look like a choirboy."

Doug pleaded innocent by reason of insanity. He was judged to be sane and guilty of second-degree murder. Before being sentenced, he yelled from the prisoner's box, "First of all, I'm not a cold-hearted son of a bitch! You're all saying I'm a monster. I've got feelings. I feel for people. I've got to get this out before I kill somebody up at the detention centre with my pent-up emotions."

Doug Worth was sentenced to life imprisonment with no possibility of parole for 23 years.

On June 1, 1990, in a Brampton courtroom the charge against Mary Kelly of being an accessory to murder after the fact was dropped.

DISAPPEARED

They dropped from sight without a trace. Are they dead or alive? If alive, what was their fate? If dead, where are the bodies?

– AMBROSE SMALL –

CANADA'S MOST FAMOUS disappearance took place way back in 1919 when Ambrose Small vanished into thin air off the streets of Toronto. The 140-pound successful entrepreneur, who lived with his wife, Theresa, in a large home on Glen Road in Toronto, has never been found.

On December 2, Ambrose completed the sale of his theatre chain and received a cheque for a cool million. Theresa deposited the cheque at her bank. At 12:30 that day she had lunch at the King Edward Hotel with her husband and M.E. Flock, one of the lawyers involved in the sale of the theatre chain. Later that day, Theresa returned home. Ambrose had a business meeting, which concluded at 5:30 p.m. Flock caught a train to Montreal.

Shortly after 5:30 p.m., Ambrose attempted to purchase the *New York Times* from newsy Ralph Savein, at the corner of Adelaide and Yonge. Due to a snowstorm, the train from New York delivering the Times hadn't arrived. Ambrose swore, leaned into the swirling snow and has never been see from that moment to this.

That same afternoon, to celebrate the sale of his theatres, he'd purchased a Cadillac and a diamond necklace for his wife, hardly the actions of a man planning his own disappearance.

— MARION MCDOWELL —

ON DECEMBER 6, 1953, 17-year-old Marion McDowell watched from her front window for her date to arrive. Jimmy Wilson pulled up in his old Dodge, and Marion rushed out the door of her east end Toronto home, shouting over her shoulder to her parents, "He's here now. I won't be late." Marion was wrong. She never returned from that date.

Marion and Jimmy parked on Danforth Road. It was 8 o'clock in the evening. They lit cigarettes and talked. Suddenly the car door flew open. A masked stranger pointed a gun at Jimmy's head and said, "This is a stick-up." Jimmy was told to get out of the car. He was struck twice on the head and lost consciousness.

When Jimmy started to come around, he found himself in the back seat of his own car with Marion's limp form draped over him. The car was travelling to a lover's lane about a half mile away.

The car stopped. The intruder carried Marion to his own vehicle. Jimmy observed the man as he opened the trunk of his car. Then Jimmy scampered into the front seat, frantically started his engine and drove away. No one, other than her abductor, has seen Marion McDowell since.

— ABRAHAM WOLFSON —

ABRAHAM WOLFSON WAS A successful South African businessman who owned an apartment building on Rathburn Road in Toronto.

On December 6, 1970, Wolfson flew into Toronto to

negotiate the sale of his building. The 65-year-old owner of Wolfson's Department Store in Port Elizabeth, South Africa, planned to retire so that he could spend more time with his invalid wife.

While negotiating the sale of his apartment building, Mr. Wolfson rented a modest bachelor suite on Jarvis Street. By December 17, details of the sale of the building, for slightly more than one million dollars, were worked out. Wolfson called his lawyer, Herbert Fruitman, advising him that he would be in his office the next day to sign the necessary documents.

Abraham Wolfson never showed up. He disappeared, leaving behind untouched bank accounts, a thriving business and an ailing wife. His glasses, briefcase and business documents were found undisturbed in his apartment. He had written a cheery letter back home to South Africa two days before he vanished.

At the time, police said they were unable to uncover any evidence of foul play. On the other hand, their investigation indicated that Wolfson definitely didn't act in the manner of a man planning his own vanishing act.

— MABEL CRUMBACK —

OLD-TIMERS STILL CALL the modest home on Willard Avenue in Toronto "The Mystery House." It's aptly named, for it's from this house that Mabel Crumback disappeared in May 1950.

Mabel was an attractive 19-year-old who sang in the choir of St. John's Baptist Church, located diagonally across the street from her home. Mabel and her boyfriend,

Jimmy Bryan, finished a tennis match that long-ago Saturday and returned to Mabel's house.

At 12:30 a.m., Jimmy left, promising to return for Sunday dinner. Mabel's parents were visiting friends in Detroit. Only Mabel and her eight-year-old brother Gary were at home. On Sunday morning, Gary woke up and couldn't find his sister. No one could and no one ever did. Mabel had disappeared sometime during the night.

A massive investigation and search ensued. Police were able to ascertain that Mabel's bed had been slept in and then made up. Oddly, Mabel's pyjama bottoms were found neatly folded under her pillow. Her pyjama top was missing. There was no sign of a struggle and nothing was taken from the house. Gary and the family dog had slept undisturbed throughout the night.

Mabel Crumback's disappearance remains one of Canada's most baffling mysteries.

– CRYSTAL VAN HUUKSLOOT –

LIKE MABEL, CRYSTAL VAN HUUKSLOOT was 19 years old when she disappeared. She had travelled from Edmonton to Toronto carrying $3,000 in a homemade money belt around her waist with the express purpose of raising bail for her boyfriend, Stacey Harris, who had been arrested on a drug charge.

She visited Harris in the Don Jail and told him about her only partially successful efforts in raising his bail of $15,000. She would raise the balance somehow. True to her word, Crystal attempted to acquire the money by legitimate means, but was unsuccessful. Harris suggested loan sharks he knew, and gave her the name of Ian Rosenberg. Crystal contacted the man. Although she was appalled at the horrendous interest rates he quoted, she accepted the deal and was promised the money within a week.

Something went wrong. Crystal told a friend that the Rosenberg loan had fallen through and that she would be flying back to Edmonton the following morning to attempt once more to raise the necessary funds. She visited Harris and told him that Rosenberg would be giving her a lift to the airport.

Crystal never took the flight to Edmonton. When questioned by police, Rosenberg claimed he had dropped her off at the airport. That was that. Crystal disappeared and has not been seen since.

If Rosenberg was lying, there is no way to prove it now. He and his girlfriend were shot to death in bed seven months later. James Bass, a friend and business associate of Rosenberg, was arrested two hours after the double murder. Bass stood trial for Rosenberg's murder.

At the trial, Crown counsel Robert McGee admitted that the case against Bass was purely circumstantial, but contended that the motive for murder was Bass's fear that Rosenberg was about to inform the police of Bass's involvement in Crystal Van Huuksloot's disappearance.

James Bass was found not guilty. No one has ever been convicted of the murder of Ian Rosenberg and his girlfriend, nor has Crystal Van Huuksloot ever been found.

– ALISON MARY THOMAS –

ON SEPTEMBER 27, 1978, Alison Mary Thomas attended a dinner party with a boyfriend and other companions at his home on Hillsdale Avenue in Toronto.

The 26-year-old attractive blonde left the house at 12:30 a.m. to hail a cab on Yonge Street. A friend offered to accompany her, but Alison refused the offer and left the house alone. She has not been seen since.

Alison's past was thoroughly investigated. She had been employed in Paris, France, for nine years before returning to her home in Rochester, New York. She had come to Toronto to visit her brother, Stephen, who was studying archaeology at the University of Toronto. There is absolutely nothing in her past to account for her strange disappearance.

– NICOLE MORIN –

ON JULY 30, 1985, 8-year-old Nicole Morin phoned her friend Jennifer at around 10:15 a.m. and suggested they go swimming in their apartment complex's large swimming pool. Nicole then went to her bedroom and put on her orange bathing suit with the diagonal stripes. Her mother gave her the key to their mailbox. Nicole took the elevator down to check the mailbox, found no mail and returned with the key.

Between 10:30 and 11:00 a.m., Nicole gathered up her swimming gear and called Jennifer. The two again arranged to meet in the lobby. Jennifer immediately left her 7th-floor apartment and took the elevator down.

Jennifer waited in the lobby, but Nicole didn't show up. Was it possible Nicole got to the lobby first? Jennifer went out to the pool and took a look. No Nicole. Maybe Nicole had changed her mind or wasn't allowed to go swimming that day after all.

Upstairs, Nicole's mother assumed her daughter was having lunch at Jennifer's apartment. She often did that, but not this day.

Nicole had walked out the door of her penthouse apartment and into oblivion. Her disappearance raised many perplexing and unanswered questions. Did she walk the 120 feet to the elevator? Was she abducted on her way to the lobby? No one knows.

– FRED JOHNSEN –

IN 1958, FRED JOHNSEN had had enough of the family farm in New Brunswick's potato belt. He hitch-hiked to Toronto. Right off, Fred liked the action of the big city. He opened a second-hand store specializing in TVs and appliances. The venture prospered in a small way.

In 1962, Fred married and bought a home in King City. He believed that nursing homes were a sound investment and purchased a part interest in King City Lodge. Within two years, the Ontario government extended the Ontario Health Plan to include nursing home care. The farm boy from New Brunswick was on his way.

During the next eight years, Fred purchased and sold nursing homes in no less than six Canadian locations, as well as in Texas, Florida and California. He also acquired an interest in Toronto car dealerships, including British

United Automobiles, Downtown Fine Cars, Vintage Grand Touring Automobiles and Coventry Motors Ltd.

Fred's holding company, Komar Investments, controlled three electronics companies. Together with his brother-in-law, Youcef Debabi, he owned Home Juice Corp.

Fred was a wheeler dealer, often using credit established by one of his enterprises to finance another. Sometimes his companies suffered cash-flow problems. Even his impressive home was heavily mortgaged. Still, Fred had come a long way from those potato fields.

One night in August, 1979, the doorbell rang at 93 Old Forest Hill Road. According to Fred's wife, Lisa, a "short, very fat and quite ugly man" claimed to have a parcel for Fred. When Fred appeared, the fat man levelled a handgun directly at his chest. In a moment, Fred was gone, never to be seen or heard from again.

When Alan Bazkur was picked out of a lineup by Lisa Johnsen as the fat man who had spirited Fred away, Bazkur was arrested and charged with kidnapping. At his trial, Bazkur was acquitted when he was able to prove that, at the time of the abduction, he was in the Hampton Court Hotel and could not have been the kidnapper.

Since the night Fred Johnsen was forcibly taken from his home, police have ripped apart a concrete wall in Toronto, checked out a burial site in Kearney, Ontario, and followed up on sightings of Johnsen in California and Arizona. These and many other leads have proven fruitless.

Where are they? The businessmen, the attractive girls, the children, who one day are leading normal lives and the next day disappear without a trace? The truth is, no one knows.